GARRATTS AND GUITARS

Volume I

The glory days, when Leicester Central was graced with Gresley's 'A3s'. No 60102 *Sir Frederick Banbury* makes a spirited exit around 11.30am on 14 August 1950 with a Manchester-Marylebone express. *Alec Ford, MJS collection*

GARRATTS AND GUITARS

Sixty trainspotting years
Volume 1: 1955 to August 1985

John Stretton

Silver Link Publishing Ltd

First published in 2016

British Library Cataloguing in Publication Data

A catalogue record for this book is available from the British Library.

ISBN 978 1 85794 469 3

Silver Link Publishing Ltd
The Trundle
Ringstead Road
Great Addington
Kettering
Northants NN14 4BW

Tel/Fax: 01536 330588
email: sales@nostalgiacollection.com
Website: www.nostalgiacollection.com

Printed and bound in the Czech Republic

Frontispiece: The spotter's Bible. This was my well-thumbed 1947 version.

Right: A Leicester City programme, from a match against Blackpool. I was blessed to see the great Stanley Matthews play.

CONTENTS

Foreword
by
Brian Morrison

My interest in railways began at school in 1942, and was due to an annoyance with school dinners. These were held in different timed sessions, each table of eight being in the charge of a sixth form prefect who undertook the serving. The prefect on my table was not a particularly pleasant person by the name of Suddards, and for obvious reasons was known as 'Soapy'. He always gave himself by far the biggest portion of the food, but chocolate pudding day on Thursdays was particularly annoying as he took off at least a quarter of the dish served for himself and distributed the remainder in very small portions to eight of us! Becoming more and more annoyed at his unfairness, I decided to join my classmates who did not partake in the school meals, and cycled out with them to the local railway line at Chislehurst, where we ate the sandwiches provided by mum and watched the steam-hauled Kent Coast expresses go by, ignoring for the most part the prolific EMUs. Our group of five 12-year-olds took the engine numbers and names of the 'King Arthurs', 'Schools', 'L1s', 'E1s', 'D1s', etc, that passed, and I was always given a cheer when 'King Arthur' No 782 *Sir Brian* went through! In the same year of 1942 the first Ian Allan *ABC of Southern Locomotives* was published, and the lists of numbers that we had in a variety of notebooks could be transferred, and underlined in the *ABC* where appropriate.

This practice continued until the end of school days in 1946, and I continued underlining in the now numerous Ian Allan *ABCs* from places all over the UK until I was reluctantly conscripted to join the Army in 1948. It had been my intention to obtain a camera and begin recording the variety of locomotives about prior to Nationalisation, but compulsory Army service delayed the move for the three years that passed until I was demobbed. With the Army gratuity received on release, I spent half on the purchase of my first camera and the other half on an engagement ring for the young lady I had met while serving!

My first photograph was taken at London Liverpool Street station on my 21st birthday in March 1951, since when I have accumulated more than 400,000 views from all over the country and from the USA and a number of countries in Europe. The first to be published was in the October 1951 issue of *The Railway Magazine*. During the 30-year period covered by this publication I travelled the length and breadth of England, Scotland and Wales, but did not manage to obtain many photographs of the Beyer Garratts, although those I did record were all worthwhile.

As you may well imagine, I have many memories of those years and so has John. By incorporating non-railway events and highlights along the way, in addition to his trainspotting activities, he has here crafted a fine evocation of the period in question – an era that we will never see again!

Introduction

Why *Garratts & Guitars*? As shorthand for railways and music, they are two of my passions and they have been a constant throughout my life since 1955. I am well aware that there have been previous spotters' memoirs from Silver Link, but this one is different, for it is an autobiography – 60 trainspotting years rather than 60 years of trainspotting. There is a difference that I hope you will appreciate as you journey with me. Opening in September 1955, when I began my second year at Loughborough College School, I present a story of my life for the ensuing 60 years, where the main linking theme is my love affair with the UK's railways, but I also include and introduce other facts and factors that I have encountered and/or been aware of along the way. This first volume covers the years 1955 to 1985, an eventful period in my young life but, while railways are a thread that links it all, outside there are additions of such subjects as world events, sport, music, writing, births and deaths, girlfriends and even my occasional reactions to things. Before you ask, this has not been prompted by Michael Portillo's TV programmes coupling railways and local social highlights, as the idea has been with me long before those, but it is a similar premise.

   The first half of the title comes from my favourite early trainspotting memories, of the massive ex-LMS 'Garratts' that I saw every day on my way between Syston station and Loughborough College School in 1955, and the fact that, although those disappeared fairly quickly, the Garratt type is still around in 2016, with ex-SAR locomotives working hard on the rebuilt Welsh Highland Railway. 'Guitars' refers to the musical content of my life but, more specifically, my passion for Duane Eddy's music. Additional passions included here are/ have been photography, writing, acting, films, theatre, sport – Leicester City and ten-pin bowling especially – and, naturally, girlfriends. So, there is a constant theme throughout, weaving in and out of my many travels to capture as many locomotives as possible; and there have been many humorous events over the

One of my favourite beasts and the reason for half of this book's title – 'Garratt' No 47981, complete with revolving bunker, stands between duties at Cricklewood in May 1955. Shedded at Toton, it was withdrawn 18 months later, in November 1956. *MJS collection*

years. Some of these are included – though others are better not in print!

These 60 years, starting when I was 12, have literally flown by but, looking back, I am happy with what I have achieved, although, like so many, it would have been good to know then what I know now! With an atavistic look at myself and others, I wonder whatever happened to the people we used to be. I am amazed at some of the things we did and some of the choices we made. There are regrets, obviously, mostly concerning what I didn't photograph, but we had to make do with what we had, not least with films and cameras. Overall, however, I would not change too much even if I had the chance.

I hope you will enjoy the journey through these particular 30 years, which saw the world change dramatically and the social mores adapt beyond recognition. I hope, also, that my stories may stir some of your own memories. There have been corners of my mind that have had a torch shone onto them in re-treading paths, and don't be surprised if this happens to you. All the photographs were taken by me unless otherwise stated. Space has dictated what has been included and, to some degree, what has been left out. It has been an invidious task whittling down the thousands of images I have to the 200-plus that you have here, and I apologise if you feel I have left out something you consider important. I have taken care to ensure as far as possible that all facts are correct, but if you do find any errors, please let me know via the publisher.

Acknowledgements

Over the years there have been many people who have encouraged me, helped me, guided me and/or accompanied me, and I would like here to thank them all. In particular, however, I would like to thank my cousin David Richards for his companionship over the years and for proof-reading this monster. He has pointed me in a correct direction on more than one occasion! Others who are/have been important to me include: Les Wade, Peter Simmonds, Brian Morrison (for his readiness to help and for the Foreword), Gill Walker, Bob Fisher, Sylvia Stevens, Mike Lancaster, Duane Eddy, Eddie Pumer, Guy Cooper, Roger Thwaites, Liz Simpson-Silva, my late wife Judi and my two wonderful children Adam and Tammy. At the publishing end, Peter Townsend is always generous with his time and advice, and Will Adams keeps me on the straight and narrow. Thank you all.

Right: Syston station as I knew it from September 1954 to July 1956, for my journeys to Loughborough College School. Seen on 30 August 1955, it closed on 4 March 1968 and the location was without a station until 27 May 1994, when a single platform was opened on the old freight route, out of sight to the right. *MJS collection*

Chapter 1
1955-1960

'No! You cannot have an Ian Allan spotter's book!'

This was dad's reaction to my request for a Midland Region *ABC* early in 1956. To be fair to him, I was apparently (although I had not noticed the trend) prone to pick up a new hobby, pester for all the gear to go with it, then three months or so later move on to something new. This was still in the post-war austerity era – rationing had only been finally abolished some 18 months earlier – and dad was not exactly bringing in a fortune each week. He decided that he had to put his foot down at some stage and he chose my recent interest in trainspotting, but his timing was not good. Sixty years later I am still at it!

Our story actually begins months earlier, during the early summer of 1955, when I became aware of several of my

schoolmates collecting and becoming excited by a mysterious array of numbers on locomotives seen during our rail journeys to and from school. In September 1954, a month after turning 11 and having been appropriately successful in the 11-Plus exams, I had joined others in the daily trip by bus and train from my home in Thurmaston, 4 miles north of Leicester, to Loughborough, to begin my education at Loughborough College School. The rail journey was from Syston station and was my first real introduction to the UK's railway system. It was towards the end, then, of my first senior year that I investigated the strange habit of my colleagues and, from the start of the second year, resolved to begin collecting engine numbers. They were neatly placed into a spare exercise book, but the collection soon became random and without form. I needed to know more and it was explained that I needed 'an *ABC*' and, preferably, one dedicated to the 'Midland Region'. Finally dad relented, I had my *ABC* but ... I had collected some numbers that began with '6', seen on the ex-Great Central line that crossed the bridge at the southern end of Loughborough Midland station, and they were not in my book! Thus I needed an 'Eastern Region' book, or, ideally, a 'Combined' version, apparently containing all the numbers of the locos running on British Railways at the time. Thus, as Christmas 1956 approached, guess what was on my present list! There were well over 20,000 numbers in that 'Combined' and, of course, I wanted to see them all. I had set myself a challenge but I was not initially to appreciate the enormity of the task!

It is said that you always remember your first love and I certainly remember my first loco. I can still visualise the moment, in September 1955, at the start of my second year at LCS, reaching the bottom step of the footbridge on my homeward platform at Loughborough Midland and watching 'Jubilee' No 45636 *Uganda* drifting into the opposite platform, slowing for the station stop on a Manchester-bound express. A 'namer' to boot! Not long afterwards No 40182 drew out of the siding immediately to the north of the station and into our platform with the 5.14pm SX to Leicester, a short train

Leicester Central at its BR height. No 61136 stands in the platform after arrival with the down 'Master Cutler' express on 21 June 1955, ready to uncouple to allow No 60855, complete with a more elaborate headboard, to take over for the last lap to Sheffield. *Gerald Adams, MJS collection*

that would provide my journey home to Syston. This and 'sister' loco No 40146 were to become familiar to us on this service over ensuing months, as was the passage of the southbound 'Thames-Clyde Express' through Loughborough just minutes before our train. Charlie, the kindly and courteous ticket collector on the gate at the station, would often advise if there were any problems with timing of our train and/or hand out free leaflets, timetables, etc. On the way home I was fascinated by the constant succession of seemingly never-ending freight trains on the two slow lines, nose-to-tail ex-LMS 'Garratts' or Stanier 8Fs. Many numbers were put into my exercise book and I was off and running.

As with many institutions of the day, there was an 'initiation' for the first-year students on the school trains. The

Chances are I am on this train! On 13 September 1955 old favourite No 40146 leaves with the three-coach Loughborough (Midland)-Leicester train that took me home after school for just short of two years. Note the GCR overbridge above the carriages, demolished after the closure of the route in 1969, but due to be reinstated in 2017. *Geoff King, MJS collection*

compartmental carriages in which we travelled had blinds for the windows, with wooden rods at their foot to slot into the groove on the carriage window frames. These 'blind sticks' were used by the 'second years' to administer punishment to the new boys (to my knowledge, the girls did not suffer this way). Whether this was to sort the 'wheat from the chaff' is uncertain, but this plus the occasional stripping of the younger boys to their underpants and throwing them, their clothes and satchels onto their destination stations – which did happen on one occasion to me! – certainly did sufficiently bully some so that they left the school. This happened to my friend from junior school, Alan, who only survived the first few months before leaving and being transferred to a school nearer to his home, without any need of transport.

In retrospect, I could hardly have had a better place to start my new hobby, with 'Midland' locos on my journeys to and from school, 'Eastern' ones on the Great Central, 'Standards' on both and, a bonus, Loughborough Midland station being right next to the Brush Engineering Works, where new British Railways diesels – later to become Classes 31 and 47 – were to be constructed. New ones could be seen as they prepared to leave the Works' complex.

As well as being a landmark year for me, it was an eventful year elsewhere, both on and off the railways. For our railways, 1955 started with a 'bang' in the shape of the British Transport Commission's *Modernisation and Re-equipment of British Railways* plan, price 3s 6d! With grand plans to drag BR out of the Victorian age, with a budget to match, sadly, as in so many aspects of life, reality did not match the vision and the modernisation saw a variant path to that originally envisaged. New steam locos were still being built, while the diesel fleet increased solely in the shape of shunters, but a vision of the future was 'Deltic' making its first test run in November, and the 1,500V dc Manchester-Wath electrification was completed. Elsewhere, Commercial TV was born, on 22 September 1955, with 'Gibbs SR' toothpaste the first advert shown, on the same day as Grace Archer was killed off in a dramatic fire in *The Archers* – rumoured to have been deliberate on the part of the BBC! Donald Campbell broke the world water speed record; Sir Winston Churchill resigned as Prime Minister, to be succeeded by Sir Anthony Eden; and Bill Haley and his Comets hit the charts with *Shake, Rattle and Roll*, then *Rock Around the Clock*.

Home, in Thurmaston, was roughly a quarter of a mile from the Midland main line between Leicester and Syston, whichever of two routes I took, as, increasingly, I spent all of my spare time by the line, soaking up the sights and smells and gradually amassing more numbers in my book. I was often late back home – for meals, bed, etc – as it always seemed that I could espy a wisp of smoke that could herald the arrival of another train; and on more than one occasion I was part way back when I heard a whistle and there was a mad dash back to the bridge to catch the number.

As time went by I began to spread my wings, either by bus or bike, and I finally found my way to the end of Hutchinson Street, in Leicester, where spotters could have a bird's eye view of 15C, Leicester Midland engine shed. How I came to learn of this Mecca I cannot remember, but I was there as often as possible. In my earliest visits the railway boundary fence was made from upended old wooden sleepers, which necessitated either standing on the crossbar of my bike or, if arriving by bus, somehow climbing up to the top of the sleepers. Potentially dangerous, something serious must have happened as, sometime during 1958, this wooden palisade was replaced by iron railings, which, joy of joys, gave us an uninterrupted view of the shed buildings and the attendant yard, and – perhaps not surprisingly – became known as the Birdcage. It was not unknown to find around 50-60 locos present, but some numbers were hidden by other locos and some were inside the adjacent

The exciting vista from the Birdcage illustrates the appeal of shed scenes in steam days. 15C (Leicester Midland) houses Nos 45267, 40452, 75059, 42372 and 44163 among others on 4 June 1957. Virtually everything in this view has since disappeared, although the shed yard still remains and in use in 2016.

covered roundhouse. An old hand showed me the way to the entrance of this building, warning me of the consequences of being caught going round it without permission. I had learned 'bunking'!

I am a creature of habit, for collecting numbers and making lists. At the close of 1955 my records tell me I had seen 857 different locomotives – 744 Midland, 100 Eastern, 7 Western, and 6 Southern – and calculated that I had a further 18,800 to complete the set!

Dad bought a TV in 1950 – a 9-inch screen in a large wooden cabinet – ostensibly ready to be able to watch Leicester City should they again reach the final of the FA Cup, a feat that had happened the year before. We had to wait for 1961 for this but, from the early '50s, dad, myself, cousin David and his dad, my uncle George, travelled to Filbert Street on Saturday afternoons, to watch both City's first team and reserve matches. Sadly, at the end of the 1954-55 season we saw the club relegated from Division 1 (the top flight), two points behind Cardiff City but 9 above bottom club Sheffield Wednesday – and this after Filbert Street had seen a club record crowd of 42,486 in October 1954, against Arsenal (result 3-3, with a goal by Derek Hines and two by Arthur Rowley). By now David had been bitten by the railway bug and we spent many hours together, initially in and around Leicester, but by the middle of 1956 we were keen to go further afield.

Our first outing was by train to Rugby, over the old Midland Counties line from Leicester. Sadly, part of my records of this trip have been lost and memories are sketchy, but I do remember that immediately on arrival at Rugby a 'Semi' ('Coronation' Class 'Pacific') roared non-stop on its way north on the fast avoiding line. It was partially hidden by coaches in between but we did see its sloping front end, a legacy of previous streamlining – the only one I saw still in this state. The rest of that day was spent racing around the station to ensure a number wasn't missed, together with soaking in the magical atmosphere of many exotic locomotives; there was a short cab ride along a bay platform on 'B1' No 61282, and there were 'visions' of SR diesel No 10203, aged No 58293, and my first unrebuilt 'Patriot', No 45505 *The Royal Army Ordnance Corps*! Other trips were made over this route until its closure to passengers on 1 January 1962. Later trips there, though, were by bike, and we also used this mode to spot at Nuneaton, which was actually closer to home than Rugby. In the opposite compass direction I would sometimes travel east by bus to sample the delights of Grantham, with its 'A4s', 'A3s', etc, and

Though taken around 1950, this exemplifies the streamlined 'Semi' that we saw on our first visit to Rugby. Captured at Symington, No 46237 *City of Bristol*, as LMS 6237, was fully streamlined until March 1947. It was renumbered to its BR state in July 1948. *MJS collection*

the constant changing of locos on the long-distance trains.

1956 had begun with an announcement in March of future electrification by 25kV overhead wires; June saw the abolition of 3rd Class for passenger travel and the introduction of a new British Railways logo – the 'Lion and Crown', otherwise affectionately known as the 'ferret and dartboard'! Yellow whiskers began to appear on the front of DMUs later in the year; No 35018 became the first 'Merchant Navy' Class 'Pacific' to be rebuilt; and the number of new diesels built was

The sort of sight that gladdened our hearts on trips to Rugby. No 46153 *The Royal Dragoon* drifts into the station at lunchtime on 5 May 1956 with an express for Euston. Note the wonderful artefacts at the end of the platform. *Geoff King, MJS collection*

greater than steam for the first time. Elsewhere, the Bill for the abolition of the death penalty was passed in the House of Commons but defeated in the House of Lords; Marilyn Monroe married playwright Arthur Miller; author A. A. Milne died; actor Tom Hanks was born; and the first Eurovision Song Contest was held, in Lugarno, Switzerland, the first winner being Lys Assia (of Switzerland) with her song *Refrain*. There were 15 No 1 records in 1956, the vast majority being 'middle of the road' and only three approaching 'rock 'n' roll' – Bill Haley's *Rock Around The Clock*, *Why Do Fools Fall in Love* by Frankie Lyman and the Teenagers, and Johnnie Ray's *Just Walkin' in the Rain* (for both November and December). These were the vanguard in what would become a perfect storm!

My first visit to Nuneaton was in the spring of 1956, by rail to Abbey Street station, then a walk to the goal, the

West Coast Main Line station, where a healthy collection of 84 numbers was amassed before the return to Leicester by the same route. Locos seen were Nos 44574, 47225, 42573, 48529, 43244, 43011, 43786, 49414, 40073, 13054, 44142, 45288, 43885, 47286, 42218, 45270, 46229 *Duchess of Hamilton*, 40104 (which I cabbed), 48743, 45536 *Private W. Wood VC*, 45249, 55515 *Caernarvon*, 48723, 46144 *Honourable Artillery Company*, 70033 *Charles Dickens*, 48056, 42956, 46236 *City of Bradford*, 45027, 46204 *Princess Louise*, 45662 *Kempenfelt*, 45527 *Southport*, 40447, 40156, 49448, 45073, 40204, 46168 *The Girl Guide*, 46164 *The Artists' Rifleman*, 48922, 49120, 44352, 45025, 46160 *Queen Victoria's Rifleman*, 45545 *Planet*, 44766, 44935, 41231, 45736 *Phoenix*, 47367, 46207 *Princess Arthur of Connaught*, 45588 *Kashmir*, 41244, 42856, 43023, 71000 *Duke of Gloucester*, 46135 *The East Lancashire Regiment*, 42186, 70047, 45541 *Duke of Sutherland*, 46245 *City of London*, 46152 *The King's Dragoon Guardsman*, 45643 *Rodney*, 46114 *Coldstream Guardsman*, 46150

My first photograph, taken with dad's camera. No 47982 heads north past Syston North Junction with a rake of empties on 1 June 1956, after coming off the Melton curve.

The Life Guardsman, 45634 *Trinidad*, 40678, 45141, 42776, 45021, 46253 *City of St Albans*, 45540 *Sir Robert Turnbull*, 44760, 46446, 45421, 40157, 45401, 58118, 45531 *Sir Frederick Harrison*, 47281, 48398, 48010, 45713 *Renown*, and 43745. Just one diesel, a shunter in the station confines. While motive power on the main-line expresses was no different From Rugby, only a few miles south on the WCML, the more prosaic fare at Nuneaton had a different and more utilitarian feel ... but nonetheless interesting for all that.

26 July 1956 saw me on holiday from school and on my way, by bus, from Thurmaston for my first visit to Grantham. Needless to say, not having seen a huge number of Eastern Region locos previously but having heard much about my destination, the anticipation was off the scale and the excitement was barely manageable. The day promised much and I was not to be disappointed. Along with a gloriously sunny day (burning one side of my face on the bus on both journeys!), the sights and sounds ... and the smell ... from the vantage point alongside the track, by the northern end of the platforms, were nigh on overwhelming. The changing of locos on northbound expresses, the variety and the sudden appearance of locos from the nearby engine shed and the vision of locos turning on the triangle next to the shed was all beyond my expectations. Suffice to say that I 'copped' the vast majority of numbers and eventually caught the bus home a very happy ferrequinologist. David and I did not enjoy the negative connotations of the term 'trainspotter', preferring, instead, to be regarded as students of the iron horse!

No 60533 *Happy Knight* was the first engine seen on my happy morning, and other locos recorded for posterity that day were Nos 60156 *Great Central*, 47300, 61580, 64218, 60053 *Sansovino*, 67362, 90038, 60153 *Flamboyant*, 92072, 63940, 67391, 90703, 47458, 60144 *King's Courier*, 60073 *St Gatien*, 60128 *Bongrace*, 60063 *Isinglass*, 69800, 60015 *Quicksilver*, 90437, 60921, 60064 *Tagalie*, 60505 *Thane of Fife*, 60011 *Empire of India*, 60126 *Sir Vincent Raven*, 60032 *Gannet*, 60051 *Blink Bonny*, 60034 *Lord Faringdon*, 90052, 64187, 60904, 69818, 60038 *Firdaussi*, 60026

Miles Beevor, 60146 *Peregrine*, 90296, 60008 *Dwight D. Eisenhower*, 60131 *Osprey*, 69814, 60896, 60821, 60859, 64263, 60061 *Pretty Polly*, 60039 *Sandwich*, 69827, 60134 *Foxhunter*, 60123 *H.A. Ivatt*, 60122 *Curlew*, 60974, 63647, 60010 *Dominion of Canada*, 60033 *Seagull*, 60047 *Donovan*, 63978, 60841, 64202, 60845, 60020 *Guillemot*, 60158 *Aberdonian*, 60918, 60117 *Bois Roussel*, 90674, 60513 *Dante*, 90269, 60113 *Great Northern*, 90211, 60050 *Persimmon*, 60924, 60893, 61203, 60120 *Kittiwake*, 60003 *Andrew K. McCosh*, 60867, 90717, 64235, 60141 *Abbotsford*, 90538, 60016 *Silver King*, and 92011. A total of 81, all cops bar a handful, and not a diesel in sight, apart from four one-year-old twin-car Derby-built E79xxx units! An additional delight was the sight of Pullman cars 76, 58, 209, 248, *Loraine*, *Avian Bar*, 107, 162, *Agatha*, *Cynthia*, *Lucille*, *Nilar*, *Juana* and *Lydia*.

The journey home was spent in reverie, and the religious duty of underlining the new haul in my 'Combined' was later undertaken with great solemnity and constant pausing to recall particular memories. It was not obvious to me that day, but my now-established hobby, through locomotive names, was later to aid my studies of history, geography, literature, ornithology and even the Sport of Kings – another reason for validity of my interest and for proving dad wrong in his initial objections! At the end of this trip, my accumulation of locos seen had risen to a total of 1,844. I had ceased recording how many were still left to see, as it was too depressing, and the constant flux of new and withdrawn locos meant that the total was really academic.

Apart from a family outing to Nottingham and a school trip to London, which presented yet more numbers to be underlined, the highlight of 1956 was racing with one or two classmates from school in William Street in Loughborough the mile or so to the Central station, in the south-east of the town, at lunchtimes to witness 'A3s' on 'The South Yorkshireman' express. Needless to say, we enjoyed a very brief window of opportunity but, thankfully, most days the express was on time! Favourites were Nos 60049 *Galtee More*, 60059 *Tracery*, 60102 *Sir Frederick Banbury*, 60104 *Solario*, 60106 *Flying Fox*, 60107 *Royal Lancer* and 60111 *Enterprise*. All were shedded at 38C (Leicester

Central) at the time, but all disappeared from the line in September 1957, transferred to either Grantham or King's Cross sheds – a sad loss to the prestige of the GCR.

One of Leicester Central shed's 'A3s', No 60059 *Tracery* stands in the shed yard at 7.25pm on 17 July 1956, about to make its way to the nearby station as the changeover engine for the down 'Master Cutler'. *Gerald Adams, MJS collection*

1957 was to see the school move out of William Street, to be rehoused in new buildings on Thorpe Hill, on the western edge of the town, well away from any operating railways. There was a line alongside the school playing field, the route from Coalville East to Loughborough Derby Road. This had closed to all traffic on 31 October 1955, but there were to be the occasional workings into the later 1950s. I only saw three, two ex-LMS 4Fs – No 44085 on 20 March and No 44103 on 25 March 1957

– and a 'Standard' 9F, though I was not in a good position to catch the number of this. The latter was very much a rarity and otherwise unheard of by us on that line.

Over the 7 months from May 1956, my tally of cops more than doubled from 1,355 to 2,730, aided by trips to Nuneaton (again) and Derby, but my first spotting outing of 1957 was not until 10 March. My first after joining the Attenborough Model Railway Society (AMR), this proved to be a very wet day in Nottinghamshire, with difficulty in keeping the notebooks dry! 16A (Nottingham shed) saw me garner 40 cops, including 11 diesel shunters, followed by 14 at 16C (Mansfield), which seemed to have more holes than roof over the locos within the shed building 16B (Kirkby-in-Ashfield) was next, with 21 locos new to me and all steam bar two, then 38B (Annesley) – 33, all steam and either ER or 'Standard' types – to be followed by 18A (Toton) with 34, including 10 diesel shunters. The final shed was, for me, the most exciting of the day. Although we saw the occasional 38A (Colwick)-allocated loco through Leicester Central, they were the exception rather than the rule, so I was delighted to witness, among the 102 cops on shed, such rarities as Nos 61726, 61768, 61763, 61738, 61732, 61777 and 61771, and a crop of tank engines that never wandered too far from their home. At the turn of 1951, Colwick had housed the fourth largest allocation on BR, totalling 206, and although it did not enjoy named express engines, its sheer size – a total of 12 tracks leading into a dead-ended shed, with two turntables in the yard – and variety was exotic to this young spotter. The journey home, by rail, seemed so mundane in comparison, but I had the delight of more underlinings and memories to look forward to.

If Colwick had seemed exotic, my next outing, on 5 May, was by many degrees more magical. For many years 30A (Stratford), in east London, held the distinction of having by far the largest allocation, with more than 380 locos shedded there in 1950. Interestingly, five of the top ten sheds for allocations in the early years of British Railways were all from the Eastern and North Eastern Regions – 30A, 35A (New England, third with

213), 38A, 36A (Doncaster, sixth with 182), and 50A (York, eighth with 176). Seen on a journey by rail direct to Stratford's shed, again with AMR, locos spotted totalled 351, with 294 being cops. Seen en route were Nos 45328, 58308, 48559, 45344, 49452, 48423, 45308, 41219, 12047, 48090, 45379, 48027, 48419, 48549, 46255 *City of Hereford*, 48359, 48754, 43089, 47500, 45331, 49414, 80040, 80082, 48898, 80042, 48716, 49287, 48951, 40672, 48195, 45398, 13174, 12050, 48681, 49070, 48128, 40069, 47475, 12037, 48688, 49671, 90015, 40016, 40125, 12035, 45726 *Vindictive*, 46458, 40051, 40068, 45532 *Illustrious*, 12055, 44860, 46168 *The Girl Guide*, 12036 and 13163.

Then 30A itself presented Nos 69632, 92070, 13064, 12051, 62618, 13019, 61569, 11103, 13298, 62611, 12107, 11112, 11507, 13302, 12110, 11506, 68529, 12109, 12104, 12130, 11135, 11134, 12105, 69614, 67738, 61609 *Quidenham*, 11123, 11132, 68571, 13051, 61820, 12111, 70039 *Sir Christopher Wren*, 69719, 69643, 13300, 11508, 64807, 76032, 90660, 61815, 61362, 68647, 64653, 46468, 65535, 70005 *John Milton*, 90256, 65450, 68666, 68665, 61235, 68574, 44669, 64693, 69669, 64652, 90551, 69642, 64775, 64663, 69652, 69601, 69728, 64681, 70041 *Sir John Moore*, 76034, 65565, 61863, 64684, 61104, 61254, 62068, 64672, 64784, 63571, 61111, 64692, 61977, 64694, 62070, 64767, 61574, 61541, 61565, 61557, 90477, 64698, 62053, 90295, 61926, 62601, 62565, 62543, 62556, 61579, 61661 *Sheffield Wednesday*, 64662, 64664, 61042, 61942, 61399, 90062, 61109, 61384, 64973, 64670, 63658, 65389, 64788, 70003 *John Bunyan*, 61663 *Everton*, 61003 *Gazelle*, 61810, 65506, 61634 *Hinchingbrooke*, 61311, 65449, 61849, 86522, 68554, 68578, 68575, 68652, 68646, 68513, 68639, 68558, 68563, 90498, 67214, 68573, 68644, 90508, 68576, 65454, 68577, 63619, 68549, 68631, 68630, 67784, 68500, 69653, 69630, 67737, 68126, 69666, 69613, 69705, 68655, 69647, 69661, 67714, 9401, 67227, 69715, 68579, 68613, 67729, 69722, 61632 *Belvoir Castle*, 61119, 69720, 69625, 68653, 68649, 67725, 68657, 69732, 67701, 67230, 69724, 68532, 68619, 76030, 61378, 64674, 70034 *Thomas Hardy*, 64800, 65546, 61164, 64675, 61957, 61973, 65476, 65446, 61610 *Honingham Hall*, 64779, 65361, 64783, 61810, 65389, 61373, 69655, 61577, 61648 *Arsenal*, 61249,

61234, 61004 *Oryx*, 61668 *Bradford City*, 64873, 11131, 15202, 13070, 12063, 13017, 12135, 13218, 69702, 80080, 11122, 61048, 67791, 64689, 61233, 67723, 61264, 69724, 61533, 61046, 68529, 32, 31, 33, 36, 13303, 61608 *Gunton*, 76031, 69708, 68660, 64780, 62613, 65523, 64660, 65464, 69640, 69679, 76033, 65531, 68588, 69618, 65562, 65523, 68623, 62606, 64658, 61672 *West Ham United*, 67718, 69683, 62610, and 61659 *East Anglian*.

Out in the wider world, Harold Macmillan became Prime Minister on 10 January and it was later in this year that he spoke those immortal words, 'You've never had it so good', at a Conservative rally in Bradford. In the air the RAF took possession of its first Vulcan bomber, and Russia launched Sputnik 1, the first man-made satellite. League Champions Manchester United made it to the FA Cup Final, but were defeated 2-1 by Aston Villa, and the UK's longest-running railway journal, *The Railway Magazine*, celebrated its Diamond Jubilee. Pat Boone's *Love Letters in the Sand* was officially the biggest-selling single of the year, but signs of the times were evidenced by hits by Paul Anka (*Diana*), Elvis Presley (*All Shook Up*), Jerry Lee Lewis (*Whole Lotta Shakin' Goin' On* and *Great Balls of Fire*), Buddy Holly and the Crickets (*That'll Be the Day*) and the Everly Brothers (*Bye Bye Love*). This was the year I bought my first record – *Singing the Blues* by Tommy Steele – a 78rpm played on my new wind-up record player! It reached No 1 in the UK early in the year.

The electric guitar was beginning to see wider usage within the popular music business, but it was one individual who grabbed my ears and really moved the instrument out of the backing group and onto centre stage in this year. In November Duane Eddy recorded an instrumental, *Moovin' n' Groovin'*, co-written by him and Lee Hazlewood, in Phoenix, Arizona. As Audio Recorders studio did not possess an echo chamber – and Hazlewood had become used to one during his time with Dot Records – an abandoned water storage tank was bought and placed on a frame outside at the rear of the building, a speaker at one end and a mic at the other! Six months or so earlier, Duane had visited Ziggie's Music Shop in Phoenix, looking to trade in his Gibson Les Paul guitar. He bought a Gretsch with an orange body, and that night took it to a gig. He and the audience were hooked. *Moovin' n' Groovin'* reached No 72 on the Billboard Hot 100 in the States in early 1958, which led in that year to a recording contract with Philadelphia-based Jamie Records, with Lester Sill and Lee Hazlewood as producers. Hit singles followed, including *Rebel Rouser*, *Ramrod* and *Because They're Young*, as did several million-selling albums. Duane made the guitar stand out from the crowd and influenced many over the succeeding years… The rest, as they say, is history, and in 2015/16 he is still recording material for a new album.

Back on the railways in 1957, No 34005 *Barnstaple* became the first of Bulleid's 'Light Pacifics' to be rebuilt; Doncaster outshopped its last steam loco, No 76116; the first Brush Type 2, No D5500, was released to the Eastern Region; the country's first diesel-hydraulic main-line loco, No D600, was completed at North British Locomotive Co's works; and from the summer, all new diesels entered traffic with a 'D' prefix. On a much sadder note, 4 December saw one of the country's worst rail disasters, when the 4.46pm Cannon Street-Folkestone/Ramsgate train, hauled by No 34066 *Spitfire*, ran into the rear of the 5.18pm Charing Cross-Hayes EMU at Lewisham in South London in thick fog. The crash brought down a 350-ton girder bridge onto the wreck, leading to a total of 90 deaths.

This was also the last year that new steam locomotives were built, apart from the 'Standard' 9Fs, and in June 1D (Devons Road Bow, East London) became the first all-diesel shed, echoing the increasing spread of non-steam operations.

On the personal front, after school broke up for the summer holidays I intensified my spotting trips, locally and also with repeat visits to Rugby, Grantham and London. The main delight, however, was to come with a two-week family holiday to Dawlish Warren, beginning on my 14th birthday on 3 August. The magnificent GWR main line between Exeter and Newton Abbot was between our lodgings and the sea and my eyes were like dinner plates at the sights of the seemingly constant stream of trains, passenger and freight, as we walked to the beach. I was under parental control and strictly limited in my spotting endeavours, being only allowed two brief sessions where I could sit beside the line and collect the numbers – on 10 and 15 August. Almost everything seemed to be named (!) and I copped a total of 257 out of 287 before we made our way back home to Leicester; perhaps not surprising, as the only ex-GWR locos that I had previously seen were on the York-Bournemouth workings through Leicester Central.

In this view from the footpath next to my grandfather's allotment, No 61975, in magnificent external condition, passes through Belgrave & Birstall station on 24 April 1957 with an up mixed freight. *Geoff King, MJS collection*

This was my first introduction to the 'Kings', 'Ganges', 'Counties' and '28xx' 2-8-0 freight locos, all of which subsequently became amongst my favourites – 16 'Kings', 20 'Granges', eight 'Counties' and six '28xxs', plus No 30450 *Sir Kay* (the first loco recorded on arrival at Dawlish Warren!), seven 'WC/BB' locos and a solitary 'N' Class, No 31839 were all eagerly witnessed. With this holiday, my tally of locos copped at the close of the year was 3,307 – 1,931 Midland, 665 Eastern, 264 Western, 64 Southern and 383 'Standards' and diesels. My

3,000th cop was No 6819 *Highnam Grange* on 8 August. On the same date, Leicester City were preparing for their first match (against Manchester United on the 24th) in the First Division, after winning the Division 2 title in April, ending 7 points ahead of local rivals Nottingham Forest. Arthur Rowley had

A ticket for a journey I made on 5 June 1957, for the grand price of 8d!

My holiday in Dawlish Warren in 1957 was one of the highlights of my young life, overawed as I was at the volume and variety of motive power and with almost everything I saw on the railway there being new to me. On one of our day trips, No 4037 *The South Wales Borderers* drifts into the wooden platform with a down train on 6 August 1957.

again been the league top scorer, with 44 goals in the 1956/57 season! Incredibly – and sadly – he was never selected to play for England!

In many ways 1958 proved to be a turbulent and eventful year, both on and off the railway. The Campaign for Nuclear Disarmament was officially launched on 17 February, at a meeting in Central Hall, Westminster, attended by 5,000 people, but a much darker event, however, occurred 11 days earlier, on 6 February, when the plane transporting players of

What will become No D5500, the first of a new class, is still Works No 71 at Brush Engineering, Loughborough, as finishing touches are made in August 1957. It was released to 30A (Stratford) shed just three months later. *Brush, MJS collection*

Manchester United – the famed 'Busby Babes' – crashed on its third attempt to lift off from the slush-covered runway at Munich-Tiem Airport. Returning from a European Cup match in Belgrade, the flight had stopped in Germany for refuelling, and 20 of the 44 people on board died. In March 1958, Elvis Presley was conscripted into the United States Army for a two-year stretch; for a fortnight from 23 August racial unrest surfaced in Nottingham, then between 29 August and 5 September greater tensions bubbled over in London, in what would become known as the Notting Hill Race Riots; 25 September saw the new Comet 4 jet airliner handed over to BOAC, enabling the establishment, from 4 October, of the first transatlantic flight from London to New York. This lead was short-lived, however, as Pan American World Airways had joined the club by the end of the month. On the ground, the first section of motorway –

the Preston Bypass, later to be part of the M6 – opened this year and construction of the M1 was gathering pace.

Although 'youth culture' was gaining ground and momentum, when the first LP chart appeared in *Melody Maker* on 8 November, it was filled with such delights as film and TV themes. The first No 1 was the soundtrack to *South Pacific* – a position it held for more than a year! 'Middle-of-the-road' Perry Como had two smash single hits – *Magic Moments* and *Catch a Falling Star* – largely due to his hugely popular TV show on UK television. Connie Francis had four hits, including *Who's Sorry Now*, but the biggest-selling artists, with their double-A side *All I Have to do is Dream* and *Claudette*, were the Everly Brothers. Cliff Richard had his first hit in October, and Duane Eddy his first UK hit in September, with *Rebel Rouser*, which enjoyed five weeks in the charts and reached a creditable No 19, after being the biggest-selling single in the summer in America. Other stand-out hits were Conway Twitty's *It's Only Make Believe* and *When* by the Kalin Twins – both enjoying five weeks at No 1. As well as savouring increasing musical highlights, I enjoyed seeing Leicester City survive in the First Division (by 1 point!), including two consecutive high-scoring home matches – 6-1 v Aston Villa on 8 February and 8-4 v Manchester City two weeks later! Arthur Rowley was again top scorer, but Jimmy Walsh scored four in the Manchester City match and was to become the top scorer the following season. By then Rowley had transferred to Shrewsbury Town after eight years, having scored 265 goals for Leicester, just eight short of Arthur Chandler's City record. Rowley is still the record-holder of the most goals scored in English league football – 434 from 619 games!

On the railways, yet another disaster happened when, on 30 January, ten were killed and 93 injured when the 6.35pm Fenchurch Street-Shoeburyness train (hauled by No 80079) ran into the rear of the 6.20pm Fenchurch Street-Thorpe Bay service, again in thick fog. The 'Bluebell Line', between Lewes and East Grinstead, closed on 17 March; a new station for Gatwick Airport opened on 28 May; North British-built

The very first photograph from my own camera, a very much more primitive one than dad's, shows No 48613 on a down mixed freight at Thurmaston on 29 September 1957, just days after transfer from Gorton to Toton. I still had a lot to learn photographically!

No D600 was delivered to Swindon Works on 14 January; a new Thornaby depot opened on 5 June; steam locomotive construction ceased at Crewe Works on 15 December when No 92250, the 7,331st to be built there over the 115 years since 1843, was released; and 1 October saw the first run of the 'Condor', the express freight service from Hendon to Gushetfaulds, hauled by the new 'Metrovicks' Nos D5700 and D5701. The last months of the year saw other new diesel types emerge, although the first main-line diesel to be withdrawn – No 10100 – was taken out of service in November. The writing was well and truly on the wall for steam.

After the summer holiday in Devon in 1957, spotting trips seemed somewhat mundane over the months into 1958, but all that was to change in April. On the 13th I was given a guided tour around 15C (Leicester Midland) shed, courtesy of a friend of Uncle Gordon. With the excitement and enthusiasm of being so 'close up and personal' with the engines present, I climbed aboard 28 of the 31 recorded, including highlights No 45641 *Sandwich* and visiting 'B1' No 61047. The following day diesel

One of my spotting memories was arriving at the Birdcage and seeing the diminutive No 41518, sadly on its way to Derby for scrapping. Though not taken by me, this view closely replicates my memory, as the loco is dwarfed by 'Crosti'-boilered No 92026 on an unknown date in 1958. No 41518 was withdrawn in February 1958 from Lower Darwen shed and is here already without coupling rods. *MJS collection*

A view from the tender of No 45064, looking towards Leicester (London Road) station on 13 April 1958, during my guided tour of 15C's shed and yard. *Doug Giles, MJS collection*

railcars began service in and around Leicester Midland station.

Just six days later, on 20 April, there was another AMR trip to London – by rail to 'the smoke', then coach to the various sheds … another magical experience. 73A (Stewarts Lane) was first, where I copped 55 out of 65 steam and two diesel shunters and delighted in seeing many exotic (to me) Southern locos, plus Nos 70004 *William Shakespeare*, buffed up and ready to haul the 'Golden Arrow', and 70014 *Iron Duke*. The former was about to leave the shed, and in his excitement David ran towards it. The group leader, affectionately known as 'Gumboot', was most concerned but, being mute and with a limp, was unable to stop the athletic youngster! The array of Pullman cars on show was also interesting.

70A (Nine Elms) was next, and just as enthralling. No 34002 *Salisbury* was the first loco seen, followed by another 66 cops, including three diesel shunters, out of the 72 on shed. Highlights here were Nos 73114 *Etarre*, 73118 *King Leodegrance*, 73110 *The Red Knight*, and 73113 *Lyonnesse* (with their straight nameplates fixed to the running plate), six 'King Arthurs', and my first 'Schools' – Nos 30907 *Dulwich*, 30904 *Lancing*, and 30903 *Charterhouse*. The next move continued the Southern theme, with a visit to 73B (Bricklayers Arms). Here it was 83 cops from 87 locos (!) and just four diesel shunters. Namers were scarcer here, with just two 'King Arthurs' – Nos 30777 *Sir Lamiel* (now happily in preservation) and 30798 *Sir Hectimere* – six 'Schools', and the rest Bulleid's 'WC/BB' Class 4-6-2s. Being punch-drunk with so many new Southern locos, it was something of a relief to next visit 14B (Kentish Town). Slightly fewer locos were present – 63 – and the excitement level was able to notch down a couple of degrees, as just over half were already known to me. I was pleased to cop the two diesel shunters, together with seven of Johnson's 3F 0-6-0s, some still with their condensing apparatus fitted. Just one 'Jubilee' was on shed, No 45576 *Bombay*.

Calmer and back on the coach, that was not to last long, with a short cross-London drive getting the adrenalin soaring once more at our last stop, 34A (King's Cross) shed. Despite my trips to Grantham I still copped 100 out of 118 on view! The gems here are too many to mention, but I was extremely pleased to cop No 60500 *Edward Thompson* and three 'A4s' – Nos 60013 *Dominion of New Zealand*, 60025 *Falcon*, and 60029 *Woodcock*.

I was a *very* happy 14-year-old by the end of the day, made even better by obtaining boxer Willie Pastrano's autograph on London Road station on our return! He was in town for a fight at Granby Halls the following day, which he won.

This was followed, later in the summer, by another visit to Nuneaton (still producing 44 cops!), then my first visit to a Derby Open Day. Famed amongst our local railway fraternity, I was keen to go. Taken by car by Uncle George, David, dad and myself were to taste the delights of this annual event on 30 August. Again the sheer number of locos seen, on Works, shed or in and around the station, at 164, is too many to list here, but highlights were cabbing No 70017 *Arrow*, seeing both Nos 10000 and 10001, *Thundersley*, D5700, D5001/2/3/4/5/8 – all on Works in various stages of construction – Nos 47003 and 47007, and logging a further 96 locos new to me. A total

The 'twins' were always favourites of mine but, of the two, I preferred No 10000. At Derby Works on 30 August 1958, it was in for attention during its allocation to Camden shed on the WCML. I now have an OO gauge model in my collection.

Left: Another view from the Derby Open Day of 30 August 1958 sees me posing at the cab door of No 70017 *Arrow*, resplendent in my school blazer! Note how everyone else is also in jackets – no sloppy dressing in those days! *Horace Stretton, MJS collection*

Below: My *abc Combined Volume*, Summer 1958 edition.

of 29 diesels were on display, including a batch of shunters due for delivery to Scotland, together with many steamers that were awaiting their final end.

Hardly had I had time to underline the new entries in my 'Combined' than I was off on another trip just eight days later. On 7 September 1958 I joined another AMR trip, this time to Leeds. An area way outside my normal sphere of access, I looked forward

to it with keen anticipation and was not disappointed. 55D (Royston) was first, with an eclectic mix of elderly and not so elderly utilitarian steam locos, including Nos 58066, 58197 and 58260, together with nine diesel shunters out of the total of 48 on shed. By comparison, 56A (Wakefield) was much more interesting, with 77 on view and including Nos 60131 *Osprey*, 61015 *Duiker*, 61040 *Roedeer*, 52044, 52133 and 52252, as well as a delightful bevy of 'Austerities' – 66 more to be underlined when I got back home. Then at 55C (Farnley Junction) 54 were present, including four rare (to us in Leicester) 'Jubilees', Nos 45581 *Bihar and Orissa*, 45646 *Napier*, 45695 *Minotaur* and 45708 *Resolution*. At 55A (Holbeck) were 55 more, with three 'Scots' captured for the first time, Nos 46112 *Sherwood Forester*, 46133 *The Green Howards* and 46145 *The Duke of Wellington's Regiment (West Riding)*; 55B (Stourton) yielded 30, with 20 cops; and finally 55E (Normanton) provided 43, with 35 cops including No 52461 and yet more 'Austerities'.

Five days later, on 13 September, the family had a long weekend away in Mablethorpe. Not much opportunity for spotting, but I did see and cop four – one MR and three ER examples – as well as noting the myriad of new diesel multiple units operating the local services. A sadly memorable part of this weekend, however, was on the way back home on Sunday the 14th, when the coach in which we were travelling was involved in a fatal road crash. We had hoped to sit on the rear seat but had been foiled by another family, meaning that we were midway up the coach. The rear of our coach was rammed from behind by another one, trying to move back into the stream of holiday traffic after an unwise overtaking attempt, and those on the rear seat perished.

By the end of the year my tally had risen to 4,148 – 2,277 MR, 768 ER, 271 WR, 237 SR and 595 'Standards' and diesels.

My 4,000th was No 46435 at Wakefield on 7 September. Leicester City ended the year with matches against Burnley, on consecutive days – Boxing Day and 27 December – both draws.

To reflect the increasing interest in and popularity of the electric guitar, instrumental records – some with other featured lead instruments – began to make inroads into the higher levels of the charts. *Hoots Mon* by Lord Rockingham's XI kicked off the trend, holding the No 1 spot for three weeks in November 1958. Between then and the end of 1963 (when the trend was effectively killed off by the Liverpool influence) the field was led by Duane Eddy (17 Top 20 hits), The Shadows (13, including No 1s for *Apache*, *Kon-Tiki*, *Wonderful Land* and *Dance On*), Russ Conway (12, including No 1s for *Side Saddle* and *Roulette*), Acker Bilk (8, with one No 1, *Stranger on the Shore*), and Johnny and the Hurricanes and Kenny Ball, with seven each.

Moving into 1959, much of the country was still reminiscent of Victorian times, with 14% of households with outside toilets, most with coal-fired heating and fewer than 10% owning a telephone, but no matter how else the year had started, for those of us of a certain generation, steeped in popular music, 3 February was a disastrous day – 'the day the music died'. In blizzard conditions, the small plane carrying Buddy Holly, Ritchie Valens and J. P. Richardson Jr ('The Big Bopper') crashed in Clear Lake, Iowa, cutting short the careers of three talented musicians. Nearly 60 years later, the day is still remembered. Elsewhere, on land in this country, Alec Issigonis's 'Mini' first appeared in August, followed by the opening of the M1 motorway in November. Raymond Chandler and Errol Flynn died, but Kirsty MacColl and Emma Thompson were born. *Ben-Hur* was the film of the year, garnering 11 Oscars, including one for Charlton Heston as Best Actor in a Leading Role; and the bestselling single was *Livin' Doll* by Cliff Richard, who also had another No 1 with *Travellin' Light*. In addition to this last title, two other records enjoyed seven weeks at No 1 – Elvis's *A Fool Such as I*, and *Only Sixteen* by Craig Douglas.

This year saw me complete my first year in the Sixth Form at Loughborough College School, after an accelerated stream taking GCE O Levels in just four years, but my studies did not interrupt my spotting outings. I had wanted to study English, French and Maths for A Level, with a view to going to university, but in those 'enlightened' days it was not permissible to study arts and sciences together, so I had to drop Maths, taking Art instead. This proved not to be a successful move! Elsewhere, something that would affect me within a few years was Barclays

Bank becoming the first UK bank to install a computer, while in Norwich a trial began of a mail delivery system incorporating what were dubbed 'postcodes'!

On the railways, the production of diesels was accelerating, from both BR and private manufacturers, a fact that I would notice as the year progressed, but, to the surprise of many, out-of-use No 41000 was restored at Derby Works and made available for special use. Also noted by me was the transfer away from Leicester of No 41268, having been an incumbent of 15C from new in September 1950. I had grown attached to the loco as it shunted stock around London Road station, and the move to 27A (Bank Hall) shed on 14 February was a very sad day. Another loco to which I was (perhaps not surprisingly) very attached was No 61665 *Leicester City*. I was sad when it was withdrawn in June 1959 and wrote to BR asking to buy one of the nameplates – splasher, ball and all. One was offered to me for £13 10s, but dad wouldn't lend me the money! To

One of my all-time favourite locomotives at Leicester, No 41268 was station pilot from new in September 1950 until transfer to Bank Hall shed in February 1959. It is seen here taking water alongside London Road station on 23 June 1955. Note the extensive sidings to the right, now buried under a car park! *Gerald Adams, MJS collection*

A booklet of diesel and other passenger services operating between Leicester and Nottingham (on both the Midland and Great Central routes) from 6 April 1959. *MJS collection*

DIESEL SERVICES

between

LEICESTER LONDON ROAD
and
NOTTINGHAM MIDLAND

Also

PASSENGER TRAIN SERVICES
between
LEICESTER CENTRAL
and
NOTTINGHAM VICTORIA

6th April, 1959 until further notice
SUBJECT TO ALTERATION
For full service between Nottingham Midland and
Trent see folder AD 266

AD 289

be fair, that was more than his weekly wage at the time! I have actually touched 'my' nameplate since, but the loss still hurts!

My first outing in 1959 was a trip to Crewe, on 4 April, just spending time on the station, without any effort to 'shed bash', but I was still graced by 98 locos, with 76 of them new to me. Highlights came with Nos 45596 *Bahamas*, WR 5167, 46221 *Queen Elizabeth*, 46200 *The Princess Royal*, five more 'Jubilees', five 'Patriots' and 41936. During the following week I went lineside at my favourite local bridge at Thurmaston to witness the 'Condor' freight, usually double-headed, and saw Nos D5708 with D5701 (on the 6th), D5707 and D5705 (the 8th), and D5712 and D5704 (the 12th). I was actually to see all 20 of the class during the summer.

10 May saw me on another AMR London trip and a visit to 30A (Stratford), two years and five days after my first exciting time there. The log this time was decidedly lower than previously, providing a total, including locos seen on the way, of 272 and, not surprisingly, only 151 copped. The diesel march was evident, with 53 of various types seen by the end of the shed visit, including Nos D8400-9, the complete class of North British Type 1s, less than a year old; Nos D5506/9/13/16/20/22/23/26, all less than 18 months old; Nos

40

One of my delights has always been sitting lineside, not knowing exactly what will come. This was especially so when new workings were introduced, such as the 'Condor' fast freight service between London (Hendon) and Glasgow (Gushetfaulds), which, in 1960, introduced the 'Metrovick' diesels to my local line. On 5 February of that year, two of the class – Nos D5705 and D5711 – pass Thurmaston but, surprisingly, on a Manchester-St Pancras express!

D203/5, just 12 months old; No D6105, a visitor from 34B (Hornsey) and destined to move to Scotland and be withdrawn at 65A (Eastfield) in 1968 and cut up by J. McWilliam at Shettleston; and the rarity No D0227. On the steam front, I was pleased to see Departmental No 43 (ex-68532), and Nos 61639 *Norwich City*, 61620 *Clumber*, 61651 *Derby County*, 61618 *Wynyard Park*, 61653 *Huddersfield Town*, 61636 *Harlaxton Manor*, and 61664 *Liverpool*, plus 70011 *Hotspur* and 70007 *Coeur-de-Lion*.

The rest of the trip could not maintain that standard but, with three other depots to call at, there still remained some delights. Next stop was 33A (Plaistow), my first (and only) visit there, which furnished me with 26 cops out of 30 on shed, most of them 'Standards', but I was pleased to make acquaintance with Nos 42500, 41981 and five 'Jinties'. 73B (Bricklayers Arms) was next and understandably, with my previous visit only 12 months earlier, I had only 25 cops out of 69 present, but two more 'Schools' were ticked off – Nos 30921 *Shrewsbury* and 30934 *St Lawrence* – and 'King Arthur' No 30800 *Sir Meleaus de Lile* was another pleasing sight. 70A (Nine Elms) was similar, with 33 cops from 68, including five 'WC/BBs', one 'Merchant Navy' – No 35014 *Nederland Line* – three 'King Arthurs', one 'Lord Nelson' – No 30855 *Robert Blake* – and one 'Standard 5' – No 73116 *Iseult*. The outing had produced 279 more numbers for me to underline.

June 1959 saw me on holiday for a week in Yarmouth, with mum and dad and Uncle Gordon and Auntie Dorothy. From memory, they had travelled over from Leicester in a 'bubble car' while we went by rail. As well as locos seen en route, I was treated to visits to the engine sheds in Yarmouth. Officially, 32D (South Town) was still (just) open – it closed on 2 November of that year – but 32E (Vauxhall) had ceased operations on 5 January and 32F (Beach) on 2 March, the latter in conjunction with the ending of passenger services on the South Lynn-Beach line the same day. However, No 61572 was on South Town on 8 June together with, over the week, Nos 68656, D2571, 70012 *John of Gaunt*, 61670 *City of London*, 62604, 62570, D2555, 61055, D5502, 70003 *John Bunyan*, 70005 *John Milton*, 70000 *Britannia* and 61971. A visit to Lowestoft on 10 June revealed Nos 65581, 69706, D2573, D2568, D2039, 65567 and Departmentals 41, 38, 39 and 40 (ex-68177, 68168, 68131 and 68173 respectively). A brief visit (in the bubble car!) to Caister on 8 June saw the station in its early months after closure and No 43145 there on inspection.

By this time David and I had often been joined by Les Wade, to form a 'Gang of Three'. David had first met Les in the Claremont Methodist Church 'Life Boys', but their friendship grew as David went to see his model railway layout. It didn't take much to introduce him to our spotting trips and an early one was to Brush Open Day in Loughborough on 8 July, where we saw new-builds Nos D5539-58, together with No 61161 on the Great Central line adjacent to the Falcon Works and No 61027 *Madoqua* at Leicester Central station. Happily, Leicester

The delightful-looking Caister station on 8 June 1959, just three months after closure, seen during my holiday to Great Yarmouth, transported there in Uncle Gordon's 'bubble car'!

Another view from the Yarmouth holiday. Two crew of DMU No E51298 engage in some deep conversation at Yarmouth (South Town) on 10 June 1959.

City had again managed (just – 19th out of 22) to stay in the First Division, with Aston Villa and Portsmouth being relegated. Over the summer they prepared for the new season, beginning on 22 August, away to West Ham United (and losing 3-0!), but with the help of their recent signing of goalkeeper Gordon Banks they were to improve over the 1959-60 season.

Eleven days on from Brush, I was to partake of another AMR trip, this time to the Birmingham area, starting with a call at 17B (Burton-on-Trent) on the way, which gave me 27 strangers out of a total of 61 present. Most of the former were ex-LMS 3Fs, but Nos 41532 and 41536 were bonuses. From there three of the next five sheds were pure Great Western and, as such, a goldmine of new sightings.

The long climb up the steep gradient to 84B (Oxley) was rewarded with 56 locos on shed, just five being not new to me. With express locos being predominantly 'Halls' and 'Granges', the mix included seven diesel shunters. Back into Wolverhampton, the next delight was my introduction to Stafford Road. I drooled over more 'Kings' and 'Castles' – my appetite whetted during the Dawlish Warren holiday – and was happy to cop 68 out of 76. Among those on view were Nos 6861 *Crynant Grange*, 6418, 5923 *Colston Hall*, 6964 *Thornbridge Hall*, 48349, 7008 *Swansea Castle*, 5947 *Saint Benet's Hall*, 42418, 5047 *Earl of Dartmouth*, 4990 *Clifton Hall*, 5031 *Totnes Castle*, 7929 *Wyke Hall*, 5022 *Wigmore Castle*, 5089 *Westminster Abbey*, 7015 *Carn Brea Castle*, 5088 *Llanthony Abbey*, 4078 *Pembroke Castle*, 6022 *King Edward III*, 5045 *Earl of Dudley*, 6001 *King Edward VII*, 5063 *Earl Baldwin*, 4918 *Dartington Hall*, 7900 *Saint Peter's Hall*, 6008 *King James II*, 4938 *Liddington Hall*, 6023 *King Edward II*, 6011 *King James I*, 73034, 5070 *Sir Daniel Gooch*, 7026 *Tenby Castle*, 5042 *Winchester Castle*, 82008 and 46524.

From there my adrenalin was allowed to fall from its spike with a visit to 1B (Bourneville). Here was a small haul of 19 cops out of 32 locos on show, with elderly Nos 58143, 58138, 58261 and 58168 of particular interest. This proved to be a slight respite, as the excitement quotient leapt once more as we reached 84E (Tyseley), my first visit, but a place to which I would return over the years. On this day my tally was 76 cops from 80 locos, predominantly freight, but with railcar No W17W, Nos 48738, 75005 and 75006, and a handful of named engines but, sadly, just one 'Castle', No 7014 *Caerhays Castle*.

The day ended with another relatively staid experience, back to the Midland Region and 3D (Aston), where 30 cops were had from 38, showing that although these were Midland Region locos, there was an operating apartheid between east and west Midlands. No 45548 *Lytham St Annes* was the only namer present but this was not new to me. Overall, including a short rail journey to end the day, the trip had produced a haul of 244 more for me to underline, and I was again a very happy spotter at the end of it.

The remaining five months of 1959 saw no let-up in my quest to capture as much of the remaining BR steam as possible, both with local outings and times spent at both Leicester Midland and Central stations, together with as much time as possible at the Thurmaston bridges. We 'Gang of Three' were now cycling to various nearby locations but still considered Grantham a trip too far. So on 21 August the visit was again by bus. This was to be another milestone for me, as I copped my 5,000th loco with the third one seen at our destination – No 63963. The last 1,000 had taken me precisely 350 days – an average of three a day! Despite this being my third visit to the area, I was still to be rewarded with 43 more cops and several Pullman cars that were new to me. Nos 60516 *Hycilla* and 60523 *Sun Castle* were delights, and No D203, the first of the class I had seen there, was a precursor of what was to come. Part of the day was spent on the platform, where, after chatting to the driver, I was allowed to climb into the cab of No 64213.

Two weeks later saw me, David, his friend Graham Reid and Graham's father on the train from Leicester (London Road) for a day trip to London, unusually double-headed by Nos 45656 *Cochrane* and 45576 *Bombay*. The day started well, with 15 cops from 43 seen on the journey to St Pancras, where I added another two from ten. After Graham's dad departed to go to an exhibition, we three lads made a quick skip across the road to King's Cross, where I garnered seven out of eight, including Nos 61652 *Darlington* and D5908. A real surprise was then to see – and cop – Nos 68982 and D3691 during our Underground journey to Liverpool Street! This location was the main target for the day and, despite having already been to 30A (Stratford) twice, 28 locos were still new to me, including three 'Britannias' and Nos 61641 *Gayton Hall*, D200 and D0226. After a happy few hours there, largely spent at the country end of the station and witnessing engines using the turntable, Nos D5315 and D5310 were copped during our Underground trip across London to reach Paddington. In only a brief stay the haul there was 18 out of 19 (!), not least including No 70016 *Ariel*. A quick pop into King's Cross again, on the way home, brought the delight of the first sight of 'Deltic'. The run back from St Pancras ticked off a further nine from 27, and another day ended with great satisfaction.

A glorious view of No 70013 *Oliver Cromwell* on the turntable at Liverpool Street station on 3 September 1959, during the visit there and to other stations within London by me in company with cousin David and friend Graham Reid. Happily the loco can still look this good, having passed into preservation after withdrawal. *David Richards*

While the last few days of the school's summer holiday, before returning for my second year in the Sixth Form, had been satisfyingly lucrative in respect of furthering my spotting ambition, the next trip, on 20 September, was to be a force majeure and one that will stick in the memory for many a long day! Yet another AMR-organised outing, but this time by rail, we were to travel to Swindon and Eastleigh, both Works and sheds. Originating at Nottingham Victoria, 'The Eastlindon Flyer' picked up David and me up at Leicester Central. We had been expecting an ER 'Director' 4-4-0 as motive power, but were very disappointed to see the train pull into Leicester behind a 'bog standard' 'B1', No 61188. This hauled us to Oxford, via a slight detour between Calvert and Claydon LNE Junction with No 41222 at the head, possibly due to engineering works on the more direct route via Banbury. A change of motive power at Oxford saw us head for Swindon behind No 7307. After arrival in the Wiltshire town, we passed through the station and into sidings alongside the Works complex, where we all detrained for the tour of the facility and thereafter on to the shed area.

One of the first sights was No 92212, literally brand new out of the Works and waiting for delivery to its first home, two weeks later, at 84C (Banbury). My notebook records 142 locos at the Works, in various stages of dress or undress, some being worked on and others awaiting their final end. Inside the Works it was interesting to see the progress on construction of Nos D811-818, the first-numbered to be released the following month, while D818 was not to see work for six months. All were named as they were released, becoming *Daring*, *Royal Naval Reserve 1859-1959*, *Diadem*, *Dragon*, *Druid*, *Eclipse*, *Foxhound* and *Glory* respectively. No 70022 *Tornado* and 70026 *Polar Star* were also present, as were Nos 1021 *County of Montgomery*, D602 *Bulldog*, just 10 months old, new-builds 92213-17, and a wide variety of ex-GWR loco types.

Moving over to the shed, 82C, we were treated to another 122 locos, all steam with the exception of Nos D3107, newly renumbered that month from 13107, D2087 and D600 *Active*,

Literally brand new and as yet undelivered, No 92212 shines in the sunshine of 20 September 1959 at Swindon Works. It was sent new to Banbury shed on 3 October, and became another BR 'Standard' loco to survive into preservation.

18 months old. After swarming like so many ants over the two locations and finally back on board, No 9740 was added to the head of the train to take us to Andover Junction, via Rushey Platt Junction, Swindon Town and the Midland & South Western Junction Railway route. Having dropped No 9740 at Andover, where we saw No 6309 in the station, the '4300' Class 2-6-0 then continued alone to Eastleigh.

No 76012 met our train in the station, then proceeded to negotiate the tracks into the Eastleigh Works sidings. Once more the ants swarmed, first into the Works complex, where we feasted on 41 locos, including four 'Merchant Navies', seven 'WC/BBs', No 30859 *Lord Hood*, several 'Standards' and the elderly and preserved Adams 'T3' 4-4-0 No 563 and 'Terrier' *Boxhill*. Thence on to the shed (71A), where the trawl over the much wider geographical area was to present 136 engines. Here the predominance was 'King Arthurs' (18) and 'Lord Nelsons' (nine from a class of just 16), with just one 'Schools'

(No 30913 *Christ's Hospital*), three Bulleid 'Light Pacifics' and no 'Merchant Navies'. For those of us based further north, however, other tasty morsels were Nos 73119 *Elaine*, 'E4s' 32579 and 32556, representatives of the 'T9' and '700' classes, plus the sole electric on view, No 20001 – a 1941-vintage design by Raworth and Bulleid. Among the handful of non-steam were four consecutively numbered shunters – D3011, D3013 and the other two interestingly still bearing their original numbers, 13012 and 13014. All new to 73C (Hither Green) in 1952, these latter two were not renumbered until February and December 1960 respectively. The return journey was a reverse of the outward run but there was little opportunity for further spotting, apart from a handful of locos noted as we passed Swindon, for most of the journey home was in the dark! However, the day was an unmitigated success and certainly one of *the* highlights of my life to that point.

Thereafter, 1959 ended with just two outings. The first, on 26 September, was the best part of a day spent on Leamington Spa station platform, with David, while our families gathered

No 6009 *King Charles II* waits for the 'right away' at Leamington Spa station at the head of the up 'Cambrian Coast Express' on 26 September 1959, during the day that David and I spent spotting while the rest of the family attended a wedding! Allocated at that time to Wolverhampton (Stafford Road), it moved to Old Oak Common three years later, from where it was withdrawn just four months after that, on 9 February 1963. *David Richards*

elsewhere in the town for a family wedding celebration. We did not mind missing that event and I delighted in copping no fewer than 40 locos, there being only three that I had seen before! Just over a year old, No 92233 was a welcome sight shortly after we had taken up position at the London end of the down platform, immediately followed by No 6009 *King Charles II*. A further 'King' – No 6005 *King George II* – came by two-thirds of the way through our stay, with a variety of 'Halls', other ex-GWR engines – more 'Kings' but only two 'Castles' – 'Standards' and four ex-LMS locos. It was dark by the time our parents came to collect us, but we were still somewhat disappointed to leave!

A third trip to Rugby, on 3 November, was the last we would make by rail before the line from Leicester closed. A little surprisingly, considering previous visits there and to Nuneaton, I still copped 44 on this trip, but 17 of these – Nos D8000 and D8001 plus 15 English Electric Type 4s – were witness to the influx of a greater number of diesels than we had encountered before. Again taking the opportunity to stay on the platform, I cabbed No D232, the only diesel on which I would enjoy this luxury for many years to come. By the time of this later trip, 15C (Leicester Midland) had taken delivery of its first four diesels – shunters Nos D3785-88 – on 24 October. This caused great local excitement and much speculation, but still no one sensed what they presaged – the beginning of the end of steam at the shed and on our main line. Seeing them brand new standing next to elderly visitor No 62612 was fascinating and incongruous.

The close of the year saw me with 5,735 numbers towards my target, with the accumulation of nearly 1,600 over the previous 12 months being evenly spread throughout the regions, with the exception of the Southern, which had grown by only 160. Leicester City had only lost 10 out of 24 matches and were roughly midway in the First Division, their highest position since the 1937/38 season! Adam Faith's *What Do You Want* was top of the charts over Christmas, but Anthony Newley was hot on his heels with *Why*, which would take over

An important day for 15C, with its first allocation of diesels. Shunters Nos D3785-88 stand in line, together with far more ancient No 62612 on 24 October 1959, with Nos 44189, 44743 and 44984 elsewhere in the yard. *Les Wade, MJS collection*

in mid-January 1960. Duane Eddy continued to fly the flag for instrumentals, being in the Top 10 with *Some Kinda Earthquake*. The experience of and disappointments with my photographs in London and at Leamington had led me to see the very real disadvantages of my Brownie camera. Happily, the year-end would have a highlight for me, as Father Christmas brought me a new Halina A1 camera. Admittedly still with a fixed shutter speed, which I had long discovered severely limited my lineside shots if trains were travelling at any appreciable speed, this took a 120 film, giving me much larger negatives and a greatly improved focal length. The results were much more to my liking, which was just as well, as the effects of both dieselisation and electrification on the WCML were beginning to be felt at my vantage point in Leicestershire.

The end of November saw the allocation of 'Royal Scot' Nos 46100 *Royal Scot* and 46157 *The Royal Artilleryman* to 16A (Nottingham) shed and these, together with rarer 'Jubilees' and 'Patriots', meant that it was even harder to prize me away from the lineside! Sadly, I still had not learned the photographic skills needed – which had been taught to me by my father, who had been a photographer during the war! I still expected to just point the camera, shoot and all would be well. I had to learn quickly.

As 1960 began, we were all blissfully unaware that this would be a decade that would dramatically change not just the UK but much of the wider world as well. Part of it was the progressive dismantling of colonialism, with Prime Minster Harold Macmillan describing a 'wind of change blowing through Africa', but the growing influence and demands of teenagers in both Britain and the USA was to wreak what some saw as havoc. Being 16 at the start of the year, I was feeling some of the hormonal pressures, but at that time our generation was still very much under the strictures of the older generations. A harbinger of what was to happen began the previous year, with the passing of the Obscene Publications Act 1959. This led to the publication of D. H. Lawrence's *Lady Chatterley's Lover* in 1960 and the successful defence towards the end of the year against the 'trial of Penguin' for obscenity. This would in turn lead to the arrival of more racy and/or earthy novels, plays, films, etc. In Royal circles, Prince Andrew was born on 19 February and the wedding of Princess Margaret and Anthony Armstrong-Jones took place at Westminster Abbey on 6 May, while in politics Aneurin Bevan, post-war Labour Minister of Health, died on 6 July, in Chesham, Bucks. An announcement in January, which has been controversial ever since, was the demolition of the 70-foot-high, 1838-vintage Doric Arch at Euston, as part of the trumpeting of the modernisation of the ex-LNWR terminus.

Musically, the year's biggest-selling single was the Everly Brothers' *Cathy's Clown*, being No 1 from April to June. In previous months the top spot was enjoyed by Adam Faith (*Poor Me* in February for one week), Johnny Preston (*Running Bear* in March for two weeks), and Lonnie Donegan (*My Old Man's a Dustman* for five weeks in March-April). In the long-player field, the soundtrack of *South Pacific* was No 1 for 47 weeks! And for the first time, EPs sold well enough to enter the singles charts – Cliff Richard's *Expresso Bongo* and Elvis's *Strictly Elvis*.

On the railway front, 4 January saw the withdrawal of through trains from Marylebone to Manchester, Sheffield and Bradford on the erstwhile Great Central Railway; No 92220

Evening Star was the last BR steam loco built, released on 18 March at Swindon Works; and new diesel depots were opened at Finsbury Park, with a code of 34G, on 24 April and Neville Hill (55H) on 17 June. No D210 became the first of its class to be named – *Empress of Britain* – on 12 May at Euston; the first BRCW Type 3s (later to become Class 33) appeared; and a record number of locos entered service in the year – 813 new diesels and electrics – including the first of what would become Classes 82, 83 and 84 (although 1,184 steam were to disappear).

This was also a year of passenger route closures, even before Doctor Beeching had arrived on the scene. 4 January saw a batch go – Northampton (Castle)-Market Harborough, Bala-Blaenau Ffestiniog and Newbury-Lambourn – followed by Newbury-Southampton (7 March) and Seaton-Uppingham and The Mound-Dornoch (13 June). On a far happier note, the Bluebell Railway heritage line ran its first train on 7 August, becoming the world's first preserved standard-gauge steam-operated railway, on a line – East Grinstead to Lewes – that had closed barely more than two years earlier.

This year BR's Works sites were becoming unable to cope with the scrapping of the literally hundreds of steam locos being withdrawn, and the fitting of all remaining engines with speedometers. No 45609 *Gilbert and Ellice Islands*, allocated to 14B (Kentish Town) for its entire BR life, became the first 'Jubilee' to face withdrawal, from 13 August, but others would meet the same fate the following year.

While I had not been overly disappointed with the trips I had been on, I was becoming a little irritated that the organisers were often not going to places that attracted me, so I formulated the idea of The Thurmaston Railway Society (TRS), a group that planned to go to new locations. It did not make it off the drawing board until 1961, so I continued joining other spotters, including trips to Manchester on 21 February 1960. I took my new camera with me and hoped for decent results!

Taking a somewhat devious route, our first stop was 17C (Rowsley)! The 32 engines on show were of varying shapes and sizes and 14 were new to me. Thankfully, despite the time of year and the reputation for snow in the higher climes of the Derbyshire Peak District, the weather was kind and we even saw several periods of sunshine. 9D (Buxton) was next, with a similar-sized presence, but I was to capture more new numbers here – 26 out of 36. Particular delights were Nos 41908, 41905 and 41906, plus several ex-LNWR 7F 0-8-0s (of both classes). 9B (Stockport) had 34 on show, with a diesel this time – No D3772 – and a slightly greater percentage of passenger types. 9F (Heaton Mersey) displayed more – 51 locos – but sadly only 21 were new to me. I was, however, pleased to see a number of Fowler and Stanier Class 3 2-6-2Ts – Nos 40059, 40089, 40113, 40124, 40001, 40057 and 40004 – plus a surprise, No 64747, which was allocated to Gorton! Being a football fan, I was aware of the name Old Trafford – home of Manchester United – so was pleased to visit 9E (Trafford Park) shed, so close to the ground; here there were 44 locos on duty, again with just one diesel – No D5070 – together with more Class 3 2-6-2Ts and Nos 65194 and 65166. 26F (Patricroft) presented 68, with one 'Jubilee' – No 45600 *Bermuda* – a wide range of freight and passenger types, three diesel shunters and, a real delight, No ED1 – a 1936 Fowler diesel 0-4-0! 9A (Longsight) was the place we really wanted see and the best was left until last, with 56 locos of a real mix that included Nos 45680 *Camperdown* and 41907, more Class 3 2-6-2Ts, No 40674 – and No E3002, my first electric. On the day, out of 323 seen, I had copped 212.

On Saturday 12 March 1960 I played cricket for LCS against a team from a Derby school. We were 'away', playing the match in Derby, on a ground that was bordered on one side by the railway line out of Derby Friargate. What with trying to concentrate on the match, whether fielding or batting, as well as the 'cleanliness' of the locos on the line, it was difficult to collect numbers and I was only successful with one – No 64405 of Goole shed – when fielding on the boundary! I am glad I did see it, however, as it was withdrawn two months later.

Eight days later, on Sunday 20 March, I went with mum and dad to the DeMontfort Hall in Leicester to see 'The Biggest Package Show Ever'! Headlined by Bobby Darin (his first visit to the UK), the show also featured Clyde McPhatter (who I was very impressed with) and Emile Ford and the Checkmates, but the main reason for me to go was to see Duane Eddy live (on his first tour of the UK). I was bowled over by his performance and also by briefly meeting him in the scrummage at the Stage Door afterwards. To counter B. B. King, the thrill has never left me from seeing Duane play on stage.

May was to see us twice cycling to Rugby, on the 6th and 22nd, my fourth and fifth visits. In the relatively short time spent alongside the line, both opposite the north end of the platforms and to the south of the Great Central bridge, 45 and 44 locos respectively were seen, with 27 and 20 being new to me, including Nos 61052 and 64669 across the GC bridge on the second visit. Five more 'Patriots' were gathered into my net over the two dates, as well as two 'Scots', one 'Jubilee' – No 45702 *Colossus* – and one 'Princess Royal' – No 46209 *Princess Beatrice*. I had taken my camera with me on the first visit but only snapped one picture, of No 45503 *The Royal Leicestershire Regiment* hauling a freight on the northbound avoiding line, close to where we were sitting on the wall. I was to learn a valuable lesson with that shot, however, as I forgot to wind on the film, so the next shot – of 'K3' No 61880 at Thurmaston, on a special from Peterborough – was superimposed onto the 'Patriot', spoiling both! From the look of the negative, both would have been decent views! Whether this had any effect on me, I am not sure, but on the next outing, to Crewe by rail on 27 July, I left the camera at home. A stupid decision but, thankfully, Les had taken his.

This was to prove another 'grand day out', with views of 23 locos as we arrived at and departed from Derby, 30 at Stoke, six at Alsager and 32 in and around Crewe station, before we made our way to the Works. This provided yet another basket of delights – 140 locos, a mix of old and new, awaiting attention or scrap, and a collection of 'Peaks' in the process of construction. Only two namers were new to me – Nos 46220 *Coronation* and 45647 *Sturdee* – but the wide variety elsewhere more than made up for this.

In steam days rakes of carriages were stabled in sidings to the north of Syston station, alongside the large triangle of lines. On 11 April 1960 No 46123 *Royal Irish Fusilier* ambles past Thurmaston with such a rake of empties, on their way to enter service at Leicester.

Just four days later I went with mum, dad, Gordon and Dorothy to Belgium for two weeks based at Ostend. Strangely, Les's parents had also booked the same trip for the same two weeks! We spent many hours together and saw several Belgian trains as we went out and about, including a total of three steam locos, but they did not hold our interest. However, the young lady manning the pitch-and-putt course did hold our interest, but neither Les nor I were able to sufficiently use our schoolboy French to impress her!

Two days after our return, the 'Gang of Three' made yet another trip to Rugby – my sixth – again by bike and, rather surprisingly, I copped another 31, still predominantly steam! No 13169 still bore its original number, despite having been officially renumbered in February 1959, and Nos 60876 and 61060 were surprising appearances, as were Nos D2153-5, brand new from Swindon and officially allocated to 50A (York)! Three days after this, my fourth trip to Grantham trawled another 32 cops, including Nos 60048 *Doncaster*, 60504 *Mons Meg*, 60112 *St Simon*, 60040 *Cameronian*, 60119 *Patrick Stirling*,

60065 *Knight of Thistle* and 60067 *Ladas*. This time I did take my camera with me.

My final major outing before a return to school (and, indeed,

Several of my days at Rugby were spent alongside the main line just north of the station, where No D212, without any yellow front-end adornment and still un-named, pauses with a Euston-Carlisle express on 6 May 1960. It became *Aureol* four months later.

At other times, part of the day at Rugby would be spent to the south of the station, close to the massive Great Central overbridge. Also seen on 6 May 1960, No 45537 *Private E. Sykes VC* approaches this structure – out of picture to the left – with a northbound special.

my last before 1961) was to another Derby Open Day, on 27 August. By rail this time, I had already copped eight before entering the Works (two at Leicester and six while on Derby station), including No 45504 *Royal Signals*. Thereafter, I recorded 260 around the Works yards and inside the buildings, of which 122 were totally new to me. New-builds included Nos D5129-31/35-42/44-46, D12-16/19-21 and D3986-92/94-D4002, with other delights for me including Nos D232 and D234, ED2 and ED6, 47000, D4 *Great Gable*, 45519 *Lady Godiva*, 41900, 40047, 40489, 40652 and 41734. On shed, there were another 60 locos (offering 24 cops, including No 45572 *Eire*), and here were the missing Nos D5132-34, D3993 and D17/18, plus 40005. This completed a marathon effort to capture as much as possible over the school holidays.

Thus ended five hectic spotting years, which had produced No 64745 at Leicester Central on 26 March 1960 as my 6,000th loco, made a total at the end of August of 6,434 – 3,073 MR, 1,093 ER, 695 WR, 384 SR and 1,189 diesels and electrics – an average of 1,287 per year, or 3½ per day!

Top left: Locos rare to the area were especially welcome during any spotting trip to my local line. On 14 August 1960 No 45120 of Carlisle (Kingmoor) shed is hundreds of miles from its home as it trudges south past Thurmaston with a down freight. Prior to December 1952 it had worked out of Inverness shed!

Bottom left: Part of the attraction of Grantham was the changing of locos on ECML expresses. On 19 August 1960 No 60067 *Ladas* drifts slowly through the station ready to take over a southbound express for King's Cross.

Chapter 2
1960-1965

My next outing was not until the following year – apart from a brief weekend in Blackpool for the lights, over 24/25 September 1960. I visited 24E (Blackpool South) on the 25th but in the dark, and was thus disappointed to only be able to record 16 numbers, although 12 were cops, including Nos 45653 *Barham* and 45584 *North West Frontier*. In other spheres, however, there were notable events prior to the end of the year.

On 10 September 1960 the very last slip coach operation on BR took place, on the Western Region at Bicester North; suffragette campaigner Sylvia Pankhurst died on 27 September, aged 78; on 29 October Cassius Clay (later Muhammad Ali) made his professional debut, after winning the Light Heavyweight gold medal in the 1960 Rome Olympics; and Clark Gable died on 16 November. Back on the railways, on 25 October, in thick fog and subject to a strong tide, two barges overshot Sharpness Dock and rammed one of the columns of the Severn railway bridge, causing two spans of the cast-iron structure to fall into the river, thus severing the line from Lydney to Sharpness and leading to the closure of the route; 7 November saw the introduction of Glasgow's famed 'Blue Trains', on the North Clydeside services; 2 December heralded a new era as No D6700 emerged from English Electric's Vulcan Foundry; and just five days later, at just 10 years old, the iconic Brown-Boveri Gas Turbine locomotive No 18000 was withdrawn from service – happily it was to be preserved.

If I had to choose a favourite year from my life, 1961 would certainly be one of the candidates. I would turn 18 in August, after leaving school the previous month; I would start work (twice), the second time with Barclays Bank in October, earning my first serious money; Duane Eddy was voted the World's Top Pop Personality in a poll for *New Musical Express*, ahead of Elvis Presley; the opposite sex was taking more of my time; and, for Leicester City, the season was going well, with the last two matches of the year at home being wins against Bolton Wanderers (2-0 on Boxing Day) and Everton (4-1 on New Year's Eve), then going one better in the first home match of 1961, 6-0 against Manchester United on 21 January! The team remained unbeaten from Boxing Day 1960 to 11 March 1961, when they suffered a defeat, 1-0, away to West Bromwich Albion; *and* they were in the Final of the FA Cup, for the first time since 1949 and for only the second time ever.

I graduated from Loughborough College School in the summer of 1961. I had been promoted to Prefect for my last scholastic year and proudly wore this insignia on the breast pocket of my school jacket, which was black to denote status, as opposed to the maroon of the rest of the school.

1961 started with Johnny Tillotson in the middle of a three-week stint at No 1 with *Poetry in Motion*, but the year's best-selling single was *Runaway* by Del Shannon, despite only being at No 1 for one week (twice) in May and June. This was the first of eight Top 20 hits for the singer between 1961 and 1965. Elsewhere, Russia was ahead in the space race, putting Yuri Gagarin into orbit in April, and the Cold War intensified with the building of the Berlin Wall. As an indicator of what would become the 'Swinging Sixties', on 4 December 1961 Enoch Powell, then Minister of Health, announced that the oral contraceptive pill could be prescribed through the NHS. The deaths were announced of George Formby (6 March), Gary Cooper (13 May) and

Ernest Hemingway (2 July), while the film of *West Side Story* was released on 18 October, winning ten Oscars.

Innovation on the railways saw No GT3 emerge from Vulcan Foundry in May and undertake testing on the former Great Central main line between Leicester and Marylebone, and the first automatic level crossing barriers began operation at Spath, near Uttoxeter in Staffordshire, in May. The first two production 'Deltics', Nos D9000 *Royal Scots Grey* and D9001 *St Paddy*, were released from Vulcan Foundry in February, and allocated respectively to 64B (Haymarket) and 34G (Finsbury Park) to cover running from the two ends of the ECML. On 16 May Beyer Peacock's No D7000 was formally handed over to BR (WR) at Paddington, but what turned out to be not such good news was the appointment of Dr Richard Beeching as Chairman of the British Transport Commission on 1 June. Passenger services were withdrawn between Buckingham and Banbury (Merton Street) on 2 January, Woofferton and Tenbury Wells on 31 July, and Ashchurch and Upton-on-Severn on 14 August, and the Midland & South Western Junction Railway route was closed from 11 September.

The early months of the year were spent on intensified study for my A Levels in the summer, but a break was had on 15 April,

Over the years the UK's railways have provided many surprises. One of the most unusual was the trialled introduction of light-brown-liveried No GT3 on the ex-Great Central main line between Leicester and Marylebone. Distinctly steam-loco-shaped, it stands under the sheerlegs at Leicester Central shed on 21 May 1961, when new. It failed to impress, however, and was withdrawn in October 1962 and cut up in February 1966. *Les Wade, MJS collection*

when Dave, Les and I cycled again to Rugby (my seventh trip). Whereas David and I had bikes with gears and could cope with the undulating topography of the 22-mile trip, Les had an old butcher's bike, with a basket on the front, a fixed wheel and no gears and, to make matters worse, the pedal crank was faulty, leading to constant slipping. We would wait at the tops of hills for him to catch us up, then enjoy the spectacle of him going up and down, like a carousel horse, on his fixed wheel! Upon arrival I copped unnamed 'Patriot' No 45551, 'Jubilee' No 45559 *British Columbia* and No 58120, but roughly half of services were now diesel-hauled, leading to Les and myself becoming a little bored. We invented a railway game, etched in biro on the face of a handy poster board alongside where we were spotting. We considered it a good game and had visions of submitting it to Waddington's ... but, somehow, we never managed it!

Personal excitement at this time was seeing Leicester City through to the final of the FA Cup. They played Tottenham Hotspur – that season's League Champions – at Wembley on 6 May but, sadly, the opponents were just too strong. In front of an audience of 99,133, City's redoubtable right back Len Chalmers was badly injured in the 19th minute. With no substitutes in those days, he stayed on the pitch for another 60 minutes but was a virtual passenger on the left wing. Against effectively 10 men, Spurs did not score until the 67th minute, but then took control of the match, emerging winners by 2-0. This appearance did, however, earn City a place in the following season's European Cup Winners' Cup.

Another 22-mile cycle ride to Rugby took place on 22 May, when the weather was as uninspiring as the railway fare, but I did at least capture cops with Nos 61154 and 5966 *Ashford Hall* on the GC overbridge at the southern end of the station. In the midst of the exam period I grabbed the opportunity to attend the Brush Open Day in Loughborough on 3 June, copping Nos D0280 and 61941 (the latter again on the GC route) and new-build Nos D5801-19. Though not a cop, I was interested to see No 46141 *The North Staffordshire Regiment* roar past the works on the Midland line with a southbound express. By now, with 17A (Derby) shed receiving large numbers of brand new

At the Brush Engineering Open Day on 3 June 1961, prototype No D0280 on show, only part way through its construction. Adorned with a *Falcon* nameplate, it emerged into the light, initially on loan, in October. It was finally bought by BR in December 1970 and allocated to Finsbury Park. Withdrawal came in October 1975, at Ebbw Junction depot, with nearby Cashmore's Newport scrapyard disposing of it by March 1976.

Another engine on display at the Open Day was No 10800. Originally built as a prototype by North British Co Ltd in July 1950, it had a chequered and none too successful career. Eventually withdrawn from Rugby by BR in August 1959, it was bought by Brush for development of AC traction equipment and was graced with the name *Hawk*. It was cut up in May 1976.

A sign of the times. Brand new from Crewe and on its way to Derby, its first allocation, No D105 stands in 15C's yard on Sunday 18 June 1961, amid Nos 43861, 44156, D3786, 44519, 43937, 58137 and 44814. *Les Wade, MJS collection*

'Peaks', it was a case of copping a new one virtually every time I ventured again and again to my favourite bridge.

A month later my exams were out of the way, for good or ill, and I 'celebrated' by attending another Derby Open Day, on 2 July, accompanied by David and another friend, Peter Lightfoot. At the station, shed and Works on this day I was confronted with a total of 185 locos, of which 74 were fresh sightings. Among the highlights were No 41173, tucked away in a woodyard adjacent to the station together with 43787, providing the opportunity for a cab visit; No 11114 still with its original number, to become D2213 within days; new-build Nos D35-52; and Nos 41835, 41103 and 61039 *Steinbok*.

A month later, on 5 August Rugby was again the destination, this time by rail, as the line from Leicester was due to close within four months. Cops this time were predominantly the latest crop of diesels, but steam still gave bonuses, in the shape of Nos 61011 *Waterbuck* and 61449 on the GC, and 45593 *Kolhapur*. Two days later came a lineside outing to Essendine with David, with Uncle George as chauffeur. There were a few cops, again mostly diesel, but one delight of the day was No 60024 *Kingfisher* roaring south on 'The Elizabethan', the Edinburgh–King's Cross non-stop express, during the last year that it was steam-hauled. We thrilled to a galaxy of Gresley express passenger locos, speeding up and down the bank and, despite their threat to our beloved steam, we also enjoyed the sight of Nos D9005 *The Prince of Wales's Own Regiment of Yorkshire* and D9007 *Pinza*.

On 12 August there was real excitement for the 'Gang of Three', though none of us would at first believe it! Standing at my favourite bridge I watched a 'Scot' approach at speed from the north. As it rushed under the bridge, shrouding me in steam, I thought I had seen the number as 46121 *Highland Light Infantry, City of Glasgow Regiment* but, allocated to 66A (Glasgow Polmadie), surely I must have been mistaken. I cycled home convinced I was wrong but, unbeknown to me, Les was by the lineside in Leicester, 4 miles to the south, and saw the train continuing on its journey. He, too, doubted his eyes and went home unsure. Meanwhile, some time later David was on a train coming back to Leicester from London and had his head out of the carriage window. He saw the 'Scot' approach, at a greater closing speed, saw the number and thought, 'No, it can't be!' So we all went to bed that night convinced that we had not seen a ghost! How happy we were when we met up on the following day, each telling his story and each becoming convinced that we had indeed since this rarity. Later, the local grapevine confirmed our apparent apparition and the underlining was done with due solemnity.

Amazingly, the following day, 13 August, it happened again! We had planned to meet up at the Birdcage but, Les being late, David and I went to the sheds. On the sloping approach road we were passed by a 'Scot' on the main line, which, in the half light of late dusk, we thought looked like No 46102 *Black Watch*. While the two of us were discussing it, Les caught up with us. A

Left top: Until the electrification of the West Coast Main Line, 'Scots' were not common through Leicester. This was to change as the 1960s progressed, but No 46106 *Gordon Highlander* was always a delight to see, with its straight smoke deflectors, unique for this class. It is seen on Wellingborough shed in August 1961, when briefly allocated to Derby. *MJS collection*

Left bottom: The gem from our day's excursion to Essendine: in its last year of steam haulage, the non-stop 'Elizabethan' express hurries south behind No 60024 *Kingfisher* on 7 August 1961. A Haymarket loco for most of its BR life, its end came from Aberdeen (Ferryhill) in September 1966.

triple chorus of 'Did you see the "Scot"?' was answered by Les, who could confirm the identification, as he had seen it from the Birdcage and the number had been clearer under the lights in the shed yard. Two 66A 'Scots' in two days – what on earth was the reason? We have never found out. However, despite all this excitement, it was the rest of the month of August that was to go to make the year so special.

In the interim between school and full-time employment (and having completed the four weeks of my first work, helping to build a new sewage treatment plant at Wanlip, between Birstall and Syston, comprising tasks alongside Irish navvies!), I was to embark, in company with David and Les, on holidays to two distant points of the UK compass – to Devon and into Cornwall (19-26 August) and Scotland (30 August-1 September). In retrospect, our timing was good, as within a year so many of the locos we were to see had disappeared and, travelling by rail throughout, apart from the occasional bus and plenty of leg work, we were often scribbling furiously to capture all that we passed. The first day – 19 August – was especially satisfying, collecting 236 numbers and copping 147 as we passed through or by Nuneaton, Saltley, Bromsgrove, Gloucester and Bristol behind No 45280. We were then pulled by Nos 6908 Downham Hall and 4935 Ketley Hall to Taunton and No 4914 Cranmore Hall thence to Dawlish, where we alighted. The day was not complete yet, though, for, armed with our week-long 'Holiday Runabout Ticket' (price £1 2s 6d!), we made short journeys, hauled progressively by Nos 7924 Thornycroft Hall, D805 Benbow, D848 Sultan and 5906 Lawton Hall. 'Tired but happy' would be an appropriate description of our condition that evening!

The following day began with us taking the train to Plymouth, behind No 4975 Umberslade Hall to Newton Abbot and No D6326 to North Road station. From there, using our trusty shed directory, we made our way to 83D (Laira) shed and recorded Nos 5084 Reading Abbey, 4658, 5532, 4679, 5511, 6873 Caradoc Grange, 5053 Earl Cairns, 5572, 4561, 3806, 5560, 6400, 6771, 3862, 7316, 3686, 6301, D2129 (my 7,000th cop),

Top: On our way to an exciting Devon and Cornwall holiday, we are passed by No 4079 *Pendennis Castle*, climbing out of Bristol with a parcels train on 19 August 1961. *David Richards*

Above left: My Holiday Runabout Ticket for the week 19-25 August 1961, giving free run of the railway for the princely sum of £1 2s 6d!

Above right: Our first day in the West and my first Class 'Z' 0-8-0T loco. No 30956 pauses between banking duties up to Central station and acts as station pilot at Exeter (St David's) on 19 August 1961.

4984 *Albrighton Hall*, D6320, D6309, D6304, D841 *Roebuck*, D866 *Zebra*, D6305, D6307, D6321, D6318, D6315, 2834, 4955 *Plaspower Hall*, 3787, 6932 *Burwarton Hall*, 3804, 6938 *Corndean Hall*, 2899, 6972 *Beningbrough Hall*, 1363 and 5069 *Isambard Kingdom Brunel*. Thence to 83H (Plymouth Friary), where we were greeted by 18 locos, of which 16 were new to me, including Nos 11227, 11229 and 11225. Our brief visit to this western outpost of Devon was then over, as we travelled back to Dawlish behind No D602 *Bulldog*.

21 August saw us at 72A (Exmouth Junction) – 30 cops from 51, including Nos 35025 *Brocklebank Line*, 30953 and 30957 – then 83C (Exeter) – 14 from 22 – and a fleeting visit to Newton Abbot station, where, including a view across to the shed area, a further 20 numbers entered the book, 14 for the first time. The following day was spent relaxing in Dawlish,

During a visit to Laira shed in Plymouth on 20 August 1961, the diminutive No 1363 was a pleasing sight among plenty of big green WR locos. Built in 1910, it was sadly withdrawn 18 months later but was to find salvation in preservation at Didcot.

before, on the 23rd, we were back to 72A, this time copping five 'Merchant Navies', and a ride back behind No 34002 *Salisbury*. The 24th was a longer trip, being double-headed by the both very new Nos D851 *Temeraire* and D852 *Tenacious*. 83G (Penzance) shed was sparsely occupied for our visit, but it did present three 'Grange' cops – Nos 6854 *Roundhill Grange*, 6870 *Bodicote Grange* and, for me more importantly, 6800 *Arlington Grange*. Our penultimate day featured a day out at Torquay, pulled to Newton Abbot by No 5994 *Roydon Hall*, then, rather surprisingly, by Nos 5020 *Trematon Castle* and 6839 *Hewell Grange* to Torquay!

And so to home on 26th, behind the wings of No D835 *Pegasus* from Dawlish to Bristol. No 44841 then took over the task of transporting us through Gloucester, Bromsgrove (with No 8402 as a banker up the Lickey Incline) to Birmingham.

Our furthest point south on this holiday was Penzance. On 24 August 1961 the smart looking No 6800 *Arlington Grange* stands alongside the coaling stage, ready for its next call to duty. *David Richards*

Another change of train saw us behind No 61318 to Leicester. No 45668 *Madden* was a welcome sight at New Street station. The trip resulted in a grand haul of 434 cops from the 659 locos seen.

With barely time to draw breath, have a meal and a change of underwear, we three again met up at Leicester (London Road) station on 30 August, David's birthday, to catch our overnight train to Carlisle, behind No D87 to Leeds, via Derby and Sheffield, then No D13 to our destination via the Settle & Carlisle line. Needless to say, being overnight, we did not see much of this iconic route or, indeed, any of the journey, so the consequent haul of numbers was distinctly limited. Before leaving Citadel station, however, we were cheered by the sight of Nos 72008 *Clan Macleod* (my first 'Clan'), 46222 *Queen Mary* and 45731 *Perseverance*. Little time was lost in making our way, on foot, to 12B (Upperby) shed, where I copped 17 out of 31. I do not remember the journey to 12C (Canal), our next stop, but 18 cops from 20 was a joy, not least with the bonus of Nos 60964 *The Durham Light Infantry* and 60093 *Coronach*. Sadly, I was just enjoying the photographic possibilities there when

Our first raid on Scotland began at Carlisle. On 30 August 1961 No 43139 stands in the yard at Canal shed. Although allocated to Carlisle (either Upperby or Kingmoor) throughout its 16-year life, it was on this shed on each of my visits on three separate occasions.

my camera jammed! No amount of gentle persuasion had any effect and, obviously, I did not want to open the back and spoil the whole film. Virtually 5 minutes into our first morning and I was without a camera; it was not fixed until after my return to Leicester!

Numerically, the next port of call, 12A (Kingmoor), was much more satisfying, and the quality of locos present was also gratifying. Of the 70 present on shed, 48 were copped, and delights included Nos 90758, 90760 and 90763, plus Nos 72006 *Clan Mackenzie*, 46201 *Princess Elizabeth*, 57653, 72005 *Clan Macgregor*, 72007 *Clan Mackintosh*, 45512 *Bunsen*, 46230 *Duchess of Buccleuch* and five 'Jubilee' cops.

Our first sights back at Citadel were Nos 46223 *Princess Alice* and 60519 *Honeyway*, closely followed by No 60162 *Saint Johnstoun*. Having consigned yet more numbers into our books, we gathered on the relevant platform for our local train for Glasgow, via the G&SW route. Imagine our surprise to see No 46230, which we had only recently left at Kingmoor, backing onto our train. To make our moment complete, we were even allowed to climb into the cab for a quick inspection before departure. Capturing more rarities (for us) en route, we washed up in Glasgow St Enoch station. A massive terminus, opened by the G&SWR, it was, sadly, to close in June 1966. A wash-up was what we needed, after the day's efforts, so a quick visit to the Gents, then, with clean hands, we searched out food in the local buffet before the evening disappeared.

Where to sleep? No accommodation had been booked, so we lay down on the station's benches. We had hardly done this than we were informed by a member of staff that we could not sleep there. On explaining where we had come from and our plight, this gentleman (in a broad Glaswegian accent) pointed to a rake of coaches in a nearby platform. 'If you were to be off that by 7 in the morning, you could sleep on there!' So, we opened the door to a compartment, where David and I took a bench seat each, leaving Les to bunk down on the parcel rack above. With not too much grumbling he accepted the challenge, though he was not so happy in the morning. With the rack construction of iron stanchions and cross strands of tough string, and no pillow, one side of his face dawned with a cat's cradle design deeply imprinted!

After breakfast on the 31st we set out on what was to be a tornado of visits and numbers and a warning of the onset of foot blisters! 65A (Eastfield) was our first stop and this was to be my best ever shed for percentage of cops – 86 out of 88! Although 33 were diesels, the majority were still operational steam and a delightful number of these were types wholly new to me, such as Nos 69183 and 67623. No 60097 *Humorist* was the third loco recorded, Nos 61764 *Loch Arkaig* and 62496 *Glen Loy* were encountered later, then, a real delight, moments before we left came the sight of No 62688 *Ellen Douglas*; whether we should have done or not, we grabbed a quick cabbing.

Cowlairs Works was not far away, both geographically and percentage-wise, and I copped 40 from 41! A catholic variety of types, steam and diesel, and largely workhorse locos, did have No 72009 *Clan Stewart* for company. St Rollox Works was next, providing 27 cops from 33, with just two namers, Nos 45691 *Orion* and 45727 *Inflexible*. Next door was 65B (St Rollox) shed, which had this time a mix of MR and ER locos and a sole 'Jubilee', No 45687 *Neptune*.

Growing weary, but spurred on by what we might see next, we negotiated our way to 66A (Polmadie), where I copped 103 from 114! Incredibly, the first thing we saw on entering the shed yard was No 46102 *Black Watch*, no longer a cop after the sighting in Leicester just 18 days earlier! Other treasures on this occasion were a healthy number of elderly ex-LMS locos beginning with a '5'. The nature of the shed's work was evidenced by the predominantly passenger-orientated engine types, covering both express and more local duties. No 72001 *Clan Cameron* brought me close to seeing all the 'Clans' on this one trip (!) and No 46231 *Duchess of Atholl* ticked off another of the class rare to us Sassenachs! The final shed of the day was 67A (Corkerhill), which yielded another 56 out of 70 present. Though rare, 'Jubilees' from this shed occasionally ventured south to Leicester, but it was still a pleasure to see No 45720 *Indomitable* – new to me. The day ended with a rail journey to Edinburgh Princes Street, passing No 62712 *Morayshire* acting as stationery boiler at Slateford Road Laundry.

From there we went to Waverley station, where, after garnering more numbers, we entered the Men's Waiting Room and prepared to bed down for the night. I had a wooden bench this time, David on the table and Les on a chair, resting his head on the table next to it. David slept well, if fitfully, but awoke twice, once to see the bearded face of a sailor next to his and once to go in search of a toilet during the night, when he saw No 60100 *Spearmint* on his travels. This proved to be one the four of the 78 'A3s' that I never did see! Les was woken once, to be tasked by a policeman as to what he was doing there and where had come from. I was not bothered by the law, so presumably Les had duly satisfied the officer that we were not rogues!

1 September dawned with the three of us less than fully refreshed but still keen to capture more. After breakfast and a brief time spotting at Waverley, we boarded a train for Thornton, by way of Dalmeny, Burntisland and Sinclairtown, and thereafter found our way to 62A (Thornton Junction) shed. This was another good shed for me, copping 34 from 35, including four of the five 'K4s' – Nos 61998 *Macleod of Macleod*, 61995 *Cameron of Lochiel*, 61993 *Loch Long* and 61996 *Lord of the Isles* – as well as No 62686 *The Fiery Cross*. A return trip to Edinburgh then led us to visiting 64B (Haymarket) shed, which did not have a huge presence but did still allow new views of 13 locos, including one of the few non-antelope-named 'B1s', No 61245 *Murray of Elibank*. With an equally small offering was 64C (Dalry Road), but No 61007 *Klipspringer* was a welcome bonus. In complete contrast to these two, 64A (St Margaret's), straddling a main line, saw me cop 55 out of 63. Three 'A3s', plus Nos 60534 *Irish Elegance*, 65224 and 68342, were greeted with pleasure, as was the overall volume and variety on view.

Back at Waverley station we gathered up a few more numbers before boarding our train for the first part of our journey back home behind No 60052 *Prince Palatine* to Newcastle, on the 'Heart of Midlothian' express. No 60034 *Lord Faringdon* then took over for the onward southbound journey. We were alert at Newcastle (especially to see No 60018 *Sparrow Hawk*, Darlington (Nos D9002 *The King's Own Yorkshire Light Infantry* and 60512 *Steady Aim*), York (Nos 70002 *Geoffrey Chaucer* and 60077 *The White Knight*) and Doncaster (Nos 70036 *Boadicea*, 60092 *Fairway* and 60121 *Silurian*) before detraining at Grantham. Here David and I caught a bus for Leicester but not before copping Nos 60009 *Union of South Africa* and 60145 *Saint Mungo*.

Meanwhile Les decided to go home by rail, to Leicester Central via Nottingham Victoria, on the face of it not a bad choice. However ... he fell asleep after Nottingham, slept through the Leicester stop and awoke at Woodford Halse, many miles to the south! By this time it was growing late and he had to wait for some time before retracing his steps. Les did seem to be somewhat accident prone on this trip, and could easily have ended with a trip to hospital. On our journey south from Newcastle, he wanted to poke his head out of the carriage window but, not wanting to risk catching something in his eyes, he put his hand out as a test, only to find a red-hot cinder from *Lord Faringdon's* boiler trying to burn a hole through his palm. His distress was very vocal!

So, I arrived back home with a fresh collection of 767 out of 920 locomotives seen, and many more gaps in my 'Combined' being filled, as well some first entries in some classes. Ten days later – either a sucker for punishment or to make up for the brief visit on the way back from Scotland – Monday 11 September saw me back at Grantham. This time the visit included a tour of the shed – my first time inside 34F – and I was rewarded with the sight of Nos 60127 *Wilson Worsdell* and 60150 *Willbrook*. Back on the station platform I copped No 60006 *Sir Ralph Wedgwood* on the 'White Rose' express together with another 20 locos, including Nos 61251 *Oliver Bury*, D9010 *The King's Own Scottish Borderer* and 60520 *Owen Tudor*.

Another first-time shed visit came just five days later, during my tenth visit to Rugby, again by rail before closure came, hauled from Leicester by No 42541. I only copped three of the 21 locos on shed there, but one was special – No 18000, presumably visiting the adjacent Testing Plant. Back on the platform, Nos 70025 *Western Star* and 46205 *Princess Victoria* were welcome sights before I sadly left the location behind me.

By this time I had been accepted by Barclays Bank, which asked me to start on 16 October 1961. Somewhat chancing my arm with my new employer, and knowing that I would be working Saturday mornings for them, I advised that I would be in Blackpool on the 21st, so could I start the following week? With some relief on my part they agreed. So, bearing in mind that my freedom, enjoyed since leaving school nearly three months earlier, was to be curbed, I determined to pack as much into the last weeks as possible.

The first outing was another AMR trip – the East Midlands Locospotters' 'Don-Yor-Dar Flyer' – by rail to Doncaster, York and Darlington, on Sunday 17 September 1961. The motive power for the Leicester-Darlington outward leg was due to be 'Midland Compound' No 1000 but, for some reason that I cannot remember, I travelled by rail from Leicester to Nottingham behind No 42331, picking up the special at Nottingham! En route, at Beeston, it was interesting to record and cop No ED10 and *Wren*. The railtour progressed through Long Eaton, Hasland, Sheffield, Darnall and Mexborough to Doncaster, where we alighted to tour the Works, immediately greeted by new-build Nos E3065-73. Thereafter, close by, was experimental blue-liveried No D5578, then further in were Nos 70038 *Robin Hood*, 60001 *Sir Ronald Matthews*, D5351/53 – brand new from Crewe – and a bevy of express passenger locos, steam and diesel. I copped 48 out of 62 recorded and immediately added No 70001 *Lord Hurcomb* on returning to the station. A batch of numbers were collected as we passed York on our way north, to Eaglescliffe, where No 62042 was attached to take us to and from Darlington.

The Works there was very busy, with 86 locos on show,

of which 68 were new to me. Among the attractive selection were Nos 61017 *Bushbuk*, 77001, brand-new D4075/76, and Departmental 54 (ex-68153), as well as Nos 62739 *The Badsworth*, 62716 *Kincardineshire* and 62734 *Cumberland* – all withdrawn and awaiting scrap. Other numbers were collected on our return trip, but progressively fewer as the night drew in. It was another successful trip, with a tally of 211 cops out of 323.

A visit to Nottingham on 20 September, by rail, to cement my employment details with the bank, saw a handful of fresh faces and haulage back to Leicester by No 44918. Eight days later David and I were in Birmingham, but for an unusual appointment.

Broadcast on ITV since earlier in 1961, *Thank Your Lucky Stars* was a British television pop music show made by ABC Television. Audience participation was a strong feature, and the 'Spin-a-Disc' section, where a guest DJ and three teenagers reviewed three singles, is a well-remembered feature of the show. We had applied to be part of this and received an invitation for an audition. Held at the ATV studios, we were in a group of five teenagers, sitting in a row on high stools, listening to some new releases. Alan Freeman, an employee of ATV, *not* the more famous disk jockey, asked us in turn for our opinions. Sadly I was the end of the row for each record and, overawed by the location and occasion, in addition to a natural reticence to parade my own views, on top of the other four basically saying all that I was going to, I was less than impressive, and we both failed the audition! It was a matter of a few weeks later that Janice Nicholls appeared on the show. A former office clerk from the Midlands, she became famous for the catchphrase 'Oi'll give it foive', said with a strong Black Country accent, and I could see what sort of impact they had been looking for! After the audition we spent time at Snow Hill station, where I copped Nos 7017 *G. J. Churchward*, 6807 *Birchwood Grange*, 6855 *Saighton Grange* and 7824 *Iford Manor*, as well as 7036 *Taunton Castle* at 6pm on a Paddington-Birkenhead express. I photographed the latter and No 6017 *King Edward IV*.

After our TV 'auditions' (see the text), David and I spent time at Birmingham (Snow Hill) station on 28 September 1961. At around 6pm No 7036 *Taunton Castle* climbs into the station with a Paddington-Birkenhead express.

Ever closer to the end of my freedom, I finally organised the first TRS coach trip. A moderate affair, to 31B (March) and 34E (New England), it was, however, successful and left those aboard wanting more. Both sheds were bulging with locos, but March especially was a revelation. Presenting 132 locos, there was truly an eclectic mix on shed, with steam and diesel, large and small, from different regions and of varying types, but just one namer, No 70008 *Black Prince*. Much of the bread-and-butter work of the shed was freight and the motive power reflected that, with a good number of 'Austerity' 2-8-0s. Many of the diesels were 'main-line' types less than a year old, but an alternative was offered in the guise of Nos 15000, 15001 and 15002. In all, 69 of the total were new to me. The percentage of new locos was roughly paralleled at New England, where I copped just 48 out the 104 present. The freight/passenger split was more even noticeable here, but with steam predominating. Though not on shed, No D9011 *The Royal Northumberland Fusiliers* was espied literally roaring past the site on the ECML.

So to my last outing of the year, that 21 October visit to Blackpool that delayed my bank employment. Again with David and Peter Lightfoot, we were there at the time of the famed lights but our real interest was the shed. Again in the dark, with the sounds of the funfair and general merriment as a backdrop, we managed to identify Nos 44778, 42294, 45442, 48227, 45377, 42481, 44889, 45502 *Royal Naval Division*, 42455, 44731, 44732, 44779, 45318, 44930, 42558, 44927, 45189, 45201, 44926, 44937, 42206, 42153, 42643, 42625, 44947, 45075, 42461, 45436, 42657, 44687, 45415, 44873, 45225, 42638 and 45435. With the shed's name, the darkness and the predominance of 'Stanier 5s', it could almost have been termed a 'black hole'!

My year-end tally was 8,579 – 3,600 MR, 1,587 ER, 913 WR, 440 SR, 882 'Standards' and 1,157 non-steam. My 8,000th was No 68040 in Darlington station on 1 September.

Now working in Leicester city centre, I regularly ventured at lunchtimes to the Birdcage, overlooking the 15C shed yard, and met and became friends with Peter Simmonds. We played tennis, he joined the ten-pin bowling team of which I was captain, and began to join us on some of our trips. The 'Three Musketeers' were now the 'Gang of Four'!

On 15 November the second of two matches between Leicester City and Atletico Madrid, in the European Cup Winners' Cup, took place, City going down 2-0 away in the second leg, after a highly creditable 1-1 in the first leg at Filbert Street. At the end of the year Acker Bilk was at No.1 with his *Stranger on the Shore*, the first week of four at the top.

1962 was to be a momentous year in many ways, not least with the 'Cold War' between Russia and the West at its height and the 'Cuban Missile Crisis' in October bringing the world to the brink of nuclear war. As if determined to save face, the Americans put Colonel John Glenn into space orbit in the Mercury capsule 'Friendship 7'. On the ground, in the UK, the modernistic Coventry Cathedral was finally completed and consecrated on 25 May, followed by the premier five days later of Benjamin Britten's *War Requiem*, especially composed for the occasion. Launched the previous year, *Private Eye* magazine featured more satire in 1962, following part-funding by Peter Cook, also coinciding with the equally satirical *That Was The Week That Was* proving a huge success on television from its very beginning on Saturday 24 November.

In the sphere of popular culture, perhaps *the* most cataclysmic event was the death of Marilyn Monroe on 5 August, from an overdose of barbiturates, at the tender age of 36! The exact cause of death has seen constant speculation ever since. Musically, the year was also notable, though not appreciated as such at the time, for the signing by George Martin of a new group to EMI's Parlophone label. On 6 June they had their first recording session, but it was the session on 4 September, with a new drummer, that produced the Beatles' *Love Me Do*, *Please Please Me* and *P.S. I Love You*. The first title was released in October and only made No 17, but the rest, as we now know, is history. The year's charts were moving away from strict rock 'n' roll and the two records with the longest runs at No 1 were *Wonderful Land* by The Shadows (eight weeks from March) and *I Remember You* by Frank Ifield (seven weeks from July).

On the railway front, I had been buying *Trains Illustrated* for some time but, from January, it metamorphosed into *Modern Railways*. This did not appeal to me at the time but, 50 years later, it is now one of my favourite reads! It also did not please me that North British Locomotive Company – a builder of so many iconic locomotives – went into liquidation in April. Two months later, Swindon Railway Museum opened, and a further two months saw the pioneer No D1500 (later Class 47) appear from Brush Falcon Works in Loughborough. One month after that, on 29 October, Dr Richard Beeching previewed his plans for British Railways, the full impact of which was not appreciated at the time.

With growing confidence now that I was earning real money, and with the success of TRS, 21 January was the next trip for the club. Venturing further this time, we headed west, first to 84H (Wellington) shed. An interesting mix gave us Nos 3607, 3792, 3744, 41204, 9639, 4178, 41241, 9741, 4158, 6429, 6421 and 41900, eight of which were cops. 89A (Shrewsbury) was next, where, between the Midland and Western sheds, I copped 39 from the 64 recorded. Especial delights were six 'Castles' (three new to me), eight 'Halls' (three new), No 1016 *County of Hants* and, appropriately, No 1026 *County of Salop* (a cop). Nos D3976, D3111 and D3193 were the only diesels on view. Oswestry provided another eclectic mix, with, on the 89D shed, Nos 3209, 1458, 1636, 7822 *Foxcote Manor*, 7812 *Erlestoke Manor*, 3789, 1668, 46521, 1447, 46524, 82009, 46505, 1432, 46401, 1628, 5421, 46526, 46515, 7819 *Hinton Manor*, 46507, 3770, 1438, 7434, 2276, 2251, 7807 *Compton Manor*, 46520, 46511 and 2236. Inside the adjacent Works were Nos 9017, 92247, 46522, 6374, 1020 *County of Monmouth*, 823 *Countess*, 7800 *Torquay Manor* and 6392 – all of which were cops for me!

Working our way back east, we travelled to 84B (Oxley) – which presented 50 locos, including no fewer than 15 'Halls' and one Stanier 'Black 5' – then 84A (Stafford Road). Here there were eight 'Kings' present, but not all in steam, as their work was shortly to be taken over by Western Region diesel-hydraulics. Several 'Castles' on show would also soon go the same way and, indeed, this once proud GWR location would close just 18 months later! The day's outing had produced 240 engines, of which 139 were to be newly underlined in the 'Combined'.

Just over three months into my banking career I was instructed to attend a course at the Barclays' training facility in Wimbledon beginning on 12 February 1962. After travelling up to London the previous day, I made my way to the address of one of the bank's Assistant Managers in Carshalton Beeches, at whose house I was to be resident for the next two weeks. Travelling to Wimbledon each day by rail, I was delighted to note the Southern steam on offer and within the first week had added to my trawl, among others, Nos 35018 *British India Line*, 35020 *Bibby Line* and 34039 *Boscastle*. The middle weekend was free so, rather than travel back home, I stayed in situ and took the opportunity, on 18 February, to 'do' as many sheds as possible – sans permit, of course!

First off was my first and only visit to the steam shed 75C (Norwood Junction). Still battling electric units and the increasing number of diesels, it would provide employment until closure on 5 June 1964. This day it housed 33 locos, two-thirds steam of utilitarian nature, and provided in total 22 cops. 73C (Hither Green) was next, which had a slightly increased complement, at 45 – all diesel – of which I saw 38 for the first time. Briefly calling in at King's Cross, St Pancras and Paddington en route, I then made my way to the highlight of the day, 81A (Old Oak Common), where 124 numbers were recorded, dotted around the large shed area; 75 were cops and 97 were steam! It was interesting to see No 90565 but, as it had been transferred to 81C (Southall) shed the previous year, it was probably not so surprising. Being the major shed at the eastern end of the GWR main line and the provider of motive power for Paddington, it was no surprise that the vast majority were passenger types, main-line and local. I was pleased to cop Nos 1507 and 6002 *King William IV*.

Gathering my breath after this experience, it was but a short journey to 1A (Willesden), which offered 77 locos, 31 of which were new to me. Just 18 diesels were on show – predominantly what would become Classes 20 and 25 – and I was disappointed not to see any of the Midland namers that I still needed; but I was not saddened by the 183 fresh cops! The rest of the bank course passed without incident and I returned home on 23 January, again a tired but happy bunny!

By this time photography was assuming a greater part of my spotting trips and I began logging exposure details, to judge against the printed results. Having been a photographer for the RAF during the war, dad was able to give me valuable advice and guidance, and I was pleased with most of my output, all done without the aid of a light meter. However, becoming 'cocky' I eschewed such material aids, which was fine in the short term, but I fell foul of my conceit a year or two later when I changed cameras. I have since lived to regret some of my abysmal failures without the instrument!

The next outing was some way off but would be the first of

a very full weekend. Saturday 28 April saw me travel to Preston by rail, via Crewe, from Leicester. Hauled by No D255 from Crewe, the usual course of head swivelling to catch as many numbers as possible ensued until arrival at Preston station. The target was the remains of 24K shed. We had been alerted by the railway press to the storage of locomotives at the site, following the destruction of the shed roof in a fire on 28 June 1960 and its closure to operations on 12 September 1961. There were just a handful on view, but quality rather than quantity – Nos D3782, 42661, 42476 (my 9,000th cop), 45549, 45533 *Lord Rathmore*, 45513 (a cop), 45546 *Fleetwood*, 45550, 45524 *Blackpool* (another cop), 45547, 45551, 45520 *Llandudno*, 45543 *Home Guard* and 44904. It was a sad and poignant visit, the dispiriting air heightened by the collection of 'Patriots'. The buildings were demolished in 1966.

Some time spotting on Preston station followed, before travelling south behind No 45289. Back at Crewe, a clandestine bunk around 5A (Crewe North) shed produced 48 numbers, but just eight cops! Two of these were Nos 45721 *Impregnable* and 70020 *Mercury*. The trip was then completed with further time on Crewe station, the highlight of which was seeing brand-new 'Peaks' Nos D156/160-163, perhaps en route to 17A (Derby), their first allocation.

The following day was the next TRS outing, by coach. We were using the same Leicester coach company by this point and Ken, the driver usually allocated, was becoming more of a friend than a mere on-duty 'servant'. 1B (Camden) was first, but we saw little of it, being refused permission, and only nine numbers were collected – all diesel. 34G (Finsbury Park) was more successful and, despite being a purpose-built diesel shed with an allocation to suit, 26 cops out of 32 was good enough for me, as well as being up close and personal with Nos D9012 *Crepello* and D9018 *Ballymoss*. Sweeping across London and changing Regions, 73B (Bricklayers Arms) was next, exactly four years after my first visit. The drastic reduction in the number, but variation in type, of locomotives was reflective of the changes locally in traffic and motive power requirements. Four of the five Bulleid 'Light Pacifics' were of the rebuilt variety and No D6500 plus four 'sisters' echoed the non-steam change throughout the country. 70A (Nine Elms) was faring better, with just four diesel shunters out of a total of 62 locos, but an interesting change was the sight of ex-GWR Nos 4681, 9770, 4672, 4692, 4601, 4616 and 4698. 73A (Stewarts Lane) was another shed with declining numbers, down to 36 this time, with exactly half being diesel or electric, as opposed to just one diesel shunter four years before.

Having had more than five years' experience with a camera, I still had much to learn, as can be seen from this image of me cutting off the front buffers of No 31588 as it stands in the shed yard at Stewarts Lane on 29 April 1962. I was beginning to realise that what I saw in the viewfinder, especially composition, was vitally important.

Having visited 81A (Old Oak Common) just two months earlier, the number of cops was not surprisingly well down, but what was a little unexpected was the collection of 'Kings' on shed being exactly the same as in February. Perhaps it was coincidence, but more likely the result of the cull of these ex-GWR locos that was beginning to gather pace. 1A (Willesden) produced almost exactly the same overall total as my earlier visit, and the number of cops was greatly reduced, with no namers. Our last port of call was 14A (Cricklewood), where 41 locos awaited us — with just nine cops! That was also the number of diesels present, the shed still oozing a steam atmosphere at this southern end of the Midland main line. Brand-new Nos D5379/80 were on view, the first of the type allocated here, which were to trek north to Scotland before too many months were out. The following day, Leicester City finished the 1961/62 season 14th in the First Division but, sadly, with no repeat appearance in the FA Cup Final, as they had been knocked out by Stoke City (5-2 in the replay) in the first round for the professional teams!

I may have seen the back of my GCE studies but I was now into the early part of my Institute of Bankers exams. I was advised that until I achieved my AIB qualifications (somewhat amusingly known as 'Another Idiot Banker'!) I would not progress far or fast through the system, but this did not stop my railway efforts, and on 27 May I travelled by rail from Leicester to Nottingham behind No 45262, before joining another trip with AMR, this time to Lincolnshire. 34F (Grantham) was first, with 37 on shed (just four cops!), including seven 'A3s', all with 'German Federal' smoke deflectors. No 61013 *Topi* was a cop, as were Nos 63941, 92189 and 90025. My one and only visit to 40F (Boston) did not disappoint. Again there was not a huge number of locos – just 30, of which 16 were cops – but many of those present, both steam and diesel, did not travel far from this outpost. 40A (Lincoln) was marginally better, with 19 cops from 43, including Nos 61026 *Ourebi*, 61405 and four 'K3s'. The cast list continued to grow with our trip to 40B (Immingham), predominantly a freight shed but needing locos that could move heavy loads and/or travel at speed, and it was pleasing to be able to underline – and photograph – No 61379 *Mayflower*. Nearby 36C (Frodingham) was akin in many ways, with almost as many engines on shed, but here the emphasis was on brute strength rather than speed, with many 2-8-0 'Austerities' on view. Our final destination was 36E (Retford), the ex-GC shed first, followed by the ex-GN site. Again the focus was on freight, but the latter shed, albeit with fewer locos to see, housed a greater number of 'B1s', evidencing some mixed-traffic turns.

Nicely away from the crowded environs of Frodingham shed on 27 May 1962, No 63973 is cleanly pictured, seemingly ready to lift the rake of 16-ton wagons from the siding. Despite looking in fine fettle, it was withdrawn, from Retford shed, in November 1963.

On the same day Nos 61379 *Mayflower* and 70035 *Rudyard Kipling* make a fine pair, poking out of Immingham shed as they rest between duties. Built as late as June 1951 – new to Colwick shed – *Mayflower* lasted only until 11 August 1962, less than three months from this view, a total waste of a valuable asset! No 70035 was even newer – built in January 1953 – but did last a little longer, until the end of 1967.

The outing on 12 June was a quick out and back from Leicester to Peterborough, to visit 34E (New England) shed. With much in common with the last sheds on my previous trip, there was, however, a greater degree of non-freight motive power, due not least to its position right next to the ECML. The sheer variety ranged from 'A2s' to more elderly 'N2s', tender and tank locos, diesel and steam, a smattering of ex-LMS 2-6-0 Class 4s, and a good mix of 'Standard' 'Austerities' and 9Fs alongside the ex-BR locos. A total of 108 were seen, from which my latest haul totalled just 23 cops, reflecting my recent exposure to ER locations, but I did cop No 60155 *Borderer*, which was very pleasing.

Bristol and Swindon were the headline destinations for the next TRS trip, on 1 July 1962, a coachload of mainly 13-14-year olds venturing towards a challenging list of venues. On a bright, sunny day and graced with two drivers (to cover the anticipated longer hours), we initially turned up at 82E (Bristol Barrow Road). An ex-MR shed, at the furthest outpost on the Midland route to Bristol but now under WR jurisdiction, the motive power was, apart from four ex-GWR locos, exclusively Midland or 'Standard' types – both passenger and freight – or diesel. No 75000 was one of 17 copped out of the 48 present. 82B (St Philip's Marsh) was next, where the flavour was well and truly ex-GWR – 83 out of 95! Among the copper-capped green passenger express locos present, I was happiest to see Nos 1009 *County of Carmarthen* (a cop) and 1365. We were severely restricted at 82A (Bath Road) and collected only 25 numbers (20 of them new to me), with just two steam – Nos 7006 *Lydford Castle* and 4959 *Purley Hall* – among the diesels, the latter mostly 'Hymeks'.

Travelling south-east along the Bath Road we made our way to 82F (Bath Green Park) shed, where I copped 13 from 24, the most satisfying being Nos 40700, 53806, 53808 and 53810. Continuing our southerly direction, 70E (Salisbury) was next, displaying 38 with a mix of WR and SR, predominantly the latter, ranging from 'M7s' to 'Merchant Navies', but for me the highlight was '700' Class No 30315 – the class was to become extinct by the end of the year.

Being around the railways of the UK from the mid-1950s, I was able to see many of the more ancient types before they disappeared for ever. One such was No 30315, of Drummond's Victorian '700' Class for the LSWR, seen at Salisbury on 1 July 1962. The tender is full of coal but the loco would only last another six months.

Hardly having a chance to enjoy our sandwiches, we briefly stopped in the centre of Swindon to peer through the doors of the Museum and espy preserved Nos 2516, 3717 *City of Truro*, 4003 *Lode Star* and broad gauge *North Star*. Then it was on to 81E (Didcot), which hosted 40 for us – with two 'Castles' and nine 'Halls' – and 26 cops for me, including Nos 1002 *County of Berks* and 6856 *Stowe Grange*. 81F (Oxford) was next, displaying 48 (27 cops) and a mix of steam and diesel and freight and passenger types. We were taking advantage of the long summer daylight, but by now sunset was threatening as we headed towards our final call, 84C (Banbury). With no permit for this location we chanced our arm and made it round most of the shed, until suddenly caught and ejected, after only 35 locos had been recorded (17 cops). No 5047 *Earl of Dartmouth* was the only 'Castle' seen, together with 11 'Halls' and one 'Grange' –

No 6833 *Calcot Grange*. The more diminutive Nos 1440, 1455 and 1453 made for interesting comparisons.

Remember, these were the days before a multiplicity of motorways and dual-carriageways or mobile phones, so by the time we arrived back at the drop-off point in Leicester, hours late, we were greeted with a bevy of irate and worried parents. Many threatened not to let their youngsters join us again but, somehow, with a promise 'not to do it again', they all relented, not least when they saw that their charges were delighted with their day! So was I, with another 198 in the bag out of 357, although I was not so pleased with dad's reception. He was not amused at us arriving back after midnight and the various parents constantly ringing him at home, asking for updates. Needless to say, I had not rung him to advise progress! His phone was red-hot and so was my ear!

Six months into 1962 and the year had been the busiest by far for me, for not only was I constantly chasing illusive locos and planning trips for TRS, but I was also studying for my banking exams, captaining a ten-pin-bowling team at the Bowling Alley in Lee Circle, Leicester, a member of the Thurmaston Methodist Church and, more specifically, the amateur dramatic group therein … and I was becoming far more interested in individuals of the opposite sex, not least within the drama group! In some ways threatening my sanity, however, the pace was not to let up for the remaining six months!

3 July saw a 'smash and grab' raid on 18A (Toton) shed and Derby Works, which yielded 43 cops from 99, but that paled into insignificance just five days later, with a second trip to Scotland. Again travelling up by rail, this time behind No 44851 on the 11.30pm from Leicester, we journeyed overnight, alternating between grabbing moments of sleep and desperately trying to record what was about at intermediate locations to Carlisle, such as No 48474 at Sheffield and 42189 at Keighley, and being pulled by No D29 from Leeds. Arriving at Carlisle bleary-eyed at just after 5.30am, we immediately (well, after a quick breakfast) retraced our steps around the three local sheds, as the year before. 12B (Upperby) was again first, which,

despite being the shed for the WCML, was still predominantly steam – 36 out of 42. Sixteen locos were new for me including, rather pleasingly, No 65321, one of just a handful of these ER locos allocated here. 12C (Canal) was next. No 43139, photographed the previous year just before my camera failed, was again present, as were glamorous ER locos, including Nos 60519 *Honeyway* and 60534 *Irish Elegance*, three 'V2s', two 'B1s', including No 61029 *Chamois* – a cop for me – and five D53xxs, ex-34B (Hornsey) and transferred north in 1960. 12A (Kingmoor) was also mostly steam – 72 from 80 – and provided cops of (among others) Nos 57568, 60824, 72004 *Clan McDonald* and 45728 *Defiance*. We also took the opportunity for another cab visit – on No 72008 *Clan Macleod*.

Back at Citadel station, we boarded a train for Perth, double-headed by Nos 46134 *The Cheshire Regiment* and 45029. We again grabbed what numbers we could on the journey, including cops for me as we swept past 68D (Beattock) shed – Nos 42130, 42205 and 54507. No 57583 was copped at Carstairs, Nos D8117, D8120 and 54502 at Polmadie, 72000 *Clan Buchanan* as we approached Glasgow, D3216, 44931 and D8114 passing St Rollox, D2739, D2742, 45084 and D2740 at Stirling, and 55260 and 45459 on the entrance to Perth. The goal here, immediately, was the eight-road ex-LMS shed, coded 63A, that had opened in 1938 to replace the previous ex-CR facility slightly to the north. We were to be based in the town for the next four days – with overnight accommodation this time! – in a private house run by a very charming lady, who was a big fan of Stenhousemuir football club. Needless to say, the beautiful game was part of our conversations!

Sixty-one locos greeted us on this first visit to the shed and it was a delightful mix – steam and diesel, main-line and locos for lesser duties, old and new, and even a WR representative – No 1646! New to 87D (Swansea East Dock) in May 1951, it had been transferred to 60C (Helmsdale) for local branch work in February 1957. Stored there in August 1960, it had moved south to Perth some time before our visit, but was not officially allocated there until 11 August. Although our permit was only for this first day, the shed foreman was gracious enough to allow us a visit every day, which we did, usually on our return to the town, to mop up what had changed over the ensuing 24 hours.

9 July saw us journey north behind No D6102 to Aberdeen, via Forfar and Montrose, where we immediately made the trip to 61A (Kittybrewster) shed. Being the furthest north that I had ever travelled, I was fascinated to see what would be in store for us – sadly, few in number (18) and just one steam, No 76108! The rest was a range of main-line and mixed-traffic engines and shunters. 61B (Ferryhill) was not much better, with 19 present, but at least only three diesels. Nos D357 and D360 were less than a year old, unlike two of my other cops – Nos 60094 *Colorado* and 60525 *A. H. Peppercorn*. During a brief stop-off at Forfar we found the shed (ex-63C but now a sub-shed of Perth) to be almost wholly consisting of nine elderly locos in store, with just No 55204 in steam and working, shunting sidings at the side of the shed. Back at Perth, the shed

There was steam on Forfar shed on 9 July 1962, but, sadly, only one loco actually in steam. No 55204 engages in a bout of shunting in the sidings alongside the engine shed. Five days after this, it was moved to Perth, from where its career ended on 19 January 1963.

contained 24 locos that had not been there the previous day!

We rounded off each day, on our return to the town, with a visit to a large local transport café for our evening meal. The ladies behind the counter were incredible and by just the second day they guessed what we would order, and after that we did not need to speak at all! They saw us in the queue and cried out, 'The usual?'!

The next day, 10 July, we decided to explore more of the Glasgow depots. Again we soaked up sights of locos en route, as we returned along the route that had brought us to Perth two days earlier. Arrival in the city saw us travelling to 66B (Motherwell), where more elderly ex-LMS fare was on show as well as mostly freight types; 58 numbers were recorded, 54 steam, of which I copped 46, including two ER interlopers, Nos 68709 and 68733, both officially allocated to 66C (Hamilton). Across the city to St Rollox next, with an inspection of the Works complex first, containing 37, 19 of which were mostly passenger diesels. Steam was predominantly passenger types, and one delightful 'stranger' was No 62686 *The Fiery Cross*, albeit in store. Moving across to the shed area, the display was nearly double that of the Works, and only 12 diesels out of a total of 69. More elderly ex-LMS stock was cheek-by-jowl with modern 'Standards' as well as numerous 'Black 5s'. 66A (Polmadie) followed, with a further 70 on view (fewer than the 114 just 11 months earlier) and only nine diesels. Otherwise the mix for motive power was much as elsewhere that day, except for a sight to bring joy to our hearts, that of No 54463 still in steam – one of only three of the class nominally still at work, and which proved to be the last, withdrawn just three months later. This shed would produce my 10,000th cop – No 42055 – midway round the visit.

67A (Corkerhill) was a shadow of its former self, with this year's crop half of what we had seen the previous year. Three pleasing cops, however, were Nos 45693 *Agamemnon*, 45677 *Beatty* and 70052 *Firth of Tay*. No 40615 was also a welcome sight, as this class was also rapidly disappearing. 65D (Dawsholm) shed was a much smaller affair, but it had the distinction of housing preserved locos HR No 103, NBR No

As described in the text, we were keen to visit Dawsholm shed and to see the preserved vintage types. Centre of attention here on 10 July 1962 is ex-Caledonian Railway 4-4-2 No 123 (ex-LMS 14010), built in 1886 for the Edinburgh International Exhibition. It was later to be moved to the Glasgow Riverside Museum.

256 *Glen Douglas*, GJR No 49 and CR No 123. Others at rest within the walls were Nos 54398 *Ben Alder* – which was set aside for preservation at the time but was, sadly, scrapped in 1967! – 56039, 68335 and 68336. Long closed, the depot site was redeveloped in 2004.

Happily our next port of call, 65A (Eastfield), was as prodigious as the previous year – the total of 91 was three more than on show in 1961 – and 51 of them were still new to me, including two rare (to us from Leicester) consecutively numbered – and named – 'B1s', Nos 61243 *Sir Harold Mitchell* and 61244 *Strang Steel*, the latter always one of the most evocative loco names to my eyes, for no particular reason! Thirty-four were diesels but the rest an eclectic mix.

For the next day we trekked east, first to Dundee and 62B (Tay Bridge) shed. Relatively restrained in numbers, the majority

One of the joys of shed-bashing was being able to be 'up close and personal' to the locomotives. Later on 10 July 1962 No 45693 *Agamemnon* stands proudly at the head of a row on Corkerhill shed. Probably biased to a degree by my first ever cop being a 'Jubilee', this class was always among my favourites and it was a special joy to see examples that did not normally make the trek south to the Midlands.

of the 32 present were of a prosaic nature, with just two 'A3s' bringing some glamour – Nos 60057 *Ormonde* and 60077 *The White Knight*. Although nominally a bigger shed, the cast at 62A (Thornton) was an increase of just eight, of which 27 were cops. Here the predominant raison d'être was freight, with a mix of ER and 'Standard' locos and just seven diesels, including as a slight surprise No D367. 62C (Dunfermline) was last before we returned to Perth and food; there were just 30 on shed, with the mix akin to that at Thornton.

12 July was mostly to locations not before visited and we were keen to see what they had in store – literally, as we had read reports of the number of locos being dumped wherever there was space, as the sheer number of withdrawals was outstripping the capability of Works to scrap them. The first four engines we encountered at 65F (Grangemouth) had rags over their chimneys – Nos 44234, 43137, 65306 and 90755.

None were officially yet deleted from stock, but would be within months, with the exception of No 43137, which would survive for a further five years, after moving south to end up at Blyth. The highest-numbered and only named 2-10-0 'Austerity' was here – No 90774 *North British* – and this would be the only time I saw it! Bo'ness Docks was known to us through the railway press as a store dump, and though we were very disappointed to see so many sad-looking locos – 49 in total – it was gratifying to see many that would otherwise have escaped us had the cutter's torch been in action. Forty-two were cops, including Nos 62691 *Laird of Balmawhapple* (another of my favourite names!) and 62693 *Roderick Dhu*. Back to Glasgow by rail, a revisit to 67A (Corkerhill), just two days after the previous one, granted me eight cops, including No 45692 *Cyclops*. The last visit of the day was east again, to 64F (Bathgate), where the vast majority on site were in store. In addition to five 'V2s', two delights were Nos 62685 *Malcolm Graeme* and 62484 *Glen Lyon*.

Our penultimate day, 13 July, was south-east to Edinburgh, first stop 64B (Haymarket). As the year before, the performers here were few in number, not reflecting the importance of the shed for the ECML's motive power requirements. However, it was quality if not quantity on show, with cops for me with

Bathgate was awash with stored locos on 12 July 1962, not least some more ancients about to disappear. No 62484 *Glen Lyon* will sadly not work again, being put to one side at Hawick on 18 November 1961, after 42 years of service.

Further along the line at Bathgate was No 62685 *Malcolm Graeme*, new in 1924 and withdrawn from Haymarket in January 1962. It had been a stationary boiler at 64B between March 1959 and January 1960, and was then used for steam heating the Caledonian Hotel in Edinburgh's Princes Street from July 1961 to 16 January 1962. Evidence of this work can be judged from the white coating on the front end and the stub of a heating pipe sprouting from the smokebox.

three 'Deltics', three of seven 'A3s' and the sole 'A4' present, No 60002 *Sir Murrough Wilson*. Quality was also on view at 64C (Dalry Road), not least the first loco encountered, No 62712 *Morayshire*. Built in 1928 and withdrawn in the summer of 1961, it had been used as a stationary boiler at Slateford Road Laundry in Edinburgh from June of that year, then dumped out of use at Dalry Road at the beginning of 1962. This had no doubt saved it and, happily, it went on to be preserved, to the delight of many private railway visitors 50 years later. By comparison to these two sheds, 64A (St Margaret's) was displaying close to 20 per cent more locos than the previous year, just over half of which (39 of 75) were yet more underlining fodder. No 60087 *Blenheim* was the highlight, but the rest were an entertaining and enjoyable mix.

Yet more 'oldies': No 62712 *Morayshire* stands in Dalry Road shed yard on 13 July 1962, sans coupling rods, after also spending time as a stationary boiler in Edinburgh. Happily, this was another loco that was to find life in preservation.

Although I grew up liking the unadorned 'A3s' on the Great Central, later I was to shift my allegiance to what I considered to be the more aesthetically pleasing members of the class with the 'German Federal' smoke deflectors. No 60037 *Hyperion* is a prime example on Haymarket shed on 13 July 1962.

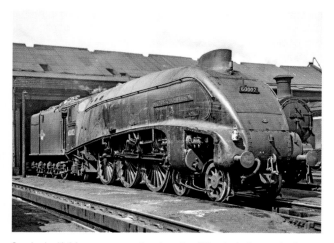

Surely the 'A4s' were among the pinnacle of Gresley's designs, looking the part that they so ably filled. No 60002 *Sir Murrough Wilson* stands majestically at Haymarket on 13 July 1962.

Our final day in Scotland was a sad affair, both because we were returning home, away from the 'exotic' delights north of the border, but also because we knew that we were leaving behind so many locos that we had either not managed to see or would never see again. So many of the exhibits we had seen on this trip had already been ragged and others were just dumped, the depots running out of sackcloth! Such a tragic waste of both steam power and past investment, and the pace of abandonment was increasing. No hot embers from the train home this time – we were pulled from Edinburgh by No D320! – but plenty of additional captures were made on our journey south, including Nos 60074 *Harvester* at York and 60135 *Madge Wildfire* after our arrival at Grantham.

Six days later saw yet another, brief trip to Rugby, with limited excitement but a tour around the shed (2A). This yielded just seven cops from 49, but included No E2001! There was, however, the sight of five 'Patriots' in store – Nos 45541 *Duke of Sutherland*, 45542, 45537 *Private E. Sykes VC*, 45548 *Lytham St Annes* and 45538 *Giggleswick*. Despite not now having a long summer school break to enjoy, this did not stop my momentum as I was still enjoying AMR trips as well as TRS outings.

The former was the next host on a trip to the Leeds area on 29 July, again accompanied by David. 56C (Copley Hill) was first but disappointingly bare of locos, with only 16 numbers collected, although it was satisfying to see Nos 61016 *Inyala*, 68925, 68988, 68892 and 68984. MR locos were the staple at 55C (Farnley Junction), a mix of passenger and freight types and just two diesel shunters out of the total of 31. Between sheds we had half an hour to kill before our permitted time at the next stop. While most of us waited on the coach, one of our number went out in search of 'talent'. Incredibly, he returned 30 minutes later with a girl on each arm, and they were in tears as we left them behind! What his secret was is unknown, but I have never found it!

After the break we moved on to 55A (Holbeck), with exactly the same results as Farnley Junction – 13 new from 31 recorded – all MR apart from three diesels (two shunters and one 'Peak') and two ER 'B1s', Nos 61165 and 61316. 55H (Neville Hill) was only marginally more satisfying (22 from 36), predominantly ER but with five MR interlopers – Nos 40193, 40148, 42188, 41281 and 41252 – four diesel shunters and one 'Peak', No D166. 55B (Stourton) was almost identical but with only six cops from 35. Here the freight bias was virtually 100 per cent. By contrast, 56A (Wakefield) was much busier, but the complement was enhanced by 11 locos most obviously in store. Otherwise, its residents were, apart from 'Austerities', a mixture of MR and ER locos, reflecting its somewhat ambivalent status, having been 25A under the control of the former region until September 1956, when it became 56A under the ER with boundary changes in and around Leeds. It would close to steam in January 1964 and completely from 25 June 1967. It was sad, indeed, to gaze on Nos 60861 and 60884, together with four

'B1s' among the stored items. The final shed on the itinerary was 55D (Royston), another exclusively freight facility, housing 49, from which I copped just 10. Tracing and tracking engines that I had not seen before was becoming ever more difficult and on this trip the percentage was lower than I would have liked – 114 from 271 (42%) – an experience that I would have to accept and would then yearn for as the years passed!

The new 1962-63 football season did not start well for Leicester City, who lost 2-1 away to Fulham on 18 August, but it would later prove to be a record-breaker, with ten consecutive league and FA Cup victories in a 16-game undefeated run, beginning with a 5-1 drubbing of Leyton Orient on Boxing Day (their only time in the top flight of the league) and ending with a 2-1 defeat to West Ham United away on 13 April 1963. They would also go all the way in the FA Cup.

On 11 August 1962 I paid yet another visit to Rugby, where I had my first sight of No DP2 and also copped No 5912 *Queen's Hall*. On the 25th I was back again at Derby Open Day. The exciting views for local fans was the brand-new WCML electrics Nos E3071 and E3087, neither of which would be released into traffic until October. Other new-builds were Nos D5186-90 and the last 'Peaks' from Derby, Nos D189-193 – none of these under construction would see the light of day until 1963, when in January the 'Peaks' went to 52A (Gateshead), their first allocation. The total for the day, in and out of the Works, was 46 cops from 145.

Another combination of shed and works followed on 2 September, when the next TRS coach outing made a bee-line from Leicester to Swindon. Both locations in this railway town, on either side of the Gloucester line, offered steam and diesel and old and new. 82C (the shed) was the more limited in number and variety but the outstanding exhibit here was No D0260 *Lion*, the white-liveried BRCW Type 4 diesel, completed just five months earlier and alone making the visit worthwhile. In the Works the spread was both across types and geographical, with locos over much of the considerable acreage of the complex. As well as recipients of loving care within the various Shops – not least the famous 'A' Shop – there were many locos that would never turn a wheel again and would soon make their contribution to many a baked-bean can! Alongside all of this was the sight of the latest builds of 'Westerns', Nos D1008-24. 83D (Laira) was the first allocation of '08', whereas the others were to be split between London (Old Oak Common) and Cardiff (Canton) sheds. By the end of the morning, on completion of our tour of this Wiltshire town, I had copped 85 out of 144 and made real inroads to the gaps in my WR collection!

70D (Basingstoke) was next, but was a let-down after this excitement, with just 22 locos on show, but I did enjoy copping 12, including Nos 30792 *Sir Hervis de Revel* and 30763 *Sir Bors de Ganis*. Reading was next, but before we reached it there was a personal delight on the coach radio. During *Pick of the Pops*, which reviewed the latest releases and was introduced by the real (!) Alan Freeman, to my absolute delight and wonder he played the new single release from RCA by Duane Eddy, *(Dance with the) Guitar Man*. In a change of style, this incorporated female vocalists whereas he had been purely instrumental previously, but the sound was stunning and I couldn't wait to buy it later in the week. That weekend had seen Duane enter the charts with *Ballad of Paladin*, which would go on to enjoy five weeks in the charts and reach No 10. *Guitar Man* would enter the charts on 17 November 1962 and stay there for 12 weeks, reaching No 4. Obviously, his new style was proving popular.

The two Reading sheds – GW and Southern – were pleasing without being overwhelming, with 14 'Halls', two 'Granges' – Nos 6842 *Nunhold Grange* and 6854 *Roundhill Grange* – a cop in the shape of No 4094 *Dynevor Castle* out of the four of the class on view,. and, most amazing of all, brand-new No D1006 *Western Stalwart*, allocated to Laira but on the Southern shed! The tiny presence of just 11 locos at Slough, with nothing particular to commend them, ended the day's visits, which had garnered 165 cops from 285.

A sad day a week later saw the final 'Pines Express' running over the Somerset & Dorset line on 8 September, bringing to an end a relationship between train and route after 52 years. No 92220 *Evening Star* was given the 'honour' of operating the last trains. Thereafter, at the instigation of the Western Region, the train was to be diverted through Oxford.

On the personal front, there was no letting up on the entertainment. A short fortnight after the Swindon trip, on 16 September, the Thurmaston gang trekked to Manchester, with 9E (Trafford Park) being first. Twenty-two prosaic locos were all that greeted us, a very quiet beginning, before we raised the stakes at 26F (Patricroft). Here the fare was not dramatically different from 9E, with the exception of a slightly greater emphasis on freight power, but at least the number was higher at 53, of which 23 were new to me. Nos 49199, 49087, 49382, 49335, 49426, 49034, 49147 and 49323 were a pleasing gaggle of 'Super Ds', and equally welcome were Nos 40453 and 40681. 26B (Agecroft) was another freight-dominated shed, with more 'Austerities' and 'Black 5s', but the special ones here were Nos 51204, 51232, 47165, 51237 and 51206 … and 30 cops from just 42. The balance for passenger strength was redressed to some degree at 26A (Newton Heath), although still a healthy contingent of 'Austerities'. With nothing outstanding on shed and a mere 28 gains from 61, this was something of a disappointment.

Happily, that was to change on entering 9G (Gorton), as we were met with an intriguing MR and ER mix, just five diesel shunters and electric No 26021 among the 100 on site. Exactly half were cops, including No 90657, which was my 11,000th cop in almost exactly seven years – an average of 1,571 a year, or a little over four for every day of those seven years! This loco was in store, as were around a third of all on shed. Electrics were also present – indeed, they were to be the focus at the next location, 9A (Longsight), where 17 of 35 were from the WCML express fleet. The gathering pace of the Modernisation Programme was most notable in effect at this depot, many more than we had seen thus far elsewhere. 9F (Heaton Mersey) was next, again almost exclusively freight types making up the 39 on view, from which I only added eight to my collection. 9B (Stockport) wound up the trail, with me copping the grand total of two from 23, Nos 44911 and 48310. It was pleasing, however, to view three 'Jubilees' still at work, Nos 45632 *Tonga*, 45696 *Arethusa* and 45678 *De Robeck*, although this last was to be discarded just three months later and cut up at Taylor Brothers, Trafford Park, 12 months after that. The day had reaped 172 new views from 380, once more below 50 per cent.

The next TRS trip, on 30 September 1962, to Crewe and the Chester area was to prove a momentously memorable one, but not just for the locos on view. Beginning at 5B (Crewe South), we were greeted by 81 locos, of which 27 were 'fresh meat' for me, including among all the MR steam No 6928 *Underley Hall* and the majestically named No 5907 *Marble Hall*! Not being the depot that provided motive power for the WCML, freight was the predominant flavour, with a wide range of types together with diesel shunters Nos 12010, 12022, 12054, D2386 and D2221. Nearby was Gresty Lane shed, a sub-depot to Crewe North, and this was to be my only visit there. Opened in 1870, the joint province of the GWR and LNWR, its size and facilities were always limited, being a two-line dead-end building; it closed on 17 June 1963. Being the servicing depot for locos on trains from the west, it housed on this day Nos 41241, 6848 *Toddington Grange*, 4923 *Evenley Hall*, 48460, 6828 *Trellech Grange*, 6831 *Bearley Grange*, 3792, 45235, 44780, 45045, 42627, 42593, 45057, 78041 and 44874. Just three of these were new to me.

With the influx of the WCML electrics, largely provided by and serviced at Longsight in Manchester, the allocation of 5A (Crewe North) had taken a knock, and on this visit the number present was down to 37, of which only six were cops – Nos D5006, 45397, 42236, 70018 *Flying Dutchman*, 45429 and 46238 *City of Carlisle*. The rest was another mix of ex-LMS types, except for Nos 78030, 80117 and 73126, and included No 45556 *Nova Scotia* and the celebrated No 45552 *Silver Jubilee* … and this is where the momentous memory comes in. Choosing to walk from North shed to the Crewe Works complex, we passed the perimeter fencing of the former, made up of 'three-fingered' spiked railings. Ever on the lookout for something unusual, Les espied the end of a finger, complete with nail but now white and well drained of blood, lodged in the top of one

Gresty Lane was the Crewe shed that maintained locos handling services to and from Shrewsbury. Often these would be ex-GWR types, but here, on 30 September 1962, No 41241 is from the ex-LMS mould, although built by BR in October 1949 – another example of a loco that evaded the cutter's torch and has been restored to steam in preservation.

of the steel uprights. Finding this fascinating, he could not leave it behind, so, sensing a trophy, he dislodged it and wrapped it in his handkerchief, to take home with him! Little did we know that, some 53 years later, as a result of a brief article by me for *Steam Railway* magazine, we would learn the facts of the mishap. We had thought that some unhappy spotter had left it behind on a frantic exit from the shed, but no, he had been trying to scale the fence to gain entry! He had travelled from his grandmother's home in York with a friend and had slipped from the fence, leaving his digit behind him. Some railwaymen had come to his aid and he spent two days in Crewe Hospital before being allowed to make his way home. Apparently one of his concerns at the time was that he did not collect the numbers of the locos on shed!

After this excitement there was distraction as we toured the Works, but the 122 locos on view soon brought us back to earth. As might be expected at such an important facility, the mix of locos was wide, with many in stages of undress and some awaiting their final end. Pleasing to see were Nos 52441, 52312, 52093, 51412, 45617 *Mauritius* and 77004, as well as 'Patriots' Nos 45513, 45551, 45548 *Lytham St Annes* and 45524 *Blackpool* (three of which we had seen on Preston shed five months earlier) and 45563 *Australia*, together with L&MR 0-4-2 *Lion*, LNWR 2-2-2 *Cornwall* and LNWR 2-4-0 *Hardwicke*. In the Erecting Shop were Nos D1041-58, which would see release progressively over the next six months, together with No D1001 *Western Pathfinder*.

Re-boarding our coach, the compass was then to the north-west, to arrive at 89B (Croes Newydd). Now well and truly in ex-GWR territory, all bar two of the 33 locos on shed were from 'God's Wonderful Railway', most being freight engines, with just No 6872 *Crawley Grange* and 4960 *Pyle Hall* of a more glamorous nature. 6B (Mold Junction) held a slightly more eclectic mix, with MR and GWR examples together with Nos D3370 and 12048. Fifteen of the 34 here were cops for me, including No 6939 *Calveley Hall*. 6A (Chester) saw a majority of MR locos, but did also house Nos 73071, 73038, 73040, D2220, 73073, 78033, 78032, 73048, 73132 and 73070, as well as 'Westerns' Nos 6915 *Mursley Hall*, 7821 *Ditcheat Manor*, 5330 and 6959 *Peatling Hall*. 8E (Northwich) was the last venue and another that was largely unremarkable in nature, with, for me, 15 cops from the 24 present. In total, the trip had not been outstanding but at least there had still been much steam to see and overall I had copped 162 from 391 – down to 41 per cent – and I was aware that this figure was likely to continue its downward trend, with only new-builds helping to stem the tide.

Over the next month, when I would often meet either David or Les at Leicester Central station for lunch – where monogrammed crockery and cutlery were still in use in the refreshment room! – I saw Nos D6754, D6753 and D6749, all new and on a test run from their allocation of 41A (Sheffield

Darnall) shed. The end of the month would see me visiting this shed, courtesy of a TRS trip to the Doncaster area on 28 October, sadly a day of dull, low cloud, although remaining dry. We began at 36E (Retford GN), which held 40 locos, all freight bar nine mixed-traffic types, from which I scored just five cops, all 'O1/O4' Class 2-8-0s. The ex-Great Central shed in Retford showed us just 17, with a similar mix, but this time with five 'B1s'; only Nos 63785 and D3619 were cops. And so to 36A (Doncaster) and the joy of 113 locos. The mix did not disappoint, but just 29 cops did! Considering its pivotal place on the ECML, the number of Gresley's express greyhounds on view was surprisingly small, massively outclassed by the freight stud. The Works did present us with a tastier menu, not least with more new-builds, especially Nos E3077-82, more English

Shots inside works were not so easy to capture, for all manner of reasons, but interesting views were there to be had. No 60045 *Lemberg* is obviously having some 'TLC' at Doncaster Works on 28 October 1962, for its very last General Repair. Emerging back to work on 1 November, it was withdrawn two years later.

Electric '3s' (later Class 37) and the very last Brush Type 2, No D5862.

41F (Mexborough) was next and presented 57 locos, all freight apart from five 'B1s'. Little did we realise from this healthy state that it would soon go downhill and close in February 1964, a mere 15 months in the future. Wath – a sub-shed to Darnall – was a delight to those of us who had had little exposure to the Woodhead route electrics. Apart from more Brush Type 2s, we noted Nos 26009, 26020, 26028, 26038, 26008, 26035, 26044, 26017, 26037, 26056, 26050, 26034, 26000 *Tommy*, 26001, 26003, 26042, 26040 and 26057 *Ulysses*. After taking our time enjoying the electric spectacle here, our next port of call, 41B (Grimesthorpe), was very short and not so sweet, presenting only Nos D8066, D8069, D8060, D8054, D8051, D8057 and D8055! Happily, 41A (Darnall) was far more satisfying, having 63 from which I copped 38. The spread of modernisation was, however, apparent, with 28 of the complement being diesels and many of the steam in store. The final drive was to Staveley, to visit the two sheds in the town. First was 41H (the ex-Great Central shed), where 54 were on view, from which only 12 needed underlining; among the total, despite it being a long-time ER shed, were stored MR express locos Nos 46164 *The Artists' Rifleman*, 45656 *Cochrane*, 45594 *Bhopal*, 45570 *New Zealand*, 45576 *Bombay*, 45725 *Repulse*, 46151 *The Royal Horse Guardsman* and 45683 *Hogue*. Well over half of the total was equally redundant. By contrast, at 41E (Barrow Hill) just one or two were out of work, the complement being exclusively MR steam with, out of the 46 on show, just three diesel shunters. I was glad to see Nos 41708 and 41763, between their duties at the local steel mills. This trip's haul was 183 from 493 – 37 per cent!

Peter, one of the 'Gang of Four', was a member of the Derbyshire Railway Society and had sung its praises, so I joined him on 10 November on a two-day trip to Leeds, Carlisle, Cumbria and the North West. As I had been to many of the sheds over the past couple of years, I was not expecting a huge haul for fresh underlining, but was intrigued to see what I would find between Carlisle and Lancaster, around the Cumbrian coast. 55D (Royston) was first, with just three cops out of 30 – Nos D2324, 42770 and 90113 – and several in store, a factor that would become increasingly obvious during the two days. 56A (Wakefield) gave me 15 cops from just 33, with store lines containing two 'V2s' and six 'B1s' among others. The score at 55E (Normanton) was just five – Nos 90664, 43114, 90487, 42083 and 90318 – from 26, with eight in store. 56B (Ardsley) housed 52, 34 new to me, but 20 in store, including four 'A3s'! 55B (Stourton) handed me just one from 12; 55H (Neville Hill) eight from the total of 27, which included eight in store, five of which were more 'A3s'; and 55C (Farnley Junction) five from 23 in store, and no cops – my first 'nil points' from a shed outside Leicester. 56F (Low Moor) was marginally better – 17 from 31 – but another 11 in store, and 55F (Manningham) had six in store from 18. We left Leeds not exactly jumping for joy, with meagre cops and seeing the state of so many much-loved locos.

We now headed north-west towards 24G (Skipton), a completely new shed for me; nine cops from 18 was acceptable, although the complement was nothing to write home about. Percentage-wise, 24H (Hellifield) was much better – eight cops from ten! – and only three in store. And so to our last for the day – 12H (Tebay). Basically fulfilling the role of banking assistance for trains attacking Shap, there were just 11 present, of which six were new to me. By this time we were all punch-drunk on sheds and locos and very relieved to be heading for Carlisle and our overnight stay. The day had produced 116 cops from 306 – 37 per cent again. Would it improve tomorrow, venturing into virgin territory?

11 November dawned with a surprise from the outset, with the fare on offer at 12C (Carlisle Canal) almost double what it had been for my last two visits. Admittedly with seven in store, the total this day was 39, against 20 in 1961 and 24 earlier in 1962! Sadly there were no 'A3s' this time, as their duties had been assumed by diesel power, but steam still totalled 31, with a higher percentage of MR types than previously and, interestingly, No 43139 again on shed. Did it ever go out to work? Glamour

was provided by No 45602 *British Honduras*, together with Nos 61064 and 60900. 12B (Upperby) also held more than in July – 56 against 42 – with just six cops this time, but sadness was great at the sight of 12 'monarchs of the main line' in store – six 'Scots', three 'Princesses', and Nos 46221 *Queen Elizabeth*, 46237 *City of Bristol* and 45588 *Kashmir*. 12A (Kingmoor) was a shadow of its former glory, and these three depots had been as disappointing as the weather from my point of view, with just 11 cops between them!

Motoring around the Cumbrian coast, 12F (Workington) promised more, being my first visit here, and it did not disappoint, with 17 new from 27 on shed. Perhaps not surprisingly, as their work kept them on more local business, eight of those 17 cops were 'Jinties', and four Ivatt '4' 2-6-0s. Barrow was even better in gross numbers – 24 from 40 – although seven were relatively new Hudswell Clarke 0-6-0 shunters, Nos D2511-17. Also present were Nos 58120, 58177 and 58182, the first two already withdrawn, but '82' was to live on, to be transferred to Coalville shed in Leicestershire, before its final end in January 1964.

24L (Carnforth) shed was next to the world-famous station, which featured so prominently in the superb film *Brief Encounter*, and it was to serve up another hike in numbers, with 52 on shed, but only 15 new to me. Our first introduction to the shed was the sight of seven dead locos – Nos 49428, 49449, 43622, 42322, 42457, 42315 and 42319 – and, sadly, elsewhere in the yard the same fate had befallen Nos 45730 *Ocean*, 45714 *Revenge* and 45696 *Arethusa*. The majority of the rest were, happily, ready to do their bit. Continuing our trek down the north-western edge of the country, 24J (Lancaster) was next, offering us 33 to view, of which 18 were cops, including seven more 'Jinties' out of the 12 on shed, the rest being a mix of types. A return visit to 24K (Preston) provided four diesel shunters resting between duties alongside 21 steam – all stored! Somewhat surprisingly, the roll-call differed from before to some degree, with the 'Patriot' representatives now being Nos 45550, 45543 *Home Guard*, 45518 *Bradshaw*, and 45507 *Royal Tank Corps*, the rest being overwhelmingly 14 'Super Ds'.

Another medium-sized shed, 24C (Lostock Hall) did not disappoint, with just two of the complement of 45 – Nos 47572 and 47002 – in store and the remainder a welcome variety of types. Next up, 27D (Wigan L&Y) had four Stanier '3' 2-6-2Ts in store – Nos 40198, 40145, 40191 and 40090 – with most of the rest in full steam, a fact that proved to be painfully obvious inside the shed building and was to be an abiding memory of the day ever since. Whether or not there was a defect in the shed's ventilation, the exhausts of those present were certainly not escaping freely, resulting in a thick green fug that hung to about head height and made it almost impossible to read the cabside numbers! We left coughing and spluttering, with the impression that the life expectancy of the shed staff could have been measured in weeks rather than years! Happily 8F (Springs Branch), the other shed in Wigan, was a vast improvement and we rapidly replaced the air in our lungs. Seventy locos were present, of a wide variety of types and including seven diesel shunters, from which I copped 28. Finally 8B (Warrington Dallam) closed the trip with a further 46 on show, none of them apparently in store. Another mix of freight and passenger types also delighted, including No 84000. So, exhausted again but happy overall with the two days, I went home with a grand total of 175 cops from 480 – down further to 36 per cent.

The days were drawing in but I was very conscious of the continuing – indeed, increasing – withdrawal and scrapping of so many steam engines, and it was becoming harder for me to achieve anything like my original goal. So, two more trips were squeezed into my increasingly busy life before 1963.

18 November 1962 was a solitary day trip to London, by rail. Seen en route were two elderly MR locos in store at Bedford – Nos 43449 and 43808 (a cop) – but I was soon recording newer motive power on the approach to St Pancras in the form of Nos D5393, D5413, D5403, D5401, D5410, D5380 and D5381. All then allocated to 14A (Cricklewood), they would soon fly north with their siblings to finish their lives in Scotland. A quick look into King's Cross and Paddington during the Underground journey preceded a visit to 1A (Willesden), where 75 locos graced my notebook – 64 of them steam, many

in store. However, Nos 45528 *R.E.M.E.* (named in October 1959), 45523 *Bangor*, 46159 *The Royal Air Force*, 46163 *Civil Service Rifleman* and 46146 *The Rifle Brigade* were still alive and kicking (three of them only just!). A short walk to 81A (Old Oak Common) had me scribbling 112 locos into my book, which would confirm the first sight of Nos 6028 *King George VI*, 5056 *Earl of Powis*, 6010 *King Charles I*, 6020 *King Henry IV*, 4961 *Pyrland Hall*, 4080 *Powderham Castle*, 7013 *Bristol Castle*, 6990 *Witherslack Hall* and 4935 *Ketley Hall*. Sadly, all the 'Kings' were in store and only 22 locos on the shed were cops. The day was rather bare, at just 44 cops from 221, but I consoled myself with having closed one or two more gaps, and it was surely once more quality rather than quantity!

Six days later, on 24 November, I went to the DeMontfort Hall to again see Duane Eddy, this time headlining, with The Shirelles and Gene Vincent and Carter Lewis and the Southerners, with Jimmy Page on guitar! Having had a ticket for the first show, at 5.40pm, I managed to sneak in for the second at 8.00pm, initially standing at the side of the auditorium but finally slipping into an empty seat!

The year's final outing was another solo trip, on the first day of December to the Wolverhampton area, but by a slightly unusual method. Leicester City was playing away to Wolverhampton Wanderers, so I hitched a lift on a football special. While the vast majority of the participants were discussing the upcoming game and the likelihood of City staying in the First Division, I was scouring the tracks to record numbers as we made our way west. Not having permits, I would try my hand at bunking, starting with 84A (Stafford Road). Failing to breech the defences of the front entrance, set in large walls, I had heard of a 'back door' entrance, so tried that. I was successful in recording 31 locos before I was discovered and escorted out! Only three were cops, but one was an outstanding 'King' – No 6007 *King William III* – in store together with 12 other locos. I was relieved to have seen this in its final days. It was scrapped at Cox & Danks' yard, Langley Green, around the end of February 1963.

The early 1960s were to see the discarding of front-line locomotives in all regions. On the WR it was the turn of 'Castles' and 'Kings' to start the trek to the exit door. On 1 November 1962, left to right, Nos 6017 *King Edward IV*, 6012 *King Edward VI*, 6014 *King Henry VII*, 6015 *King Richard III* and 6022 *King Edward III* are ragged and abandoned at Wolverhampton (Stafford Road).

Having 'climbed the mountain' into 84B (Oxley), my visit was even shorter, capturing only nine locos, but three of them cops. 21C (Bushbury) was next, a MR freight shed that housed several 'Super Ds', including a cop in the form of No 48895 in the yard, which would go on to be preserved. My haul was 15 from 28 on shed, then it was time to return to the station for the football special home. Having copped 34 during the day I was happy, as were the City fans, but they seemed bemused when I had to ask them for the score! I was relieved to hear that we had won 3-1, two goals by Gibson and a Flowers own goal.

So this mammoth and momentous year ended, with a tally of 3,198 cops. Surely, I felt, I had reached a peak, with so many locos being withdrawn and few parts of the country still virgin to me – and could I stand the pace? I settled down to see in Christmas and wait to see what 1963 would bring.

On Boxing Day it started snowing… Looking back over 50

The ex-LNWR 'Super Ds' fought a rearguard action right into the later years of BR. No 48895 is determined to show that it is ready for anything at Bushbury shed on 1 December 1962. Reallocated to Bescot in October 1964, it was laid aside just two months later, the last of the class, with three of its sisters.

years, memory tells me that it carried on snowing right through to March 1963! Facts might tell a different story, but I certainly remember trips inches deep in snow during the first three months of the year.

As well as the snow, 1963 was to prove a momentous year in all sorts of ways, but probably the most outstanding globally was the assassination of US President John F. Kennedy on 22 November in Dallas, Texas, by Lee Harvey Oswald. Reverberations of the shooting circled the globe and many were the stories of people remembering where they were 'when JFK was shot'. Earlier in the year, in March, Martin Luther King Jr gave his famous 'I have a dream' speech during a protest march on Washington. On the 21st of the same month the infamous Alcatraz penitentiary in San Francisco Bay closed, and the 27th witnessed the publication of Dr Richard Beeching's infamous report on the future of the UK's railways. John Profumo resigned as an MP on 5 June after admitting his affair with Christine Keeler; the Great Train Robbery took place on 8 August, when £2.6 million was stolen from the Glasgow-London TPO hauled by No D326; and Henry Cooper floored Cassius Clay (as Muhammad Ali was then known) in the dying seconds of the fourth round of a fight at Wembley Stadium, only to be denied by the bell and a delay in starting the next round.

Those born in 1963 include José Mourinho (26 January), Julian Lennon (8 April) and Johnny Depp (9 June), while deaths included composer Francis Poulenc (30 January, aged 64), Patsy Cline (in a plane crash on 5 March, aged just 30) and Medgar Evers (a civil rights activist and subject of a Bob Dylan song, on 12 June, aged 37). Musically, the 'Mersey Sound' really took off, with *How Do You Do It?* by Gerry and the Pacemakers at No 1 for four weeks from 6 April, followed by The Beatles' *From Me to You*, for seven weeks from 4 May, then Gerry and the Pacemakers back again with *I Like It*, for four weeks from 22 June. The Beatles ended the year holding the No 1 spot for seven weeks with *She Loves You*, then *I Want to Hold Your Hand*. I would spend much of my time queuing to buy their records and listening to them but, sadly, this would also be the year that Duane Eddy did not reach the UK Top 20 since his first hit in 1958!

My year effectively began with another Barclays Bank course at Wimbledon, from 29 January, again staying with a more senior member of staff in his home and travelling to Wimbledon by rail, gaining some useful Southern cops on my wintry commute. As in the previous year, I stayed in London for the weekend and, despite the snow, decided to visit more sheds. My first destination was the platform end at King's Cross, where I struck up a conversation with another enthusiast who apparently worked for the railway and who expressed a desire to accompany me. 34A (King's Cross) was first, and I recorded 42 locos as we scurried around as fast as we could, including a healthy presence of Gresley 'Pacifics', but only eight cops! The highlight of these was No 60017 *Silver Fox*, and it was also interesting to see No 61912 as a stationary boiler. From there we travelled by Underground to 30A (Stratford). Having been there twice before, I was not expecting to net many steam cops but, from the 105 locos on view, I was pleasantly surprised to record 64 new to me. Most of these, not surprisingly, were diesels, but eight were not – Nos 69632, 90034, 90653, 69461, 69621, 65469, 65445 and 65462. As far as could be judged all the steam on shed was in store and this year would really see an explosion in past servants being cast to one side.

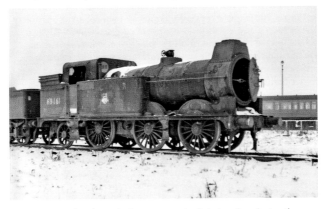

During my trudge through the snow to sheds in London during the middle weekend of my two-week banking course, No 69461 was seen at Stratford on 3 February 1963; withdrawn from Ardsley shed on 1 June 1954, it was then employed as a stationary boiler for carriage heating at Shoeburyness between November 1954 and December 1962. It was cut up at Stratford just a month after this view. Note the remains of part of the 'LNER' legend on the tank above the 'cycling lion' BR totem.

By now my banking shoes were very wet but we persevered and went to 1D (Devons Road, Bow), where all was diesel apart from, incredibly, three 'Royal Scots' in store – Nos 46154 *The Hussar*, 46146 *The Rifle Brigade* and 46147 *The Northamptonshire Regiment*. Back across to west London took us to IA (Willesden), where only about 10 per cent of those recorded were out of work. I only managed six new numbers out of 85 (four of them diesels), but was not too surprised. It was a similar story at our final venue, with just 14 cops from 118 at 81A (Old Oak Common). Happily, three of these were steam namers – Nos 6943 *Farnley Hall*, 5939 *Tangley Hall* and 5041 *Tiverton Castle* – as well as one other steamer, No 3853. 8 February was my final course day and my journey home, now with shoes back to something akin to normality!

Shoes were the least of my concerns, however, as TRS had planned a weekend in the North East for the following weekend, 16/17 February. Snow had fallen heavily since the beginning of the month and the trip looked in doubt as we watched both forecasts and actuals as the week went by. The bus company was still prepared to undertake the journey, if we were prepared and if Ken – their driver – was also prepared. He was! More snow fell during the preceding couple of days before the tour, but we were still being given a green light so … at the crack of sparrows on the Saturday morning we rounded up the 11 participants, all with hats, gloves, thermals, war rations and enthusiasm, and the minibus set off for the frozen north!

This 'Newcastle Weekend' was to prove one of those of which I still have vivid memories, of all those that I undertook over the years. Excitement and anticipation, jaw-dropping visuals, anxieties, setbacks and cops! Having toured the snowy streets of Leicestershire, picking up the various young hopefuls, we headed towards Grantham with the aim of picking up the A1. Then just a normal dual-carriageway, this presented our first problem … only the left-hand single carriageway was passable, its neighbour being the recipient of bulldozed snow, sometimes to a height of around 8 feet! Fortunately, with traffic being lighter in those days and with the weather deterring other less foolhardy travellers, we made decent progress north to Darlington Works, our first destination. The look on the face of the Supervisor on our arrival was a mixture of shock, amazement, incredulity and admiration for our perseverance (and perhaps thinking also of our stupidity?), and he was only too pleased to reward us with the run of the place. In all, 105 locos were in various stages of undress, either new, under repair or awaiting scrap, and 58 were new to me. An immediate sight was the construction of more of the 'enemy' – Nos D5176-85. There were other diesels around, including Type 4s, but steam was in abundance, even if much of it was a collection of boilers on the ground outside, still with their smokebox number plates! I was, however, delighted to see elderly No 65033, the last of the class but still whole, having been withdrawn ten months earlier and slated for possible preservation.

51A (Darlington) shed was only just behind in presentation and cops, with 41 out of the 91 on show, but the main difference here was just seven diesels! An eclectic mix of types saw 'A3s' cheek-by-jowl with elderly freight types, and even 12 MR locos and seven 'Standards'. One of the main hopes for this trip, to an area not visited by me previously, was a boost for cops and a closing of some gaps in the 'Combined', and soon after arriving at 51A I recorded my 12,000th cop – No D2590. 51L (Thornaby) was next, and confirmed my hopes, with 64 new from 77. A varied mix was again present, but with a greater percentage of diesels this time; 19 had been in store at Darlington and a further 11 were at Thornaby, not huge percentages but certainly thin edges of larger wedges to come. Six of the nine BRCW (later Class 27) diesels allocated here early in 1962 were on shed, later to be shipped south to the MR before reversing their trajectory and ending up in Scotland. 51C (West Hartlepool) was next, and the last of the day; only one of the 46 on show was obviously stored, and I was to cop 40, all freight or mixed-traffic.

We had booked accommodation in Consett and after 51C we made our way there, under darkening skies and threatening clouds. Eight of us were to bed down in a local youth hostel, while Les, Ken and I had slightly more salubrious fare in a small hotel in the centre of the town. We went to bed satisfied with the day and wondering what the morrow would bring…

Sunday 17 February brought more snow and a lost minibus! Where it had been parked the night before there was now just a large mound of snow, and it took some clearing after breakfast to discover the bus beneath it! Fortunately the day dawned clear with blue skies, cold but cheering, and the bus started first time! Having gathered our flock we set out up an icy, snow-covered hill from the hostel. We were halfway up when our progress was interrupted by a snowplough going down the hill, halting our momentum. We lost grip and no amount of pushing or bouncing by all of us prevented a slide back down to the bottom. A couple of runs and some more pushing and bouncing and our wheels managed to grip sufficiently for us to crest the brow and continue with our planned itinerary, but an hour behind time.

52C (Blaydon) was first, where we were greeted by sidings containing 27 locos in store, including six 'A2s', three 'A3s' and two 'V2s' To see these magnificent express engines abandoned was disheartening. Elsewhere there were six more, including No 61038 *Blacktail*, but I was consoled to some degree with 41 cops from 57. Arriving at 52A (Gateshead), we were only allowed a limited inspection, from which 23 numbers were taken (six of them steam), of which I copped 15, including all the steam. The next journey was further north-east to visit 52F (both North Blyth and South Blyth), with a freezing boat trip across the River Blyth separating the two railway locations. In total the shed housed just 30 locos, more or less equally distributed in number. South was exclusively 'J27' 0-6-0s apart from one diesel shunter – No D2055 – and all apparently still in use, whereas North had seven of these together with four 'Q6' 0-8-0s and Nos 61238 *Leslie Runciman*, 62022 and D2105, with again none in store.

In complete contrast, all the locos at 52E (Percy Main) were in store apart from No D2248; those idle were 15 'J27s'. 52B (Heaton) upped the ante, presenting 39 from which I copped 21, 12 steam and No 26501 as well as No D6786 and a handful of diesel shunters. As well as a freight contingent, this was a shed catering for main-line motive power, hence the presence

More evidence of the great snows of 1962/63, together with the wastage of so many good engines. Abandoned, never to work again, are, left to right, Nos 64852, 67657 and 67687, among others, together with No 60521 *Watling Street* at Blaydon on 17 February 1963.

of five 'A3s', three 'B1s', two 'V2s' and Nos D357, D260 and D393. 52H (Tyne Dock) was next, home of seven specially modified '9Fs' to work the Consett iron ore workings but, sadly, none of them was at home on this Sunday! However, I did cop 38 from the 42 locos on shed, more closely living up to my hopes and expectations from the trip. With both a roundhouse and straight shed, Tyne Dock was similar to 52G (Sunderland), our next port of call, and the last before our long return journey home. With locos confirming the heavy freight duties undertaken by the shed, it was identical to Tyne Dock in housing 42 locos, of which 38 were new to me, but here only seven were out of use compared to 17 at Tyne Dock.

So, despite the tricky weather conditions, we all survived without slips, trips or falls, no sprained ankles and certainly no complaints from the assembled throng on the way south. Personally, I recorded 571 locos seen and 394 cops – 69 per cent – and a truly memorable and satisfying weekend. Sadly, the prospect was work the next day!

A fortnight later, the next TRS outing was back to Leeds, kicking off in glorious sunshine on 3 March. Incredibly, considering the amount of snow we had received over the past two months, it disappeared rapidly as the thaw set in at the beginning of the month and all was clear at 55G (Huddersfield). Another shed handling freight and passenger turns, there were only 23 on shed, 11 of them 'Austerities'. 56D (Mirfield) was another mostly freight facility but this time the range included both MR and ER locos, including two 'B16s' – Nos 61449 and 61477. Back once more to 56A (Wakefield), the immediate surprise was to see No 70002 *Geoffrey Chaucer* in plenty of steam in the shed yard. Nine locos were in store, including Nos 60115 *Meg Merrilies*, 61309, 40147 and 42862, and littered around the complex was a bevy of 'Austerities'. From 79 recorded, my personal tally was, not surprisingly, only 14 cops. 55B (Stourton) held 28 – only six diesels – but disappointingly all had been seen previously. 56B (Ardsley) was only marginally better, 25 from 71, with 20 in store, including No 60069 *Sceptre*. 55H (Neville Hill) had a further 17 in store, including Nos 60038 *Firdaussi*, 40193, 60081 *Shotover*, 40148, 60084 *Trigo*, 60074 *Harvester* and 60086 *Gainsborough*, and four 'Royal Scots', Nos 46117 *Welsh Guardsman*, 46109 *Royal Engineer*, 46161 *The King's Own* and 46113 *Cameronian*.

A revisit to 55C (Farnley Junction) was to serve up thin gruel, just four cops from 40 (three of them 'Austerities') and nine

No 60069 *Sceptre* stands in Ardsley shed yard on 3 March 1963, with a full tender of coal, even after five months since withdrawal and with the rag on the chimney so loosely tied that it hangs limp atop the smokebox!

stored – Nos 42766, 46103 *Royal Scots Fusilier*, 90726, 46145 *The Duke of Wellington's Regiment (West Riding)*, 42713, 42798, 42771 and 46130 *The West Yorkshire Regiment*. Fourteen of those seen at 56F (Low Moor) had ragged chimneys, being condemned MR, ER and 'Standard' types, but it was pleasing to see both Nos 45565 *Victoria* and 45694 *Bellerophon* still ready for action. Seven cops here out of 43 brought my day's total to just 86 from the mustered 392 – down to a meagre 21 per cent.

The north was again our target for the TRS on Sunday 31 March, starting at 50A (York South), where there were just 12 on view, seven in store – all steam – including Nos 60146 *Peregrine*, 60138 *Boswell* and 60154 *Bon Accord*. York North was a relieving lift, showing us 93 locos, but only 20 cops. Although Gresley 'Pacifics' were absent, their places were taken by a number of other ER front-line types, fighting off the interloping EE Type 4 diesels. Freight servants were also in good numbers, not least yet more 'Austerities'. From there the compass pointed virtually due east as we travelled towards the coast and 50B (Hull Dairycoates). Here I copped the first 21 locos

This wonderful line-up around the Hull (Dairycoates) turntable on 31 March 1963 comprises, left to right, Nos 61475, 61454, 61472, 90695 and 61420. They are all still in service but to be discarded over the ensuing 12 months, apart from the 'Austerity', which lasted until 1967. *Les Wade, MJS collection*

seen – all diesels – and added another 13 of these towards the end of the visit. Between them was exclusively steam, of which only five appeared to be out of use. Again a mix of ER, MR and 'Standards' – predominantly 'Austerities' – the variety was far from disappointing, as was the 63 copped from 97 on shed. If we were excited with that, however, even more was to come, of a most unexpected nature.

The walk to 50D (Goole) shed was well over a mile from the road and our bus, and it was nigh on half an hour before we finally reached the edge of the shed yard but ... we were not to proceed further. Standing guard, blocking our way, was an irate gentleman (who proved to be the shed foreman) in a 'they shall not pass' stance, who advised us that we would not be allowed our visit as some time earlier someone had set fire to one of the diesels! From where we stood we could see No D6733 at the entrance to the shed building, still simmering. Having expressed our horror and explained where we had come from, he relaxed enough to let one of us collect the numbers of the locos we could see and another to

The momentous visit to Goole! Centre right, No D6733 still smoulders after the vandalism attack (see text), and this was the only photograph allowed to our party by the shed foreman. Surrounding the unfortunate loco are Nos 90186, D2598 and 90704. *Les Wade, MJS collection*

take 'one photo'. Needless to say, this was the sole subject of discussion on our long walk back to the coach and speculation as to exactly what had happened. By serendipity, late in 2015, I learned of a rumour that three 'undesirables', in a party visiting earlier that day, had been the culprits, but nothing has ever been proved. The nine locos that we were allowed to record were Nos D2610, D2614, 46415, 90186, D2598, D6733, 43125, 90704 and 43098, and I am eternally grateful to the shed foreman, as eight of these were cops!

Coming back to earth with a bump, we arrived at 36C (Frodingham) to be met by 60 locos, all freight, some of which were in store and of which only seven were new to me. Here the main balance was held by ER 'O1s', 'O4s' and 'Austerities', but with two Stanier 8Fs, Nos 48060 and 48376, present. Once more going almost due east, but this time on the south of the Humber Estuary, our last destination was 40B (Immingham). As at Frodingham, 'Austerities' proliferated, but this time with a number of 'Standard' 9Fs in competition and a small collection of 'B1s' flying the mixed-traffic/passenger flag in the place of 'Britannias', whose absence was noticeable since the cessation of the fast freight runs over the erstwhile GC route to Banbury. Just a handful were in store, including 'B1' Nos 61082 and 61408, and nine cops from 66 here gave me a final total of 116 from 338.

By this date I had been promoted by the bank and had opened a new sub-branch at Blackbird Road in Leicester, which prevented my daily visits to the Birdcage, leaving me to major on weekend visits almost exclusively. I had recently passed my driving test and had bought a car – for £100 and with a loan from the bank of £50 – delivered to me at the sub-branch by a customer. This caused me some problems… Not unusually for a driving school, I had learned in a car with four gears and the engine was always warm and primed ready for the lesson. My new prize was a 1956 'sit-up-and-beg' Ford Popular, with three gears and a 6-volt battery, and by the time I was ready to drive home, the engine was cold. So I pulled out the choke, put it into what had been first gear in the driving school car and careered backwards, nearly hitting a Corporation double-decker bus! I had forgotten that where first was in four-gear cars was reverse with three gears!

Resuming some calmness, I began my journey home and reached traffic lights on Belgrave Road, opposite the old GNR station. They were red as I reached them, so I stopped at the head of a large stream of traffic. For the first and only time that I saw, the inwards stream of traffic for the city centre was halted, to allow the sheer volume of outward traffic to have a free flow. The lights changed to green but I didn't move. I had forgotten to push in the choke and the engine flooded, refusing to fire. I was hastily approached by a policeman who, having learned of the situation, helped push me across the stream of traffic and on to the pavement, advising me to wait there until the engine and traffic flow had cooled before trying to restart the car. This I did, but I still feel the embarrassment even after all these years!

Also at this point Leicester City were in the midst of a run of 16 games unbeaten, as already mentioned, climbing the First Division table as a result, and they had also reached the FA Cup Semi-Final, by beating Norwich City away 2-0 on 30 March. They would go on to defeat Liverpool 1-0 at Anfield on 27 April, earning their place in their second Final in three years – a record for the club. Ken Keyworth and Mike Stringfellow were the goal-scoring heroes of this season, accumulating 46 between them in all competitions.

As stated before, one of the reasons I formed TRS was to go to locations where I could (hopefully) garner the most cops. So it was that on 21 April we made our way as a club to the Lancashire/Manchester area. I had obtained permission to make my first (and only) entry to Horwich Works. Not knowing what to expect, I was delighted to be greeted by Nos 11324, 11305 and 11368, three Aspinall 2F 0-6-0STs that worked as works shunters and had escaped renumbering on Nationalisation to 51324, 51305 and 51368, although they were denoted as such in my 'Combined'! Other joys came from Nos 52515, 51207, 40083, 40073, 40120, 47402 – since preserved at the Great Central Railway – L&Y 2-4-2T 1008 (withdrawn in October 1954 as No 50621), and diminutive works shunter *Wren*. Though perhaps fewer than I had hoped, the 25 cops from 87 was balanced by the rarity of some of the locos on display. I was, however, more prepared for the lowering of my sights as we approached 26B (Agecroft), so just eight cops from 41 was not wholly unexpected. A varied mix of large and small – including Nos 51232 and 51237 among the latter – one diesel shunter and one ER loco, No 61256, kept the interest alive as we toured the facility. 26F (Patricroft) lowered the bar even further – just two from 36! – but by now my interest was veering more towards photographic records than purely numbers. 9E (Trafford Park) gave me just No 42434 out of the 25 present, mostly passenger or mixed-traffic types, but thankfully, on each of these three sheds, there were only small knots of abandoned locos.

9A (Longsight) I knew would be different and so it proved, with 14 WCML electrics alongside 11 diesels – nine shunters – and 13 steam, of which 'Austerity' No 90142 was my only fresh sight. No 46115 *Scots Guardsman*, since preserved, was seen as we toured the shed. A little further south brought us to 9B (Stockport Edgeley), which had none of the 22 on view apparently out of use; and 9F (Heaton Mersey) was almost as good, with just Nos 40113 and 40105 in store among 36. My five cops here were all steam – Nos 48323, 48094, 42675, 90212 and 44494 – and, indeed, only one diesel shunter was present, No D3853. 9D (Buxton) was all steam and still apparently healthy, and my cops here rose to 10 from 27. A final dip into Derby on our way home brought us up short, seeing brand-new Clayton Type 1 Nos D8507/14-19/21/27-29. All with initial allocations at 66A (Polmadie), they would never be seen here again after their impending delivery north.

Just one week later, on 28 April, we had swung the compass to again face south, beginning with the relatively short hop from Leicester to 84C (Banbury). With 'virgin territory' now becoming rarer to find, the haul of just seven new from 39 was accepted, but it was interesting to see still in situ five of the six diesel shunters that had been allocated to the shed in 1955 – Nos D3105-9 on this day – and No 6027 *King Richard I* among the seven locos in store.

Another visit to 82C (Swindon) was next. First sight there was three brand new 'Hymeks' from Beyer Peacock – Nos D7070, D7074 and D7075 – but elsewhere many of the steam contingent were out of use, including cops Nos 4909 *Blakesley Hall* and 1029 *County of Worcester*. Sixty-six locos were logged before we moved into the Works complex, where a further 112 were on show. Happily, 54 of these were cops, not least the latest batch 'Westerns' under construction, Nos D1020-29. One factor regarding establishments such as this, unrecognised at the time, was the contribution to physical health by walking the large acreage across which the locos were scattered!

East along the GW main line brought us to 81E (Didcot). Though 42 locos were on display, sadly 17 had been put to one side, including six 'Halls', two 'Counties' and No 5025 *Chirk Castle*. 'Halls' and a 'Castle' – No 7030 *Cranbrook Castle* – were also in store at 81F (Oxford), but one delight here was the cop of No 92220 *Evening Star*, the last steam loco built for BR and

A celebrity throughout its BR life and on into preservation, No 92220 *Evening Star*, the last steam locomotive built for BR, is here on more humble service at Oxford shed on 28 April 1963, standing face-to-face with a WR visitor.

just 13 months old. The inter-regional nature of the location was evidenced by the presence of Nos 48207 and 45292. No real surprises thus far on this trip, but that was to about to change!

The next venue was 2F (Woodford Halse), roughly midway between Leicester and Marylebone on the erstwhile GCR. There were only 36 on shed, with 14 in store, but there were eight cops for me, including No 64875, which was to provide the shock. Boldly chalked across the smokebox door, in capital letters a foot high, was the name 'DUANE EDDY'! And, no, this had nothing to do with me, but it was gratifying – and inordinately pleasurable – that someone else should share the appreciation of the man and his music. This was not to be the last time I came across this 'graffiti' and, again by serendipity, I was to learn of the culprit some years later. This proved to be a satisfactory end to the day's outing, from which a further 109 numbers needed to be underlined, from a total of 349.

Over the past few years my long-distance trips had all been taken in the company of others, but Tuesday 30 April was to be a solo expedition. I had been tipped off that a visit to a certain shed in Liverpool would be to my advantage, so on that day I boarded a train at Leicester (London Road) station and was pulled north by No 45667 *Jellicoe* – perhaps appropriate, as Admiral of the Fleet John Rushworth Jellicoe was someone else who had set sail for battle! On my way to the north-western port I collected numbers at 17C (Rowsley) – three cops from 14 – 9E (Trafford Park) – one from eight – Manchester and Liverpool Exchange. Using the suggested itinerary in *The British Locomotive Shed Directory*, I caught a tram outside Liverpool's Lime Street station and alighted at Bank Hall station. According to my informant, 27A (Bank Hall) shed was to be my Eldorado, but it was not to prove so easy! Passing through the gate acting as the shed entrance in Stanley Road, I immediately stepped into a passage with the foreman's office on the right. With no permit but a courteous and polite request, I was met with a flat 'No!'

Emerging onto the street, feeling and no doubt looking downcast, I almost literally bumped into a railwayman.

Explaining my plight, he offered his help. He would engage the foreman in conversation, while I was to creep, Red Indian-style, along the passage behind his coat-tails, to then descend the flight of steps into the shed proper. Moving as quickly as possible, not wanting to be ejected before reaching my goal, I recorded 22 locos, mostly in steam and including Nos 45657 *Tyrwhitt* and 45698 *Mars*, but not what I was looking for. Having recorded all inside the shed building, I was losing hope, but there was a siding alongside the far wall and there was a loco, in store, its tender towards me. With heart beating I approached, hardly daring to hope, but on reaching the cab I read 45719. *Glorious* – my 'jackpot', my last 'Jubilee', which had been withdrawn the month before. Truly, a *glorious* sight – I stifled a cheer but did exercise a little leap-kick to celebrate! Now to try and escape without detection. Back up the stairs, slowly at first, along the passage, then a dash for the gate. A booming voice came from the foreman's office, but I was not about to stop!

The rest of the day was something of an anticlimax, but I pursued the suggested itinerary and completed visits to 27E (Walton-on-the Hill) – four cops from ten, the latter including No 61031 *Reedbuck* – 27B (Aintree) – five from 19 – and 8A (Edge Hill) – nine from 37, including Nos 49375 and 46241 *City of Edinburgh*. Returning to Tiverton Road from the last-named shed, I caught a tram back to the city and retraced my way home, by way of Manchester (Central), from where I was pulled by No 45441. The haul for the day was 49 out of 154, but the trip had been a *glorious* success!

It's strange how things work out. I had long before booked a TRS trip to Liverpool, and this took place on 12 May, revisiting some of those locations so recently viewed. 8B (Warrington Dallam) began the day and presented us with a variety of motive power, including Nos 45530 *Sir Frank Ree* and 45638 *Zanzibar* and five elderly 3F 0-6-0s in store – Nos 43657, 43240, 43615, 43282 and 43257. Only five were new sightings from 40. 8D (Widnes) was more thin gruel, showing us only 13, though seven were cops. 8C (Speke Junction) was far better, with 66 on shed and 24 new numbers for me, many of them ex-LMS

Derby-built wartime diesel shunters in the '120xx' series. No 51253 was also a pleasing addition, albeit in store. Next it was back to 27A (Bank Hall), only this time with a permit! There were still 23 on view, just 12 days since my lone visit, and many common to both days, but all the 'Jubilees' had vanished, including *Glorious*. How close I had come to not closing the gap in my collection of the class! 27E (Walton-on-the-Hill) nearly doubled its presence from 30 April, but still had little to offer, as opposed to 8A (Edge Hill), which was next. Here I copped 11 from 55, most of them still in service, but there was a dearth of ex-LMS main-line express engines. 6C (Birkenhead) was the final call and my first visit there. There were 77 on shed and I collected a further 23 cops for my 'Combined'. Nos 47005, 47009, 47164 and 47160 were especially good to see, as were Nos 68066 and 68065. We had been warned to beware of certain unruly elements in this part of the Wirral, but had seen nothing until we began to drive away from the shed, when we were pelted with half-bricks from a gang of youths, seemingly intent on smashing the windows of this bus carrying foreigners!

Between this and the next trip, Leicester City would play the last two matches of the season, after which they would end fourth in the First Division, with Everton as Champions. They would also meet Manchester United in the FA Cup Final at Wembley. Special trains ran from Leicester (Central) to Wembley, taking hundreds of fans, and with United finishing the season 19th out of 22, City had the advantage on paper, not least as they had beaten this opponent 4-3 on 16 April. Sadly it was not to be and – in front of a crowd of 99,604! – they lost 3-1, Ken Keyworth again being Leicester's scorer.

Line closures had slowed over the past six months, but during this summer, before the 'Beeching Axe' was savagely wielded, passenger services were withdrawn between Redditch and Ashchurch and between Chesterfield (Central) and Nottingham (Victoria) on 17 June, and the Uffington-Faringdon branch closed completely on 1 July and Coleford Junction-Speech House Road on 12 August.

Before the next TRS trip, I took the opportunity of briefly returning to the Town Hall Square branch of Barclays on 25

May to have lunch with Les and Peter at Leicester Central. This was enjoyable, for the company, a refreshing pint of Double Diamond and for a convoy of locos seen heading through the station. Where Nos D6815, D6816, D6798, 92229 and 92244 were going is unknown, not least as the diesels were allocated to 41A (Darnall) and the 9Fs to 88A (Cardiff Canton, as it then was)!

For the next trip, we again travelled to the North West, but this time to a conglomeration of sheds to the north of Manchester, after opening in the city at 26A (Newton Heath). Sixty-two locos were seen here and, although I only copped seven, the variety of types retained the interest. During my time visiting various areas, there are some that, for no good reason, have become favourite places. 26E (Lees [Oldham]) is one of those, despite only copping nine from 17 and there being just that small number on shed – I cannot explain the reasoning. I have fond memories of the shed itself and its residents, but I also recall an (as it turned out) amusing event as we were leaving. Obviously, as tour organiser, I had to be aware of what would today be called 'health and safety', but I also had to ensure that I had regular head counts, to make sure we didn't lose anyone. Somehow, however, we were over a mile into the journey to our next destination when a cry came up from the rear of the coach, 'Where's Chirp?' The headcount revealed that John Bird (hence his nickname) was missing! Doing an about-turn, we retraced our journey back towards the shed, to discover 'Chirp' resolutely striding out down the street towards us. Where exactly he thought he was going I know not, but there was relief all round that we were again a complete group!

26D (Bury) was virtually identical to Lees in number on shed and my cops, but the mix was different, being almost exclusively 'Austerities' and Ivatt Class 2 2-6-0s, affectionately known as 'Mickey Mouses'. Travelling a few miles broadly south-west took us to 26C (Bolton), where we were entertained by yet more 'Austerities' among the 39 locos on view, together with the delightful collection of Nos 84025, 84019, 84014 and 84013, three of which were new to me. Due north, towards

Taking a few moments away from our visit to Lees (Oldham) shed on 9 June 1963, I took the opportunity to look at the long-closed Lees station in Greater Manchester. Opened in 1856 as part of the LNWR route from Oldham to Greenfield, it closed in May 1955, when the 'Delph Donkey' passenger train service to Delph was withdrawn.

Despite the nearby station having been closed for more than eight years, the shed at Lees remained open until May 1964, and on 9 June 1963 had a healthy collection of motive power, including Nos D2869, 90671, 90718 and 90708. It is ironic that the shed should have been rebuilt in the same year that the station closed!

Blackburn saw us end up at 24D (Lower Darwen), where we were back again to the levels of Lees and Bury – 17 locos. The same number were again new to me, three of them being Nos 76080, 76081 and 76084. Travelling north-east towards Burnley, 24B (Rose Grove) was next, where 34 were present, of which 15 were cops; the largely freight mix was again predominantly

One of the small handful of Stanier 'Black 5s' that were graced with names, No 45154 *Lanarkshire Yeomanry* presents a fine portrait at Lower Darwen shed on 9 June 1963.

'Austerities'. The day finished with a stretch west for yet another visit to 24K (Preston) and the burnt-out shed. Just nine this time, but two of the 'Patriots' seen before – Nos 45543 *Home Guard* and 45550 – were still in situ. Other than two 'Super Ds', the rest were diesel shunters. Added to my collection was another 72, from 196, the percentage remarkably holding up at 36.

Still looking for uncharted waters that could be navigated within a day's outing, the ever-willing patrons of TRS were taken south-west from Leicester, towards South Wales, on 23 June. A windy 85C (Gloucester Barnwood) was first stop, with 23

One of the saddest sights, of a row of abandoned unrebuilt 'Patriot' Class locos, in the burnt-out Preston shed on 9 June 1963. No 45543 *Home Guard* heads the row in the bright sunshine.

mostly MR locos, this being an outpost of the Midland empire. Seven 'Standard 5' 4-6-0s predominated, joined by Nos 78006 and 78009 and WR locos Nos 1409 and 6437. We then walked across the road by the level crossing and into 85B (Horton Road) shed, WR territory. The first sight that met us was 15 locos in store, including two 'Castles', three 'Halls' and six '5100' Class locos. The remaining 32 were in various stages of rest before their next duties, including a further two 'Castles', seven 'Halls' and one 'Grange – No 6866 *Morfa Grange*. Crossing the River Severn as we left the city, we then skirted the western shore of the widening expanse of water and mud flats and motored to 86E (Severn Tunnel Junction). Being a hub for a variety of work in a number of directions, the 66 locos on shed reflected this, being predominantly freight but including mixed-traffic types that could handle the lighter passenger turns. Interestingly, standing close by each other were Nos 2861, 2807 and 4277, all of which went on to see life in preservation! The glamorous highlight was No 7034 *Ince Castle*, plus, I was later to discover, No 3851, my 13,000th cop.

On this day our Mecca was 86A (Newport Ebbw Junction), and my hopes and expectations were not dashed as we saw 89 locos and I copped 69 of them! Again the vast majority were of the non-passenger variety, both ex-GWR and 'Standards', but four 'Halls' and No 6813 *Eastbury Grange* did their bit to redress the balance. Sadly, 29 of the locos were in store! Close by was 86B (Newport Pill), a shed largely overlooked by many enthusiasts intent on amassing numbers at the larger local sheds. Admittedly only 24 engines were on view, but the nature of the shed's work load was such that I copped 22 of them – 10 of them diesel shunters! One of the local 'more important' sheds was our next port of call, 88L (Cardiff East Dock), where 83 locos were scattered around the shed building and yard and were of a truly mixed variety – and only two diesel shunters, Nos 15106 and 15102 (the latter a pleasing addition to my list). Thirty-six were cops, including No 7016 *Chester Castle*. Our final shed, 88B (Radyr) did lower the numerical excitement a little, down to 54, but for me, copping 45 of them, it was a very satisfactory end to the day, especially as one was No PWM651. It was also gratifying to see a number of the class exclusive to this shed – Nos 3405, 3401, 3409, 3406, 3403, 3400 and 3402. So, as we travelled back to the Midlands I looked forward to underlining a further 232 from 387 and enjoying raising the bar to a 60 per cent success rate. I definitely echoed the title of Gerry and the Pacemakers' No 1 hit that had entered the charts on the day before our trip – *I Like It!*

Spotting trips in June 1963 all seemed to be graced with sunny conditions and Ebbw Junction (Newport) was no exception, as No 7224 stands outside the large repair shop on the 23rd of the month.

With availability dictated by my employer, my 1963 summer holiday was early this year and consisted of a trip to study South Wales from 29 June, based at a guest house in Barry and accompanied by another friend, Keith. Travelling down from Leicester by rail, we departed from Central station behind No D7012, overnight! Not surprisingly, we had a compartment to ourselves in a corridor coach, and to our amazement found an abandoned football in the luggage rack! Too excited to spend much time trying to sleep, we indulged in heading practice with the ball for much of the journey, except when we reached station stops, when we hung from windows to try and see what locos we could note. At Banbury there were Nos D3110 and 6960 *Raveningham Hall*; Oxford produced Nos 92207, 45020,

75022, D3195, 4154, 75055 and 6154; and between Swindon and our final arrival at Barry station, with daylight dawning, we logged just over 100 more!

Having dropped our bags at the digs, we made a bee-line for the gathering of stored locos in Dai Woodham's yard. We could hardly believe our eyes, as we scanned and recorded Nos 5182, 5547, 9445, 9449, 9499, 7723, 5422, 9491, 8419, 5510, 9462, 5558, 7722, 9468, 5794, 5557, 5552, 5553, 5542, 5538, 5572, 5539, 4566, 5521, 4561, 5193, 4588, 5532, 5526, 6023 *King Edward II*, 6024 *King Edward I*, 5541, 4270 and 4253. But if they were a shock, an even greater one was the legend on the smokebox of No 6023 – 'DUANE EDDY'. The chalk fiend had struck again! Over subsequent years I was to see other locos similarly adorned, one with Duane's name spelled backwards and others with different names!

Next door to the yard was 88C (Barry) shed, and a visit was de rigueur. In and around the shed were 29 engines, five

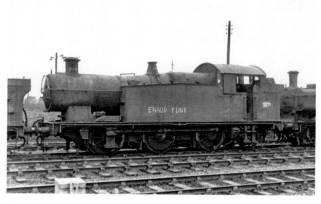

Captured evidence of the 'Duane Eddy' chalker (see text), but this time with the guitarist's name spelled backwards, to siimulate a Welsh location. The loco was copped by me when spotted on Barry shed on 29 June 1963. *MJS collection*

in store, almost exclusively 0-6-0 or 0-6-2 tanks. A brief trip out and back to Bridgend brought us another 21, including two 'Hymeks' and three 'Halls'. Straight after breakfast on 30 June we set out for a visit to 87D (Swansea East Dock), collecting more along the way, with several more 'Hymeks', not least Nos D7064, which pulled us from Cardiff, and D7034, glimpsed on 87E (Landore) shed as we passed. Of the 48 on shed only three appeared to be out of work, and of these together with their neighbours only ten had been seen before. Treasures for me on the visit were Nos 1338, 48434 and 1151. Three locos were trawled from those we glimpsed as we passed 87A (Neath) shed, on our way to see what gems 87B (Duffryn Yard) held. Fifty-five locos there were hoovered into our notebooks – 39 of them cops – and ten in store. No 6832 *Brockton Grange* was a pleasing sight among the otherwise freight stock. On that day

South Wales was always a joy to visit, not least for the sight of such small shunting locos as 0-4-0ST No 1151, seen on Swansea (East Dock) shed on 30 June 1963. Originally a Peckett design from 1907 for Powlesland & Mason – railway contractors – and numbered 779, it was withdrawn shortly after this view and cut up at R. & S. Hayes (later Bird's Commercial Motors) at Bridgend in September 1964.

110 were new to me, on top of the 108 the previous day.

So where to go the following day? After some discussion, we decided to revisit 86E (Severn Tunnel Junction), despite having been there only eight days earlier. Our reasoning was that, with the shed situated on the main line, there would likely be changes on the shed; we could also observe some of the main-line workings. Forty-three locos were recorded en route (18 cops), and 63 were on shed. Despite being a weekday, the reduction from the earlier visit was just three locos! Two of the three locos mentioned earlier, which were to see preservation, were still on shed, in store, and No 4277 was there, but still in service. A total of 25 were abandoned.

Back again to 86A (Newport Ebbw Junction) saw 74 gathered for inspection, with a good percentage stored. Just nine were new to me, including Nos 6852 *Headbourne Grange* and 92006. A noticeable feature of this period in South Wales was the number of EE Type 3 diesels at so many locations; Nos D6826, D6827 and D6856 were seen in quick succession at Cardiff station on our way to 86G (Pontypool Road) shed. My first visit there, the cop percentage rose again, with 27 out of 47, including some of the nine in store. 86F (Aberbeeg) was our next destination, a smaller shed, with just 16 on shed, including No 8417 as a stationary boiler. Twelve were cops, including Nos 4246, 5260 and 9444 in store. Passing Dowlais we finally arrived at 88D (Rhymney) shed – six cops from just seven – then planned to visit 88E (Abercynon). Waiting at a wayside halt, I asked the driver of the DMU that we were planning to board if this was the train for 'Abersinnon'. The look on his face was indescribable as he corrected my pronunciation, and I suddenly felt about 2 feet high! The view of 18 on shed, of which 14 would need underlining, did help me to recover some self-assurance, and my face regained its natural hue on our journey back to Barry! Another 127 was the haul that day.

For 2 July we headed back to the capital city and 88L (Cardiff East Dock) shed. Despite not having a permit, we still had a haul of 43 locos, 18 of them in store … and just three cops, Nos 2887, 92241 and 5617. From there we were back into the city for 88M (Cardiff Cathays) – eight cops from 15 – then made our way towards the valleys, via 88B (Radyr) – one from 25! Then followed 88E (Abercynon) again – three from 11 – 88D (Rhymney) – three from seven – and west to 87C (Danygraig). Another virgin for me, the 23 on what appeared to be a deserted shed were interesting, though virtually all tanks, with just Nos 2283 and 2248 as tender engines. Eighteen of them were obviously in store and it is conceivable that the others were as well. Back to Barry and a quick look into the shed, in case there had been arrivals, producing a tally for the day of 68 cops. There was now no stopping our momentum or ambition, and our landlady was now used to our unusual hours and making us packed lunches.

3 July took us to 87A (Neath Court Sart) shed, via Cardiff station, where 47 locos greeted us, with yet more in store – a total of 14, including No 4967 *Shirenewton Hall* – and 27 cops. 88H (Tondu) was next, another first visit, but this was to become another of my favourite locations, for no real apparent reason! The place had a peaceful air about it and it seemed at home, nestled in its location, but 25 cops – from 30 – obviously helped, including No 1422, hiding away in store. Further into the hills, 88F (Treherbert) was the last of the day, producing eight cops from ten and helping towards the 71 of the day.

The following day was a case of more travelling than pure shed-bashing, as we set out to travel north towards mid-Wales – we were determined to make the most of our 'Runabout' ticket! Still collecting numbers en route, our first stop was 86C (Hereford). The first five locos on shed were in store – Nos 7446, 2214, 7437, 9665 and 9717 – and there were four more further in. No 45283 was a MR interloper among the 27 on shed, and I copped that together with 15 more. Our furthest goal on this trip was Craven Arms shed, by then a sub-shed to Hereford but previously with its own 86G code. We didn't expect great numbers and we knew we were too late to witness ex-LNWR locos there, but the 11 on shed were interesting, not least the 'Castle' and three 'Counties' in store – Nos 5015 *Kingswear Castle*, 1017 *County of Hereford*, 1026 *County of Salop* and 1022 *County of Northampton* (a cop). On our way back south a break was made at 88J (Aberdare) to see the nine stored out of a total of 38 – all of which I copped, together with 10 others. Another drop-in at 88E (Abercynon) – red face forgotten now! – produced three cops, then we were back at 88C (Barry), but there was nothing new there to add to the 63 for the day.

5 July was our last full day and we decided on another long and challenging trip … to the far west! Setting off early for Cardiff, we then had the joy of being hauled by No D7017 to Swansea, where we would have to change. We had checked the timetables and it was obvious that timing at the various sheds we had planned needed to be controlled and the whole trip operated in military style. By DMU, past Llanelly, Carmarthen and Whitland, we finally made our first destination at Milford Haven. The tiny one-road shed, merely a sub-shed to Neyland and passed on the final approach to the station, had closed the previous December, so we had no intention of venturing there, especially as the only loco present – No 4654 – was seen from the train. Our next leg, to 87H (Neyland) shed, was to be by bus, and we were warned that our task should basically be in and out of the shed premises, as the buses were not that frequent to connect with our return train. So off we set. Our task was made easier as there were only eight on shed, but quality again overcame quantity in the form of four cops, including No 7825 *Lechlade Manor*, as well as the vision so far west of No 1001 *County of Bucks*, sadly in store together with No 3639. Literally working up a sweat, we reached the bus stop in time, then after the return from Milford Haven we settled in to relax on the journey to Carmarthen, for our visit to 87G.

Lineside numbers since Cardiff were regular and included eight 'Castles'. Another 'Castle', No 4081 *Warwick Castle*, was one of the three first locos seen on shed, all in store, after which the remaining 14 all seemed to in working order. Mostly freight or mixed-traffic types, they were accompanied by Nos 6804 *Brockington Grange* and 7811 *Dunley Manor*. Gradually making our way back east, 87F (Llanelly) was next. The two-road roundhouse did not disappoint, with 59 present and 32 cops. Sadly, 21 were in store, including Nos 4096 *Highclere Castle*, 5080 *Defiant*, 4076 *Carmarthen Castle* and 5051 *Earl Bathurst*. Back home to Barry, via a cop of No 5039 *Rhuddlan Castle* at Cardiff and No 6670 on Barry shed, the tally for the day was another 89 for the 'Combined'.

Our last day, 6 July, involved the return journey to Leicester, the whole time spent with eyes peeled for even the slightest glimpse of a locomotive! Sixty-one were captured in this way, but not surprisingly only gifting 14 new to me, but these assisted in rounding up the total for the holiday to 650! I would need yet another new biro by the time I had finished the underlining!

Although I was now not spending so much time at my local bridges, bonuses were to be had there following the diversion of some Manchester-London trains to the Midland main line, in connection with the WCML electrification, and in the week following the holiday I was pleased to cop Nos 45516 *The Bedfordshire and Hertfordshire Regiment* and 45508 (an un-named 'Patriot') on those workings.

One might think that the South Wales exertions would have been enough for a while, but no! Just a week later, on 14 July, TRS had another trip, this time to the Shropshire/West Midlands area. Another visit to 84B (Oxley) was first, with 47 on shed but just eight cops and six 'Halls' clustered in a group that looked mightily akin to locos put to one side. Bushbury was next, where six were definitely in store. Only three of the 22 on show were new, but it was gratifying to cop No 49407, still very much in steam. Travelling west to 89A (Shrewsbury), the stock at the two ex-GWR and MR sheds totalled 49 and the integration of the two regions' types led to constant variety. Two in store were, side by side, Nos 45575 *Madras* and 1005 *County of Devon*, and my cops consisted of Nos 45298, 46525, 45143, 41209 and D3194. My first visit to 84H (Wellington) provided 11, with four cops, all WR and just two in store. The two MR representatives – Nos 41241 and 41232 – were both in steam. Towards the Potteries, 5C (Stafford) was next, with

22 and four cops, together with a clutch of five in store, four 'Jinties' and No 49357. 5D (Stoke) upped the ante with 57 present and increased my haul by another ten cops, including Nos 76020, 76075, 78017 and 78056. 5F (Uttoxeter) was another first for me; a three-road shed, close to the station, it did not have an enormous allocation and was to close on 7 December 1964. Just eight locos were on hand, mostly Fairburn and Stanier Class 4 2-6-4Ts, together with a couple of 0-6-0 4Fs, ideal for the more local duties asked of the shed.

Gradually moving further east, 17B (Burton) had 47 for us but only ten new to me. Seemingly none were in store, despite the influx of a handful of diesel shunters, as well as No D5389. Only No 44132 was new steam for me and, despite having an allocation of 'Jubilees', only Nos 45557 *New Brunswick* and 45620 *North Borneo* were on show. Both were to enjoy another year of life. 15D (Coalville) had only 14 (and no cops!), but

No 42542 stands inside the roofless roundhouse of Stoke shed on 14 July 1963. Although still wearing a 5D Stoke shedplate, it had officially been transferred to Buxton five months earlier, from where it ended its days in July 1965.

of interest were Nos 58148 and 61119. And so, finally, to 2B (Nuneaton). The progress of dieselisation and electrification on the WCML had made inroads into the allocation there, and 25 was all we saw. Together with three cops, it was good to see an equal number of 'Jubilees' – Nos 45647 *Sturdee*, 45655 *Keith* and 45624 *St Helena*. Although the vast majority of locos on display that day were not new to me, it was still satisfactory to add another 55 to the book and close yet more gaps, not least towards recording the next 1,000 landmark.

Having enjoyed my week in South Wales, I now considered how to amuse myself during the second week, albeit separated from the first by 14 days! On Monday 22 July 1963, Sonny Liston retained his World Heavyweight title, against Floyd Patterson; Vee Jay Records released The Beatles' first album – *Please Please Me* – in America, but without two of the tracks from the UK version; and I made another visit to 2B (Nuneaton). Sadly, compared to the shed's complement eight days earlier, the occupation level was greatly reduced and the one cop, No 42969, was no counterpoint to a feeling of a day wasted. Hope was high the following day, though, as I travelled in the opposite direction for another visit to Grantham. Managing to successfully bunk the shed, I collected 30 numbers but only secured two new ones – Nos 63974 and D3451 – and it was extremely disappointing to see 16 in store, including seven 'A3s'. Thoughts of when the class hauled 'The South Yorkshireman' expresses through Leicester Central did nothing to lighten the gloom surrounding them. Happily, back on the platform, one of those celebrated from the past – No 60106 *Flying Fox* – worked in on an express and I said a quiet prayer of thanks.

By this time I had become more confident in my motoring abilities and this was eating into my railway attention, not least as girls were also impinging more into my life. One especially was about to enter my life, but more of that shortly.

I took a decision to expand my spotting horizons by eschewing public transport and enjoying more flexibility and freedom by road travel. Thus on Thursday 25 July I set off for

31B (March) shed. Parking in the shed yard, I approached the foreman's office and was given permission to tour the shed, which contained 39 locos, 10 in store and 12 new to me. Again, it was front-line locos that were in store, including Nos 70030 *William Wordsworth*, 70013 *Oliver Cromwell* and 70002 *Geoffrey Chaucer*. Thankfully, although I was not aware of it at the time, this storage was but temporary, for they were to be transferred to the MR by the end of the year. '13' was, of course, to last until the very end of steam in 1968. On my way back to Leicester I called in at 34E (New England) and rejoiced at seeing 59, but recoiled at the number and type in store! Of the 12, there were two 'A3s', five 'V2s' and 'A2' Nos 60520 *Owen Tudor*, 60523 *Sun Castle*, 60500 *Edward Thompson* and 60533 *Happy Knight*; with No 61912 standing in the yard awaiting its fate, having travelled up from King's Cross, where I had seen it, after its work as a stationary boiler. It was rapidly dawning on me that I had probably seen the best years and that I should accept that the future would neither be so bright nor productive.

It was to be a month before I made my next outing, on 25 August, the day after Leicester City had begun their new season, after doing well in the previous one, with a 1-1 draw away to West Bromwich Albion. 5D (Stoke) was first, having a healthy complement of 49 and only three obviously in store. It was becoming ever more difficult to be certain of status, as depots were running out of rags for the chimneys and not everyone discarded the unwanted locos to the side-lines. The complement echoed the duties expected of this important location, with a complete range of types but, somewhat surprisingly, no diesels! That was not the case at 5B (Crewe South), but at least the vast majority was still steam, including WR visitors Nos 6850 *Cleeve Grange*, 6855 *Saighton Grange* and 6826 *Nannerth Grange*; 76 were on show and while only 10 were new for me, the number and variety were satisfactory. 5A (Crewe North) had a wide variety among its 49 residents, not least with WR interloper No D859 *Vanquisher*. Several 'Jubilees', 'Royal Scots' and 'Duchesses' were present and added glamour to the eclectic mix around them. At the nearby Works complex the 94 on site represented a completely different ball game! As well as five of the new-build 'Westerns' – Nos D1030-34 – and 19 'Brush 4s' – Nos D1550-68 – surprise delights were No D202 and electrics Nos 27004, 26036, 26024 and 26012. The steam presence was a mix of maintenance and withdrawals, and even visitors Nos 63901, 63869 and 63867, together with Nos 84053, 84021, 84012, 78003, 82038 and 82030.

Striking west for a return visit to 89D (Oswestry) brought variety with both WR and MR locos alongside five 'Standards' and five of 27 in store, including No 7033 *Hartlebury Castle*. The adjacent Works was disappointing, with just Nos 73026, 3630 and 3865 in residence. 89A (Shrewsbury) again saw MR and WR cheek-by-jowl among the 52 on view, including No 51218 in steam, but three had been put to one side, including No 1005 *County of Devon*. 84H (Wellington) provided me with one cop – No 3776 – from 11, of which two were in store. Another attempt to access 84A (Wolverhampton Stafford Road) from the front was unsuccessful, so again an attempt was made at the rear. Sadly, this was short-lived, leading to the recording of only eight locos and at least five in store, including No 6012 *King Edward VI*. Another climb to 84B (Oxley) was rewarded with 51 engines, with only one – No 4906 *Bradfield Hall* – in store, but four cops, including No 7012 *Barry Castle*. And so, again, to 21C (Bushbury), where No 48895 was still in service, as was No 49446, but No 49452 was stored, having been withdrawn in December 1962. Although the sheds were no longer new to me and my tally had grown substantially over the past two years, I still garnered another 84 for the 'Combined'.

Derby Works Open Day on 31 August 1963 ended eight years of spotting and the transformation of our railways, and my reactions to it meant that I only recorded diesels there, apart from Nos 63725 (for repairs), 42212, 75014, 46447, 75011 and 41537 (on the point of being withdrawn after its departure from its Gloucester stamping ground). New locos under construction were Nos D5233-50 and D7571-77, aiding my tally of cops to 43.

The eight complete years – August 1955 to August 1963 – had provided me with the opportunities to see 14,069 different locos, 11,737 of them steam, with the 14,000th being No 49395 on Crewe Works, awaiting its fate – happily preservation – after withdrawal from 9D (Buxton) in December 1959, four years earlier! The space of the last 12 months had provided 3,392 new ones, an average of just over nine per day, a rate that just could not continue.

Into my ninth year, the next TRS trip was a return visit for me to London, on 22 September 1963. 1B (Camden) was totally devoid of steam with the sole exception of No 46240 *City of Coventry*, stored on a siding at the side of the shed. Out of use as far as this shed was concerned, it was nominally returned to steam and sent across London to 1A (Willesden), officially two weeks before this date. It remained there until a move to 5A (Crewe North) in August 1964, from where it was withdrawn the following October. 30A (Stratford) was a shadow of its former glory and, although there were 53 locos present, all were diesel apart from five in store – Nos 65464, 65469, Departmental 33 (ex-68129), 65462 and 69621. Withdrawn from this, its home shed 12 months earlier, the last-numbered, a 1924-vintage 'N7' 0-6-2T, was to escape the torch, being saved for preservation by the National Railway Museum. Similarly, 70A (Nine Elms) was a skeleton compared to previous years, with just three Bulleid 'Light Pacifics', but I did cop Nos 82022, 33009 and 73115 *King Pellinore*. By contrast, 75D (Stewarts Lane) was bulging with 30! Sadly, all the steam, with the exception of No 35006 *Peninsular & Oriental S.N. Co*, were in store, including cops Nos 32347, 32343, 32337 and 32340. Also present, to add glamour for this Midlands spotter, were Nos E5002, E6006, E5006, E5003, and E5013, together with Nos 20001 and 20003 and Pullman cars *Niobe*, *Rosamund*, *Agatha*, *Iolanthe*, 35, 167 and 166. To complete the Southern sheds on this outing, 70B (Feltham) was surprisingly busy, holding 51 locos. Although 14 steam were in store – including Nos 30497 and 30499 – the rest were more than holding their own against the 17 diesels.

Crossing to the north of the river, the 46 locos at 81C

(Southall) were predominantly steam with just eight obviously out of use, but including Nos 5917 *Westminster Hall*, 4944 *Middleton Hall*, 4987 *Brockley Hall*, 90630 and 90693. Although greater numbers were in store at 81A (Old Oak Common) – including many 'Kings' and 'Castles' – these still only presented a relatively small percentage of the 112 on shed! Though there were diesels, mostly 'Hymeks' and 'Westerns', the vast majority was steam. The same could largely could be said for nearby 1A (Willesden), for only 11 diesels stood among the 69 in total. A handful were in store, including No 46101 *Royal Scots Grey*, newly withdrawn from 16D (Annesley) shed. Again, despite previous visits, my cops still reached 101!

As the years progressed and musical fashions shifted, a greater number of records were hitting the No 1 spot but staying there for a smaller number of weeks. Trends in music following the 'Mersey Sound' also heralded the slide from the charts by many previously highly successful artists. After success with *(Dance with the) Guitar Man* at the beginning of 1963, the rest of the year saw Duane Eddy's chart heights go from 27 (with *Boss Guitar*) to 35 (*Lonely Boy, Lonely Guitar*) to 49 (*Your Baby's Gone Surfin'*). Although other records followed from him, he was not to reach the UK charts again until 1975.

As this was happening, I undertook a weekend trip to South Wales, staying again with the landlady in Barry. I began furthest west at 87G (Carmarthen), then to 87F (Llanelly), 87D (Swansea East Dock), 87C (Danygraig), 87A (Neath Court Sart), 87B (Duffryn Yard), 88H (Tondu), 88F (Treherbert), 88J (Aberdare), 88D (Rhymney) and finally on day one 88E (Abercynon). Having visited during the summer, I did not expect magic, but it was interesting to see shifts in loco numbers compared with my previous visits, not least at Danygraig and Tondu, which both seemed to be housing more than previously. Needless to say, there were many locos in store, but the predominant sights were still steam and this day had provided another 51 cops for me.

Day two began with a further visit to Barry Docks and Woodham Brothers' yard, with all the scrap locos – still 34, as seen before. So on to 88C (Barry) shed, then 88L (Cardiff East Dock), 86A (Newport Ebbw Junction), 86G (Pontypool Road) and homeward bound via 85B (Gloucester Horton Road) and 85C (Gloucester Barnwood). The experience was much as the first day, except that the cops tally was only 24. A lot of miles for little return!

On Monday 21 October 1963 both the country's musical and my working landscape were to change. The term 'Beatlemania' was first used in print in the *Daily Mail*, to describe the reaction to the 'Fab Four'; and I was transferred from Town Hall Square, Leicester, to the Syston branch of Barclays, 6 miles or so to the north of the city but actually closer to my home in Thurmaston. From a staff of around 30 I was to be in a team of just five, but this I didn't yet know as, the day before, Sunday 20 October, I took the TRS back down to Swindon. Calling at 84C (Banbury) en route, the scene was as I had found in South Wales – 37 on shed, a third in store, including No 5926 *Grotrian Hall*, no outstanding flavour and just two cops. 82C (Swindon) shed was much the same, but with 'Halls', 'Castles' and No 1006 *County of Cornwall* in store together with more prosaic stuff. The Works was better, but largely due to the locos that had previously remained elusive and had come from far corners to be scrapped here. I gratefully accepted 13 for the pot, mostly steam but including Nos D7082, D1063 *Western Monitor* and D833 *Panther*. A long trek east took us to 81D (Reading), where again main-line express locos were in store together with lesser mortals and, although I only copped five out of 35, three were these ex-mighty warriors – Nos 7818 *Granville Manor*, 6991 *Acton Burnell Hall* and 5908 *Moreton Hall*. A bonus from

Right top: One of the many delights of a trip to Swindon Works was seeing locos fresh out of the shops. Here No 7803 *Barcote Manor* waits to return to work at Machynlleth on 20 October 1963. This shot was 'Highly Commended' in a Syston Camera Club competition in 1964.

Right bottom: My one and only visit to Reading (South) shed saw No 31857 in light steam on 20 October 1963, with the massive GWR building at Reading General in the background.

the visit to the town was my first and only opportunity to visit the Southern shed (ex-70E), next to the GWR station but at a slightly lower level. Nine Southern locos were on view, with five new to me. Next up was Didcot, with the same mix as elsewhere, and the same applied to 81F (Oxford). It was, indeed, proving more difficult to find locations that could present worthwhile fare, with only 35 cops for the day.

On my first day at Syston I took the opportunity to wander to the nearby junction at lunchtime and was rewarded by copping No 90492 and no fewer than five BRCW Type 2s! A good start! The staff seemed pleasant enough, not least the young female machinist, with whom I was to forge a relationship a year later. I had had girlfriends before, but Gill seemed something special. After a few months there, I would begin to give her a lift home after work and our friendship grew.

I had to work most Saturdays, but I was able to arrange to have 26 October off, so I could join Peter on a two-day trip with the Derbyshire Railway Society, beginning at Eastleigh. The great attraction was to be visiting places thus far foreign to me, with someone else managing things and in the company of Peter.

Like so many locations recently visited, there were many locos stored on the shed (I recorded 48!) but they were of types new to me and seeing 86 in one place was back to the magic of earlier days. No DS233 (ex-30061) was the first number in the book here, and this set the seal. In the Works I was met with another 56 receiving various stages of attention, from which I added 22 to my collection, including Nos E6003, 34055 *Fighter Pilot* and 30923 *Bradfield*. 70E (Salisbury) was next, with 28 on shed including Nos 4626 and 42273, as well as the Southern stalwarts. Moving to the South Coast, 71B (Bournemouth) followed, where the mix was express passenger and mixed-traffic and no diesels! 71G (Weymouth) was similar, except that Nos D2295, D7008 and D2083 spoiled the clean sweep and I copped a higher percentage than I had become used to – 12 from 17 – including two WR locos, Nos 4610 and 7780. The final destination of the day was 72A (Exmouth Junction). Not being new to me, I was not overly disappointed with just a few cops, but was grateful for Nos 6430, 4694 and 4655 among the Southern and 'Standard' majority. So, a total of 104 on this first day and a feeling of satisfaction.

The second day dawned dull but dry and the visit to 83D (Laira) provided a veritable feast of variety but, sadly, all but three of the steam element – Nos 2822, 6988 *Swithland Hall* and, strangely, 34024 *Tamar Valley* – were in store, a total of 16, including three 'Counties', a 'Hall', a 'Castle', No 1363 and eight members of the '4500' Class. Into the wilds of Devon, Okehampton shed (sub-shed to Exmouth Junction) was another first (and last) for me but, unfortunately, there were only four on shed. However, three were cops – Nos 41238, 31849 and 31812. So we were quickly back on the coach and off to 72E (Barnstaple Junction), where 15 awaited, ten of which were Ivatt Class 2 2-6-2-Ts. Half of these were cops, together with Nos 34107 *Blandford Forum* and 34030 *Watersmeet*. Bypassing 83C (Exeter), as this was to close within days, 83B (Taunton) was next. Thankfully all was steam bar three diesel shunters, but 15 of the 34 had been put to one side, including three 'Halls'. 72C (Yeovil Town) was yet another virgin shed for me and, although only 17 were on shed, it was a rich mix of SR, MR and 'Standards' and eight cops. 82D (Westbury) was last before returning north, and this echoed the situation of much in store but, happily, 38 of the 41 in view were steam. My total to be added to the 'Combined' came to 66 for this day, and 170 for the weekend, which was gratifying.

The last trip of 1963, on 1 December, was to 34E (New England), 31B (March), 34F (Grantham), 40E (Colwick), 16B (Kirkby-in-Ashfield) and 16D (Annesley). While the day was to provide evidence of yet more inroads by dieselisation and the casting aside of former steam stalwarts, there were some surprises. As well as the influx of the new 'Brush 4s' at the Peterborough shed, the presence of 14 MR locos was not expected. Eight 'Britannias' in store at March was not a pleasant vista (although life on the MR beckoned), but No 61181 in

A visit to March, in the heart of the ER, on 1 December 1963 strangely features two MR locos! No 48719, from 3D (Aston) shed, is shoulder-to-shoulder with No 44260 from 17C (Coalville). Note that both have already been manually adorned with the new codes to be allotted in 1964 – 2J and 15E respectively.

One of my final shots of the year was from my final b&w film for many years. In store at New England on 1 December 1963 are, right to left, Nos 60017 *Silver Fox* (complete with fox motif on the boiler casing), 60029 *Woodcock*, 61122, 60032 *Gannet*, 60025 *Falcon* and 60021 *Wild Swan*.

steam as a stationary boiler was more enjoyable; not so an empty 34F, which had just closed. Pluses to end on were No 61943 as a stationary boiler at Colwick, No 41844 still in work at Kirkby, and 'Jubilees' and 'Royal Scots' at Annesley. The day provided 65 cops, which helped towards my total for the year of 2,768 and a grand total of 14,545 (11,665 steam) to date.

1964 was to prove a pivotal year for me. David took over running TRS, and I turned 21. I would have a new camera and, no less important, I would have a new girlfriend! Thus far I had been visually recording on 12-exposure b&w film and felt this too restricting, but I had also noticed the greater attractiveness of colour in publications. As 1963 had progressed, hints like bombs were dropped, leading to me receiving a new Minolta SLR for Christmas. With 35mm film and the proposition of 36 exposures per film, I could not wait to try it out but, with interest being much slanted to railways, I had to wait for my first trip.

The year began relatively slowly for line closures but, reflecting the Beeching Report, with its proposals for abandoning some 6,000 route miles, the pace would quicken. On 6 January the Bewdley-Tenbury Wells line closed; exactly three months later both branches from Kemble – to Tetbury and Cirencester – lost their passenger traffic; 4 May saw the closure from Caernarfon to both Llanberis and Afonwen, the same day as the local services ceased on the Edinburgh (Waverley)-Berwick-on-Tweed route; and on 1 June came the closure of the ex-GN line from Humberstone to Melton Mowbray North. Each succeeding month to the end of the year saw a rapid abandonment of so many others.

But while the railways were contracting, music output was to expand from this year, with Radio Caroline born as a 'pirate station', broadcasting from a ship offshore to circumvent the control of broadcasting popular music by the record companies. Merger with Radio Atlanta on 2 July created massive competition for the BBC. 'Auntie' was hitting back, however, with the launch of BBC2 on 12 April, with *Play School*. On a personal note, one of the later presenters of this programme was Carol Leader, alongside whom I had earlier performed in the Thurmaston Methodist Church amateur dramatic group!

Nelson Mandela was sentenced to life imprisonment in South Africa; Winston Churchill made his last House of Commons appearance; 'Mods' and 'Rockers' fought 'on the beaches' during the summer; the trial began of the Great Train Robbers; and Britain won four Gold Medals in the Tokyo Olympics. The Beatles appeared on *The Ed Sullivan Show* in America; Malta gained independence from the UK; and Jack Ruby was found guilty of killing Lee Harvey Oswald. Born this year were Nicolas Cage (7 January), Christopher Eccleston (16 February) and Sandra Bullock (26 July), while deaths were Alan Ladd (29 January, aged 50), Jim Reeves (31 July, just 40), Gracie Allen (27 August, of a heart attack aged 69), and Sam Cooke (11 December, shot at the age of 33). Leicester City could not emulate their feats of the previous season and drifted around mid-table for much of the season, despite one of their biggest wins, 7-2 against Arsenal on 13 August 1963. They began 1964 with a 2-1 win at home against Stoke City and did go on to claim silverware, beating Stoke City in a two-leg League Cup Final on 22 April, played at Filbert Street in Leicester.

It was becoming increasingly obvious that I had seen my best years on the railway. There were fewer locos around that I had yet to see and, with ever more rapid withdrawals of steam, fewer opportunities to see them, and fewer locations that were still virgin territory. With girls playing a greater part in my life – and I could photograph them as well as the trains! – my new camera was going to be put to great use, with the collection of numbers taking something of a back seat. Still important, but less so.

My first outing was on 2 February, revisiting sites in the Birmingham area. In bright sunshine I began with renewing my acquaintance with Nuneaton, which still housed 16 steam locos and only two diesel shunters. I then moved on to Saltley (now coded 2E, as opposed to 21A previously, following wholesale re-coding of depots still operating in the Midland Region). My first visit here was rewarded with 61 on shed, including a slightly unusual occupant in No 6813 *Eastbury Grange*. A small number of 'Jubilees' were present, but No 45709 *Implacable* was not living up to its name by being in store! Aston shed was another first for me, but had little of note to offer other than the number of engines and the sight of No 49430 still in service. A return to Bushbury saw two of three 'Super Ds' still in steam; Stourbridge had seven Stanier 8Fs and two 'Standard' 9Fs as well as a healthy complement of WR locos; Kidderminster was home to a mere 12, with two, Nos 4114 and 6317, in store; and Tyseley rounded off the day with 33 on shed and 27 mostly in steam – a broadly satisfying day with 55 cops.

I had decided that my new camera should be christened with its first colour slide film on my next day away, which was a Derbyshire Railway Society tour of Manchester sheds on 9 February. Sadly, the glorious weather of the previous weekend was not to be repeated, as we set out from Derby in decidedly dull conditions. I proposed to continue my pig-headed approach to exposures, which had, by and large, served me well with b&w film, but that, together with the slow-speed Kodak film, proved to be my undoing.

Stockport was our first call, which again was still flying the steam flag against the influx of diesels and electrics. Three 'Jubilees' were present, but No 45732 *Sanspareil* was already ragged although official withdrawal did not come until the following month. Heaton Mersey did have a reduction in motive power compared to previous visits, as did Longsight, with the exception of an increase in the presence of WCML electrics. Gorton did us proud with 54 in view and relatively few in store among the mix of MR, ER and 'Standards'. 1926-vintage No 47406, allocated to Gorton, was to go to Edge Hill shed in Liverpool within a year and lasted until the end of 1966, before being eventually saved for preservation. Newton Heath was again to prove to be an important shed still, housing 63 (60 steam) of varying sizes and power categories and with just a handful in store. Trafford Park was much as previous visits, as was Patricroft, but a pleasing visitor was No 45558 *Manitoba* of Fleetwood shed, which would move to Leeds (Holbeck) within two months. Agecroft had more of its complement in store than previously, including No 45716 *Swiftsure*, which would also move to Holbeck later in the year, for just a three-month stay before withdrawal. Bury housed 21 including No 42700, another loco destined for preservation. Horwich Works was reduced in numbers, but No 11305 was still in situ, as was No 1008 (ex-50621), while Nos 52458 and 52289 were both cops. Bolton, Lower Darwen, Lostock Hall and Rose Grove completed the day that, despite previous visits to the area, still provided me with 67 more for the 'Combined'.

I was not to fare any better with the weather when, on 1 March, I was out at Thurmaston photographing No 35003 *Royal Mail* on a Home Counties Railway Society 'Derby & Burton Special', slightly late at a few minutes past 11am; and much was the same when using the camera on a TRS trip to Darlington (Works and shed), York and Doncaster six days later. While it was pleasing to see colour, the film did not cope with the conditions to my satisfaction and the overall blue cast certainly was not to my liking. Asking around, I was recommended to try Agfa and this I did. The trip did present 'fresh meat', but otherwise the locations had much of what had been seen 12 months earlier, and even more in store. Only 43 were new to me.

The extra exposures gifted to me by the 35mm camera did not, unfortunately, improve my basic photographic skills in the short term, and I still had much to learn about framing and composition, as well as exposures! The results were teaching me lessons, not least to look more closely at what was in the frame, but it took me too many years before I became more fully satisfied. In the wake of the 'Beeching Axe', lines, stations and locomotives were disappearing at an increasing rate but, inexplicably in hindsight, I showed no interest in chasing these before they went. My loco bias was so much ingrained, while also being an active member of Thurmaston Methodist Church I gravitated to the drama group within the church and this, as well as the ladies, demanded more of my time and interest.

There were still the shed-bashing trips and the next was on

22 March, to Rugby, Woodford Halse, Banbury, Swindon (Works and shed), Gloucester (Horton Road and Barnwood) and Worcester. Each had its own delights and still plenty of steam around, but so many were now in store, not least on the WR sheds, as the Region moved towards becoming the first to be rid of steam. Of interest was the sight, on Swindon Works, of the construction of Nos D9500-07, the first of the Type 1 0-6-0 diesel-hydraulics. Designed and built to replace traditional locos on pick-up freight and shunting duties, the need for them was disappearing as fast they were being built! Fifty-six were finally built, but none lasted even five years before withdrawal. Some did find other work on industrial railways and thereby lasted long enough for a number to be retained, as Class 14s or 'Teddy Bears', into preservation. My first visit to Worcester shed did provide a few cops, but the day was limited to 61.

Spring continued with trips on 19 April and 3 May – to Stoke, Crewe and Liverpool, then to Yorkshire. Rather strangely I did not take my camera on these trips and at this distance in time I cannot think why! The first three sheds, including Crewe North (still coded 5A), all had on show a fare similar to previous visits, including a WR presence at Crewe South, following the closure of Gresty Lane shed in June 1963. This day had Nos 6817 *Gwenddwr Grange*, 4916 *Crumlin Hall*, 6803 *Bucklebury Grange* and 6851 *Hurst Grange*. The biggest change on North shed was the influx of 'Britannias' transferred from the ER. There were 11 of them, together with six 'Duchesses', four 'Jubilees', No 45534 *E. Tootal Broadhurst*, and even another WR loco – No 6825 *Llanvair Grange*. The highlight of the day was, however, within Crewe Works, where the main show was the array of new 'Brush 4s' under construction – Nos D1574/5/9-81/6-1616. What had happened to the missing numbered locos was never discovered. Nos 26024 and 26011 were also within the Works complex. Mold Junction, Chester and Birkenhead sheds all had reasonable incumbents, but without locos of note, and the day ended with 81 cops – and no bricks at Birkenhead.

On 3 May began a jaunt to the north at 55G (Huddersfield), which had a poor showing of just 13; 56D Mirfield was even worse at 12; but number and variety picked up at 56B (Ardsley). Locos seen in store here previously had all gone, with just Nos 43136 and 60148 *Aboyeur* obviously out of work, although the latter was not to be withdrawn for more than a year. Three cops out of 40, however, was not overly exciting! Farnley Junction had three 'A1s' in store; Stourton was a shadow of its former self; Normanton was sparse at just 14; but Wakefield was as busy, in numbers, as before, with 66 and a large percentage of 'Austerities' and 'B1s'. Royston had more than expected, again with numerous 'Austerities'; Langwith Junction – another first for me – was obviously still very much 'in work', and from 411 I accrued 27 cops, a percentage way out of line with what I had become accustomed to and a great welcome. Most of these were ER 'O1/O4s'. Hasland was the last before home and, with its five cops from 15 – including No 47004, in store – my day's tally had risen to 47.

A sunny 9 May was to see me witness the incredibly rare sight of a 'Duchess' on the ex-GCR route through Belgrave & Birstall station, but only just! The RCTS (East Midlands Branch) 'The East Midlander No 7 Rail Tour', from Nottingham (Victoria) to Eastleigh and return, was due here around 8am, but was running at this point some 2 minutes ahead of schedule. It had taken me longer than I had planned to cycle to the station and as I arrived on the footpath approach I heard the loco whistle for the station. Leaping from my bike, I clambered on to the fence and raised the camera to my face just in time to snap No 46251 *City of Nottingham* as it roared southwards. Happily, the shot turned out well and was used in 1989 as the cover of my *Leicestershire Railways Memories* book; unhappily, the publisher then lost my slide!

The following day, 10 May, I would follow south, with another coach outing to WR sheds. Oxford was followed by yet another investigation of Swindon shed and Works, with the former housing three 'Counties' in store and the latter having progressed on its new-builds to Nos D9508-13. There were also several MR locos on the Works, which was something of a surprise. I had taken my camera with me this time and took advantage of the bright sunshine for most of the day, not least at our next port of call, Bath (Green Park), where we were greeted by Nos 53809 – the last of the class still working – 53806 and 53808 (in store). St Philip's Marsh shed was a delight in the sunshine, with plenty of green-liveried and copper-capped express engines, but, sadly, too many in store, including two more 'Counties' – Nos 1027 *County of Stafford* and 1006 *County of Cornwall*. Unfortunately we were only able to view Bristol (Bath Road) shed from the raised area by the shed entrance, but it was all diesels anyway! Nearby Barrow Road shed was all steam bar five diesel shunters but, despite it being an ex-MR facility, it was crammed with WR locos and not an ex-MR example in sight! This may have been my return visit to many of these locations, but the day still produced another 43 cops. Among the musical entertainment on the coach radio was *Don't Throw Your Love Away* by the Searchers newly at No 1 and the Rolling Stones' *Not Fade Away* not far away.

And so into my 'Technicolor' world of transparencies! Many of our TRS trips were undertaken in this coach, owned by Graham (seated) and driven by Ken (standing). Resting outside Swindon Museum on 10 May 1964, the latter was ever present and was almost a member of the group!

No 8102 has been deprived of something vital as it stands outside Swindon Works 'A' Shop on 10 May 1964! Allocated to Worcester and perhaps in for attention, it was withdrawn just two months later, so perhaps the attention was not cost-effective.

From Swindon we visited Bath (Green Park) where No 82004 was seen outside the shed on the same day.

Although I was still enjoying the shed-bashing trips, the rewards, in cops and the sheer number of locos on view, were diminishing, while the closure of depots throughout the UK was reflecting the trend. In addition, with BR Works sites becoming unable to deal with the flow of locos for scrap, industrial scrap merchants were increasingly joining the cull, adding to the locations to capture locos. Thus it was that I tracked down the rumoured 600 Group yard in the depths of the countryside near Kettering, and on a sunny 24 May I drove Dave and Les to investigate the site. Various items had already received attention from the cutter's torch, including some ex-London Underground stock, but for us the interest was to be focused on the handful of ex-BR locos present, including Nos 5018 *St Mawes Castle*, 30507, 30921 *Shrewsbury*, 31922, 33024 and 30935 *Sevenoaks* – rare diet indeed for this Midlands location. Thereafter, a pilgrimage to the site would be a frequent occurrence.

It was now obvious to me that my original ambition, of seeing all the locos in the country, was a forlorn hope, but I was still determined to mine whatever untapped seams I could discover. So, on 14 June, I was out again, with Peter as companion in my car, closer to home than some of my travels, with a mix of return visits and new locations. Nottingham shed opened the day, followed by my first sight of Colwick shed, predominantly steam, mostly freight types and, incredibly, long-withdrawn No 61912 that I had earlier seen as ex-stationary boiler at King's Cross and would see later in New England shed yard. The two facilities at Retford were much as seen before, as, to a degree, was Doncaster shed, although here the percentage of diesels had increased and much of the remaining steam was in store. Mexborough shed had closed four months earlier but, incredibly, contained No 61050 receiving attention on the wheel drop! It was later to be moved to Retford in April 1965, Doncaster two months later and, finally, Langwith Junction a month after that. Withdrawn officially in February 1966, it became Departmental No 30 before being finally dispensed with in October 1968. Situated at the eastern end of the

Woodhead route from Manchester, Wath depot housed the iconic locos from that route and gladdened the eye, in company with several 'Brush 2s'. Controversially closed to passenger services from 5 January 1970, freight survived over this non-standard electrified line until 17 July 1981, by which time many of the locos had already been withdrawn. The shed closed in 1983.

I only made one visit to Wath depot and I am mighty glad that I did. At the eastern end of the Woodhead Tunnel route from Manchester, it boasted a phalanx of the line's iconic electric locos. On 14 June 1964 No 26022 heads a long row of its sisters.

Canklow was another first for me, predominantly populated by ER 'B1s' but also home this day to Nos 45620 *North Borneo* and 45721 *Impregnable*, on diagrams from Burton-on-Trent! Staveley (Barrow Hill) housed few in number but happily, for me, presented Nos 47001, 41734 and 41528, all still hard at work. The ex-GC shed here still contained much of interest but had lost the forlorn contingent of stored 'Jubilees' that had been the gloomy vision on a previous visit. Langwith Junction was a delightful mix of ER and 'Austerities' in steam and diesel shunters among the 51 on shed, and certainly overshadowed the impressions from Westhouses, Kirkby-in-Ashfield and Annesley that finished the day; but, still, another 58 into the book. The other delight from the tour was the collection of cop number 15,000 – No 26055 at Wath.

Above: Although its nameplates are missing, No 45620 *North Borneo* is very much in steam, on a roster from Burton-on-Trent, heading a line at the back of Canklow shed on 14 June 1964.

Right: My second visit to Staveley (GC) shed was in much kinder weather conditions than the first, allowing me to calmly snap Nos 63701 and 63725 resting on shed on 14 June 1964.

The following weekend, 21 June, was another TRS trip, this time to the Southern Region. Salisbury was a pleasing and varied mix, as was Bournemouth, and Eastleigh was its usual productive self, though this time with more in store than I had remembered from previous visits. Obviously, the roster of locos had moved considerably since my last time here, as I garnered another 27 cops, not least 'Terriers' Nos 32646 and 32650. Fratton was to be last and was eagerly anticipated, as we had heard of the store of some preserved locos. 'T9' No 120 and Nos 30926 *Repton*, 30245, 30925 *Cheltenham*, 30587, 30850 *Lord Nelson* and 30777 *Sir Lamiel* were, indeed, all here, together with 13 other engines, six of them steam in store. Another enjoyable summer's day and another 45 added to the collection.

After the recent rather frantic pace it was another three weeks before my next exploit, and one that was to provide many memorable moments, not least at the outset at Derby on 12 July, a day of excellent weather after a period of rain, when, accompanied by David, I watched the almost unbelievable sight of No 60114 *W. P. Allen* drift into the station at the head of our

A TRS visit to Bournemouth shed on 21 June 1964 sees No 82027 at the head of a row of locos in the yard, with, to the right, Nos 34104 *Bere Alston* and 41312.

A period of transition at 15C, with two MR 4Fs in company with rather grimy looking Nos 92102, 92104, 92121, D5227 and D5405 on 27 June 1964.

train, the Derbyshire Railway Society tour from Sheffield to Cardiff. The excitement of both tour participants and local, non-travelling enthusiasts was palpable. With the train filled with enthusiasts, it was relatively easy for David and I to be kept up to date with identities of locos that we saw en route, including on shed at Burton-on-Trent. There was little major excitement, though, until we approached the top of the Lickey Incline, where our road was partially lifted and under the control of a permanent way gang. Reversing onto the adjacent running track at Barnt Green, we then travelled down the bank on the up line. At the foot of the bank we saw Nos 8400, 9493, 8405, 92230 and 8403, all ready and waiting to assist the next trains to go north. The '84s' would only see a further three months here before being withdrawn from service. Delayed by the movement at Barnt Green, we eventually reached Worcester (Shrub Hill) station at 11.25am, some 35 minutes late. Here we were met by No 5054 *Earl of Ducie* and there was more excitement, both on and off the train. Before our onward journey we were guided to the nearby Works and shed, where we were 'let loose' for a quick shed bash. The Works contained three 'Castles', Nos 3683 and 5932 *Haydon Hall*, four diesels and three stored ex-GWR railcars, Nos W23W, W26W and W20W. Almost the first loco on shed was No 1661, fitted with a large, US-style spark arrester chimney; elsewhere, the other 27 on shed were again a mixed variety, with four in store, including No 6992 *Arborfield Hall*.

A sight to gladden the eyes of all enthusiasts at Derby Midland on 12 July 1964, as No 60114 *W. P. Allen* draws into the platform with the Derbyshire Railway Society railtour that it would haul to Worcester, via 'wrong line' working down the Lickey incline!

Back on our train, we reversed direction as No 5054 hauled us around the sharp curve towards Foregate Street and on towards Great Malvern. Hereford was next stop, for another detraining to visit the local shed. We arrived only 16 minutes down, after some spirited running from No 5054. Twenty-one locos greeted us on shed, including Nos PWM656 and 5092 *Tresco Abbey* in store. Sadly our onwards journey slipped again in timing and we arrived at Pontypool Road – for another shed visit – a little over 30 minutes behind. Almost literally at a sprint, 43 locos were recorded in less than half an hour and, re-boarded, we set off having regained a couple of minutes on schedule. We sailed past Cardiff (Canton) shed and negotiated our way into the yard of our destination at Cardiff East Dock shed, only 35 minutes late.

While the layout of the shed was not particularly expansive, herding a train-load of enthusiasts keen on seeing all 43 locos on shed – and perhaps taking time looking at and/or photographing the last 'County' in service, No 1011 *County of Chester* – was a challenge for the tour operators and final departure at 5.35pm put us 45 minutes behind time. But we were not yet finished, as we still had a visit to Severn Tunnel Junction to savour. Twenty of the 56 on shed were in store, including Nos 33014 and 31825 on their way to Barry scrapyard. Another unexpected sight, but this one still in steam, was No 45598 *Basutoland*. Leaving there 55 minutes late, at 7.05pm, there was little of note on the journey back, until we arrived at Worcester. No 60114 had been declared a failure after a prang on Worcester shed while we had been away, and alternative motive power – No 45263 – had to be found for us. Arrival at Derby was around 11.20pm, 80 minutes adrift! Needless to say, both David and I were much later back home than anticipated, but, for me, 43 more cops was reward enough. It had been a very well organised tour let down by operational constraints.

The following week was another TRS outing, heading towards London on 19 July, for a mix of virgin and return visits. The former was first, at Guildford, with its half-roundhouse and yard accommodating 26 locos, including No 30064 enjoying the summer sunshine with No 34093 *Saunton*. It was my first visit here, and I gained 11 cops. Redhill was another shed new to me and, although only providing five cops, it did present the spectacle of 'B1' No 61313 amid a galaxy of SR locos, having failed on its working into the region. It had arrived in the area, at Eastbourne, by 26 June and had got to Redhill on 3 July. It

While I personally favour the unrebuilt, original versions of Bulleid's 'WC/BB' 'Pacifics', I must admit to preferring the rebuilt 'Merchant Navies'. No 35013 *Blue Funnel* has obviously been well cared for by the shed staff judging by its condition on Nine Elms shed on 19 July 1964.

Looking rather as it if has stopped suddenly, shooting its innards forwards, No 31400 is temporarily parked at Redhill on 19 July 1964, with, behind it, ER interloper No 61313. See the text for more of the story of why it was there.

would not leave to return home, via a working to Reading, until 1 October! Feltham was now mostly diesel, with, like Redhill, a clutch of steam in store. Southall briefly changed the regions and presented us with a healthy quantity of mostly steam, but too many in store for real comfort. Nine Elms also held a good number – with just five diesel shunters out of 70 – but again too many in store, including No 35015 *Rotterdam Lloyd*. Visits to Cricklewood and Willesden completed the roster, with more diesels and steam in store, but No 46163 *Civil Service Rifleman* on the former (just a month before withdrawal from Annesley) and a handful of 'Duchesses' and 'Jubilees' on the latter added to the appeal. My last venture before an annual holiday had provided a further 53 cops.

My fortnight's holiday from Barclays at Syston was booked from Saturday 22 August 1964. With the 'Gang of Four' all available for that period, we had discussed at some length where we should go, plumping for a return visit to Scotland for the first week and a trip around the South Wales valleys for the second … in my car! While I had long become used to driving it, this was to be a whole new test and I wondered whether 'the old girl' would survive! With the innocence and certainty of (our relative) youth we set out by loading the car onto a van at Nottingham station, to be attached to the rear of our train to Carlisle over Friday night/Saturday morning. I put my trust in BR but slept fitfully on the journey over the Settle & Carlisle route. The shunter took an hour to put the van into a siding alongside Carlisle (Citadel) station around 6am, and I was greeted with a slight dent in one wing … the restraining bars within the van had not been properly secured! There would be several months of arguments with BR on my return home. Also, when back on terra firma she would not start! Not a good beginning to our week! Happily, after a liberal spray of Holts' 'Damp Start' onto the plugs and a few hefty swings of the starting handle, we were up and running, with bodies and luggage crowded into the passenger compartment and boot of my little vehicle. The 6-volt battery and the underpowered engine struggled to cope with our weight. I was the only one with a full licence, with David still a learner and the other two not able to drive!

One of the first sights at Carlisle (Kingmoor) was No 70002 *Geoffrey Chaucer*, last seen in good shape at Wakefield, in a line of stored locos that also included Nos 45696 *Arethusa* and 45613 *Kenya* – a sombre start on a dull morning that was to be further depressed with another five obviously in store, including two 'Royal Scots'. Upperby shed was no better, with ten in store including Nos 46226 *Duchess of Norfolk*, 46200 *The Princess Royal*, 45640 *Frobisher*, 45532 *Illustrious*, 46110 *Grenadier Guardsman*, 45545 *Planet* and 46118 *Royal Welsh Fusilier*. With Canal shed closed for more than a year, we left Carlisle behind and motored to the spot with the magical name of Beattock; sadly, the complement on shed was not magical – Nos 42688, 42060, 42169 and 42693 and no cops! Swinging south-westward, we headed for the capital town of Dumfriesshire … and into the rain! Only 17 on shed, but it was our first introduction to the 'cathedral' styling of the

And so to another visit to Scotland, but this time with more films and with colour! No 80076 stands in the rain, dumped alongside Dumfries shed on 22 August 1964, the day of its withdrawal. Just ten years old, it had begun its early life working in and out of East London on the Tilbury line.

G&SWR. We had just one more to visit on this day – Stranraer – which was fortunate as the heavy rain was causing problems as we negotiated the road undulations. When I pressed the accelerator the windscreen wipers stopped, resulting in a pantomime of foot on and off the accelerator to enable a sweep of the windscreen! Four cops from 12 there was not the greatest return, nor was just 20 cops for the whole day. I had hoped for more … and for better weather!

23 August was no great improvement, but at least the heavy rain had stopped as we made our way from our digs in Ayr to the local shed, another of the very attractive 'cathedral' type. The main content was a collection of MR 'Crabs', and although the majority of locos were ex-LMS there were, rather strangely, three 'B1s' in store – Nos 61355, 61197 and 61396. A *very* brief entry to Kilmarnock Works delivered to us just No 80111, but at least it was a cop! Hurlford was a fascinating place, with a street of derelict houses near the shed. Les took great delight in climbing the outside steps to a door that stood virtually on its own, to be photographed knocking on it! He also enjoyed posing with a wheel-less pram! The content of the shed was a mix of MR and 'Standards', with 13 cops out of 33. Ardrossan was last and contained one of the old school – No 57566 – as well as a mix similar to Hurlford. I cannot recall how we found accommodation, but we landed at a B&B run by a lady who had recently lost her husband. She was, understandably, rather nervous at taking in four Sassenachs, and it took her friend to persuade her that 10pm was too early to expect us to come in, so we were given a strict curfew of 11pm. We spent the evening at the local ten-pin bowling alley, where the wooden pins were reset by hand! As we slept the night away, the Beatles were playing the Hollywood Bowl in Los Angeles!

Happily the following day saw an improvement in the weather and things began to look more cheerful, except at Greenock, our first call on 24 August. There was just No 42216 inside the shed building, with five steam in store outside and two Andrew Barclay 0-4-0 diesel shunters, Nos D2426 and D2427. Motherwell and Carstairs both had many in store,

'Any old rags and bones?' Les plies his forlorn trade outside the derelict railway workers' houses close to Hurlford shed on 23 August 1964!

including Nos 54463 and 60512 *Steady Aim* at the latter, which also housed No 60522 *Straight Deal*, in steam. Our return to Bathgate again saw rows of stored steam, including No 60042 *Singapore*, but also, on a happier note, a clutch of 'J36' 0-6-0s still working – Nos 65234, 65297, 65282 65243 *Maude* and 65267. Corkerhill was a shadow of its former glory, with over half in store, so it was a pleasure that Polmadie was well stocked, albeit with plenty of diesels, not least the relatively new Clayton Type 1s. No 60535 *Hornet's Beauty* was the only thing of beauty!

Planning to concentrate on Glasgow sheds for the next day, we checked into a cheap hotel and I parked outside. We found a local bar in which to spend the evening, but noticed the silence that descended as we walked in and the total absence of any females therein. We had hardly settled with our first pint when the landlord called 'time' – it was 10 o'clock! Walking back to the hotel, I noticed I was parked in a restricted zone, so resolved to arise very early in the morning to move the car. The alarm went, I dressed and went outside, walking straight into a monsoon!

With the nearest available parking around a mile away, I was

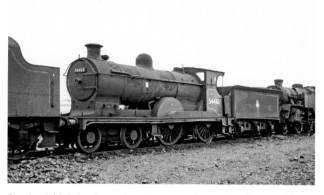

Another 'oldie' that I was pleased to see and record on film was No 54463 in store at Carstairs on 24 August 1964. It would sadly be scrapped at Motherwell Machinery & Scrap Co, Inshaw Works, Wishaw, three months later.

soaked before breakfast on the 25th, and not amused! I was doubly less than happy to be soaked for a second time when I was despatched to fetch the car and pick the others up from the hotel! Fortunately, the onslaught stopped within an hour or so, for which I was grateful … it is not pleasant or easy trying to write numbers in a soggy notebook! The rain had stopped by the time we reached Cowlairs Works and this proved to be a very interesting location. A mix of operating types was common to both MR and ER locos present, and a further delight was No 55189. The number of cops was not huge, but the visit was still enjoyable, as was the collection at Eastfield. The many diesels present had placed much of the resident steam into store, but there was still pleasure to be had from seeing 66 locos in one place. Dawsholm was, like Fratton earlier, home to preserved locos – this time HR 4-6-0 No 103 (ex-57916), CR 4-2-2 No 123 (ex-54010), NBR 4-4-0 No 256 *Glen Douglas* (ex-62469) and GNoSR 4-4-0 No 49 (ex-62277). In addition there were 12 others on shed, mostly 'Standard 4' 2-6-0s. High with the excitement of seeing these, we packed back into the car and I began showing off my driving skills in cavalier fashion … and reversed straight into a set of buffer stops! This did nothing for my ego, the confidence of my passengers or the boot of my car. Fortunately, we were still just able to lift the boot flap to access our luggage!

After Parkhead we were due at St Rollox Works, but because of the altercation at Dawsholm we were running a little late. The Works' party leader was waiting impatiently for us at the entrance of the Works and he shouted in no uncertain terms for us to hurry up. We were hustled, somewhat breathless, into the building to view 15 diesels and absolutely no steam! We were glad to leave the confines and make it into the shed and yard, where there were 26 locos, roughly half and half steam and diesel. The highlights here were No 45374 (of Aston shed) in the yard newly out of Works, and No 45742 *Connaught*, alongside the main line by the coaling stage with a good head of steam. Kipps and Stirling were hoovered before we reached hallowed territory at Perth. Here there were 39 on shed – yet more in store – but seven cops from a well-farmed location was acceptable and we also had the sight of No 46166 *London Rifle Brigade* simmering in the twilight before making its last ever revenue-earning journey, back to its home in Carlisle. We had planned to stay at our old haunt but it had changed hands, and the new incumbent directed us around the corner to a bank manager's house! He was away but his wife agreed to let us stay, again with some nervousness!

26 August dawned bright and improved as the morning progressed. We were not to visit many different locations this day, in view of the distance we were to travel, and we were not to capture many numbers, but the sights and sounds at the locations made up for this. First stop was Hilton Junction, where the lines from the north split to go either to Glasgow or Edinburgh. Parking close to the signal box, we spent a happy couple of hours watching and photographing and, in my case, copping No 61350. I took the opportunity to write a card to work, but though it was addressed to all, my thoughts were really for it to be for Gill.

While we did much frenetic travelling around Scotland, we also took some moments out to relax, as at Hilton Junction, where the routes for Glasgow and Edinburgh from the north diverged. Nos D5327 and D5132 swing towards Edinburgh, past the junction signal box, on 26 August 1964.

Our first shed was to be Aberdeen (Kittybrewster), and this was reached without too much difficulty, apart from a slightly hairy drive down a hill into Aberdeen with a large lorry on my tail. With my steering still acting up and describing zigzags as I drove rather than straight lines, the downhill speed pushed it towards its limits and effectively prevented the lorry from overtaking me. By his closeness and constant horn sounds he must have thought that I was doing it deliberately. I was mighty pleased to arrive at the shed, although not so happy to see just a handful of diesels, mostly shunters. Ferryhill was an improvement but only just, as the handful, albeit steam, was no larger and the only saving grace was to see Nos 60023 *Golden Eagle* and 60034 *Lord Faringdon*. So, only five cops in the day, but it had been more relaxed and we stayed overnight in Aberdeen, to cut down on unnecessary driving late into the evening.

We began the 27th with a return to Ferryhill. Few locos had changed with the exception of the appearance of No 60019

Bittern. A detour to Montrose saw No 64597 doing some shunting; Dundee presented us with 28, including Nos 60532 *Blue Peter* and 60528 *Tudor Minstrel*; then we moved on to Thornton Junction. This was an attractive mix of ER types, with only a handful in store and a rather precarious-looking ash pit! Dunfermline and Grangemouth presented yet more variety and some cops, with not too many in store; and we ended with a fleeting return to Bathgate before finding lodgings in Edinburgh. We did the tourist bit to the Castle in the evening, but just missed a performance of the Tattoo. In contrast to the earlier days, we were now being graced with magnificent sunsets.

All too soon we were on our last day in Scotland! The 28th was another sunny day as we ventured to Haymarket, which was now all diesel, again with many Clayton Type 1s. Dalry Road was mixed in favour of steam, and I was pleased to cop two 'B1s'. St Margaret's was again a very busy shed, still predominantly steam but the number of diesels was on the increase; the highlights were No 69128 as a stationary boiler – surrounded by timber for the firebox! – and No 60116 *Hal o' the Wind*. The journey south took us to Hawick, for just three on shed (Nos 78047, 78048 and 76049), Tweedmouth (incredibly housing four 'A1s'), Alnmouth (to cop five out of the six on shed, all 'K1' 2-6-0s), and Blyth, North and South. The presence and mix here was as before and only a handful were in store. We stayed the night at Whitley Bay and awoke on the 29th to a flat battery and a flat tyre! The former was my fault, as I had left the lights on all night! Happily, being a Friday, we were able to sort out matters fairly quickly and resume our journey, beginning with a return to Heaton. The transformation was dramatic – 29 on shed, 21 in steam, but only Nos 60940 and 60946 not in store! It was very sad to see No 60002 *Sir Murrough Wilson* side-lined together with No 60070 *Gladiateur*. Gateshead was showing similar signs, with seven in store including Nos 60040 *Cameronian* and 60083 *Sir Hugo*, whereas Tyne Dock, Sunderland, Consett and Darlington were still, thankfully, largely operational steam. The latter saw David in paroxysms of joy at the sight of No 60530 *Sayajirao*, ex-works and sparkling in the late afternoon sunshine! So, on the day that saw the release of Roy Orbison's *Oh Pretty Woman*, we arrived safely back in Leicester and I prepared to underline 281 new numbers.

We granted ourselves two days of rest, then on 1 September we were off on 'Round Two', calling in at Worcester shed on our way to South Wales. We nearly did not reach that hallowed ground, however. We somehow found ourselves in the midst of an Army convoy, travelling at some speed down country roads on our way to Hereford. Being a very hot day, I had the car window down and was suddenly being attacked by a wasp. Slightly panicking as it buzzed around my head, I caught the steering wheel as I tried avoiding action and drove off the road, up a grass bank, along a bit and back down again, into our place in the convoy, in a matter of seconds. How the car stayed upright or I did not hit anything I shall never know. The wasp disappeared, probably in fright at my manoeuvres.

Pontypool Road, where we saw brand-new No D1615 on a test run from Worcester, followed Hereford, then across the Heads of the Valleys to Aberbeeg once more. Then followed Rhymney, Dowlais (with just No 5618 present), Merthyr, Abercynon, Ferndale (for No 5613), Aberdare, Treherbert, Llantrisant and Barry, where we lodged at my favourite place. Leaving Treherbert to go to Llantrisant, we were faced with a steep climb and the car was not pulling well. I was rather concerned, as the gradient did not seem that steep, so flagged down a car travelling down the slope. After explaining my fears, the driver pointed out that everything was probably all right, as the steepness of the hill was an optical illusion, in that it was actually worse that it appeared. He also confirmed that it was not far to the brow of the hill, so, having thanked him, we restarted and continued without further hitch. Happily these sheds housed very few diesels.

Our obvious goal after breakfast on the 2nd was the expanding Dai Woodham collection. Engines on the Docks had moved around a little since previous visits, but the greatest change was the sight of locos seemingly everywhere there was a railway line, to accommodate the latest influx. As well as the hordes of ex-GWR types, there was now a sight of SR and MR locos – including No 48431, 53809, 53808 and 45690 *Leander*. The adjacent engine shed's allocation had dwindled to just nine steam (three in store), while No D6935, just four months old, was a precursor of what was to come. Dragging ourselves away from the incredible vistas, Neath was next on the menu, with a healthy presence but, again, many in store, including No 51218 inside the shed. Llanelly was similar, but Swansea East Dock was effectively dieselised, as all 14 steam were in store, including SR locos Nos 33010 and 31917 on their way to a scrapyard. Tondu was now an all-diesel shed and a great disappointment, as was Danygraig.

We took a day off on the 3rd, so it was on 4 September 1964 that we returned to the valleys, beginning at Radyr, with 33 on shed, 31 steam, but, sadly, 18 of them in store. Cardiff East Dock closely mirrored this, as did Newport (Ebbw Junction) before we rang the changes by examining Cashmore's scrapyard

One never quite knew what would appear, and this short convoy was a huge surprise, as No 48354 arrives with yet more locos for Barry scrapyard on 2 September 1964. Some of the existing residents can be seen to the right of the train.

– containing No 31623 among others – before again visiting Severn Tunnel Junction. Another SR loco, No 31913, was here pending its very last journey.

The 5th was another day of non-railway pursuits, before our final day out on the 6th, to just Llanelly and Neath. We were obviously feeling the strain … or at least I was, being the only driver! We took a quick look at Barry shed, where we were surprised to see No 15101 away from its home at Cardiff (Cathays) shed, then home. Another 87 cops made a grand total of 368 for the two weeks. Little did I know that this was to be my last railway-only holiday! The reason was to crystallise on 4 October. I had worked with Gill for a year and we had become very close. She announced that she would give up her boyfriend for me and would do the deed over the weekend of 3/4 October.

On Sunday the 4th Peter and I travelled to Grantham, to witness (I hoped) No 46257 *Sir William A. Stanier FRS* at the head of the Home Counties Railway Society 'York Special'. Sadly,

In 1964 I worked at Barclays Bank, Syston, with Gill Walker, and by the year end we would become what would later be termed 'an item'. Four months prior to this situation, on 15 June, she is snapped during her machine work on customers' statements.

I had gone to Grantham, then fully dieselised, on 4 October 1964 to see No 46256 *Sir William A. Stanier FRS* on the Home Counties Railway Society 'York Special', but it had been withdrawn the month before so we had to be content with No 70020 *Mercury*. The 'Britannia' is seen here preparing to restart from the station stop.

the powers that be saw fit to withdraw it the preceding month and we were graced with No 70020 *Mercury* as a substitute – at least it was still steam, on a line that was now very much diesel-operated. I drove home wondering if Gill had done the deed and went to work the next day with heart in mouth as to the outcome. She kept me in suspense for some time before confirming; I was greatly relieved and we were now, as the term would later be, 'an item'.

As well as the opposite sex, I had developed a real interest in what would become my favourite sport – ten-pin bowling – and I captained the 'Gondoliers' team in the Dakota League at the alley in Lee Circle, Leicester. Playing once a week in a league, studying for my bank exams and participating in the church's amateur dramatic group, railways were facing stiff competition, but I was booked on another trip south on 11th – and Gill came with me! What she thought of it all I am not sure, but she seemed content enough.

She had a gentle enough baptism at Didcot, apart from the sight of an obviously damaged No 48734, standing at the rear of the shed with a bent running plate, widespread discolouration and obvious evidence of its withdrawal after being involved in an oil train fire! Gill's education was to gallop ahead, however, with our next location as we revisited Swindon. The last of its class, No 1011 *County of Chester*, was in steam in the shed yard, but would be withdrawn within a month. Three other 'Counties' were on the scrap line, together with three 'Halls' and No 6804 *Brockington Grange*, but plenty of the other non-diesel locos were in steam. In the Works the usual wide variety was on show, but surprises in the form of 11 ER 'V2s'! In 'A' Shop more 'Teddy Bears' were under construction – Nos D9516-29 – and in the extensive yard stood No 6000 *King George V* and TVR No 28 (GWR No 450) awaiting full restoration. Bristol (Barrow Road) had 58 crammed into its yard, both MR and WR, but with the latter in the majority. Gloucester (Horton Road), our last call, was almost as full, with some MR locos, as the adjacent ex-MR shed at Barnwood had closed five months earlier. Despite none of the locations being new to me, I still managed a trawl of another 37 cops for the 'Combined'.

My last outing of the year was a return to the scrapyard near Kettering on 18 October, which now held Nos 44109, 44540, 41326, 6839 *Hewell Grange*, 41327, 3852 and 33029.

My tally at the close of December was 15,584 – 12,285 steam – an increase of 1,039 over 1963, very much fewer than the previous two years, but that was to be expected. The Beatles stood at No 1 with *I Feel Fine* and I echoed that sentiment after my first Christmas with Gill. Leicester City were still holding their own in the First Division, having beaten Coventry City 8-1 on 1 December in the 5th Round of the League Cup!

1965 did not start well, with the price of platform tickets increasing by 50%, to 3d! Then on 24 January the death was announced of Sir Winston Churchill, aged 90. Representatives of 112 countries attended his funeral, after which his

Right top: Seen from Waterloo signal box, No 34051 *Winston Churchill* backs into Waterloo to work the special funeral train on 30 January 1965.

Middle and bottom: The platform ends are thronged with people wishing to pay their own tribute as No 34051 eases gently away from the station and onwards to Hanborough. *All Ray Ruffell, Silver Link Archive*

funeral train was hauled by No 34051 *Winston Churchill* to Handborough station, for his burial in St Martin's, Bladon. The Beatles were awarded MBEs for services to music in the New Year's Honours; the year's biggest-selling single was *I'll Never*

Find Another You by the Seekers, entering the charts on 27 February and eventually spending two weeks at No 1; and *Mary Poppins* was the second-highest-selling LP, with Julie Andrews winning 'Best Actress' for her part in the film. Later in the year, on 8 October, PM Harold Wilson opened the Post Office Tower in London and the GPO introduced 'numbers only' telephones, allowing international direct dialling. On 11 November Ian Smith declared UDI for Rhodesia. More personally, the 'Gondoliers' became the Dakota League Champions that year at the Leicester bowling alley, and I also broke the league's record, with a 618 series, made up of 183, 217, 218 games. They were the first of what would become many trophies.

On the permanent way, the after-effects of Beeching were still being felt. On 4 January the death knell sounded for passenger services between Leek and Uttoxeter, local services between Swindon, Bristol (Temple Meads) and Worcester (Shrub Hill), Lostwithiel to Fowey and Glasgow (Central) to Carlisle, followed on 22 February by Carmarthen-Aberystwyth, Scarborough-Whitby (Town) on 8 March, and Dumfries-Stranraer from 14 June.

By the end of the year, the WR would officially be steam-free, and it was this progression, together with the increasing difficulty in finding new places to chase steam, that was to dent my enthusiasm for constant outings. Although my camera was light years ahead of what I had been previously used to, I had no interest in capturing diesels or electrics on film. As well as not being as aesthetically pleasing as steam, my thought was that they would be around for many a long year. I was wrong in this assumption, and in adopting this selective approach to my hobby. I was to rue my decisions in future years and it took many years for me to learn the error of my ways! Thus, I didn't venture forth until 7 March, when Gill and I travelled in my car to Norwich by way of New England. By now I had graduated from the basic Ford Popular to a slightly more luxurious Morris 1000, complete with four gears, heating, a proper floor, independent windscreen wipers and predictable steering!

There was just a handful of 16 bedraggled-looking steam on

New England – all in store, of course – including Nos 60112 *St Simon*, 60062 *Minoru* and 60106 *Flying Fox*, but the most interesting was yet another sight of No 61912, the ex-Kings Cross stationary boiler, the third location at which I had seen it since its last working duty! There was no steam to be found at Norwich – or at least none that we saw before we were chased from the shed! Before leaving the city, on our way back west, we called in at King's scrapyard in Hall Road, where the foreman was the opposite of his counterpart at the BR shed, allowing us a free roam around the yard. Awaiting their appointment with the oxy-acetylene torch were Nos 33033, 30546, 33006, 33003, 33030, 31827 and 31400. The last two were interesting, as I had seen them both on shed at Redhill on 19 July the previous year. To complete the day we called in at the Kettering scrapyard, to record Nos 44182, 44581, 6808 *Beenham Grange* and 33028, and Leicester (Midland) shed, always known to me simply as 15C. Happily, this was

Seen during one of my first trips accompanied by Gill, No 61912, the former stationary boiler at King's Cross shed between May 1962 and June 1963, awaits its fate at New England (Peterborough) on 7 March 1965. It was cut up at Cashmore's Great Bridge yard in May 1965.

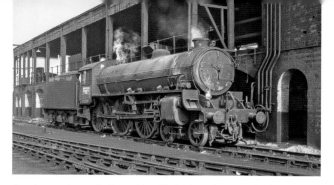

Another stationary boiler at New England on the same day, but this time still in operation. Departmental Locomotive No 25 (ex-No 61272) is most obviously in steam and still earning its keep. It was finally dismantled at Garnham, Harris & Elton, Lockerford Sidings, Chesterfield, in March 1966.

Our furthest point east on that day was King's Scrapyard in Norwich, where we were kindly given the run of the place to take photographs (unlike our hostile reception at Norwich depot!). No 30546 waits patiently in the sunshine for the acetylene torch to be summoned!

predominantly steam – 12 from 18 – but it was to proffer a surprise cop in the guise of No D3776.

The next TRS outing was on 28 March, once more to the Manchester area. Entertainment on the coach that weekend included the Rolling Stones at No 1 with *The Last Time*. This was to prove prophetic for me, as, with the decrease in live steam, it was now virtually impossible to tell which locos were in store or active, as they tended to be dumped, often with tenders full of coal. Gill, however, seemed to be something of a lucky charm as regards the weather, as for these two early trips and for the rest of the year we enjoyed bright sunshine for much of the time! The locations at Stockport, Longsight, Trafford Park, Patricroft, Agecroft, Newton Heath, Gorton, Reddish and Buxton served up much as before but, with the help of my first visit to Reddish, I managed to accumulate 38 cops. Two locos that were most definitely in store were Nos 45522 *Prestatyn* and 44425 on Buxton shed, both sans chimneys! Ringing the changes, Gill and I went to see Bob Dylan at DeMontfort Hall on 2 May, which was most enjoyable.

With external interests now taking a greater hold, it was

Gorton was a very satisfying shed to visit and the reason is clear from this view of the locos on view on 28 March 1965, including later-to-be-preserved 'Crab' No 42700.

Top: Another portrait from Gorton on that day: No 78023, complete with appropriate shedplate, quietly pollutes the local atmosphere alongside No 42978. A vertical cut of No 78023 was used as the cover shot for my first book, *Steam on Shed*, in 1984.

Middle: Little is known of my brief career on the footplate. Here I scan the road ahead from the cab of No 45522 *Prestatyn* at Buxton on 28 March 1965! *Gill Walker*

Bottom: A little over 12 months to closure, the former Great Central Railway line from Nottingham to Marylebone assumed a far more bucolic atmosphere compared to its heady days with 'A3s'. On 5 June 1965 No 48035 lazily makes its way south through Belgrave & Birstall station with a mixed rake of wagons, some tarpaulined.

The South West-North East inter-regional trains on the ex-GCR are still clinging to life as No D6817 passes Belgrave & Birstall box on 5 June 1965 with the 1N83 service. Fifty years later at this point the loco would be standing in Leicester North platform on the private Great Central Railway.

three months before Gill and I set off again, this time for a weekend at Barry on 20/21 June. By then the 'common user policy' introduced by BR on the MR in January — whereby locos were allocated to areas rather than individual depots — was in full swing; GWR speed records had been broken, on 3 June, by Nos D6881 and D6882 running from Paddington to Plymouth and back, with ten XP64 coaches, at over 100mph on several occasions; Reading's power signal box was open; and Stanley Matthews became the first footballer to be knighted. Elsewhere, Liverpool won the FA Cup for the first time and Leicester City ended the 1964-65 season at 18th (out of 22), securing a further year in the First Division. While the shed at Barry was now completely dieselised, the accumulation of more locos by Dai Woodham meant that engines were literally strewn around every conceivable spare stretch of track in and around the Docks area. We toured the collection on the Sunday, photoing at appropriate places, before paying a visit to Cardiff East Dock, to bathe our eyes on 66 steam, many of them in full working order, then driving back to Leicestershire. Only 24 new locos to underline this time — but two steam, Nos 3738 and 5655!

It was becoming increasingly difficult to find steam actually working, certainly in any numbers, or to find locations close enough to make a meaningful tour itinerary, and the increasing number of 'last of' events was depressing. So, to access our fix of steam in any form, many of the burgeoning scrapyards were added to the journeys. One such was Cashmore's yard at Great Bridge, visited between viewing Nuneaton and Bescot sheds on 25 July. Interestingly, Nuneaton was all steam apart from one diesel shunter. Though there were only 16 in the scrapyard, the variety was wide, with eight 'Austerities', three ER 'O4s', Nos 43037, 43067, 42556, 6906 *Chicheley Hall* and 5056 *Earl of Powis*. Bescot had a healthy complement of 47, with only four diesels. Oxley was similarly stocked, with a mix of WR and MR locos and 'Standards' but with nine diesels, including one 'Hymek', No D7046. Stourbridge and Tyseley played their part in quantity and acceptable quality to close the day, with my haul this time being 21. We had been 'evicted' from both Bescot and Oxley, and when I asked Gill some years later for her overriding impressions of our trips, her immediate reaction was 'Being chased out of sheds'! I had not realised that it had been that often!

Little did we know that, on this day, British boxer Freddie Mills was found shot in the head in his car, parked in a cul-

BR was taking some revenue from selling number and name plates into the 1960s, leading to No 4168 needing to have its number stencilled onto the smokebox! It is standing at Tyseley on 25 July 1965, at the head of Nos 5606 and 5658.

When access was granted, scrapyards yielded not just numbers but interesting vistas. Here the smokebox door from No 90383 lies on the ground at Cashmore's, Great Bridge, complete with number, on 25 July 1965.

Appetites for numbers were often satisfied by shed visits, such as Bescot on that same July day, where Nos 44139 and 48101 are at the near end of two long rows of similar types. Both were still active on BR's books.

de-sac behind his nightclub. He died later in the Middlesex Hospital. The inquest determined that he had committed suicide. Other deaths this year were Nat King Cole (15 February, aged 45), Stan Laurel (23 February, aged 74, following a heart attack four days earlier), Dr Albert Schweitzer (4 September, aged 90), and Richard Dimbleby (22 December, aged 52).

Out of some consideration for Gill's patience in being dragged round scruffy engine sheds, we planned to join my parents' holiday in the Isle of Wight. It was sheer coincidence that the island still had steam and that it was also virgin territory for me! We set off by rail from Leicester (London Road) on Friday 13 August behind No D1574, aboard a Holiday Special for Portsmouth, via Northampton, Bletchley, Oxford (with a change of motive power to No 6991 *Acton Burnell*

Hall), Didcot, Reading, Basingstoke and Eastleigh, then by ferry to Ryde Pier and train to Shanklin, our base for the next two weeks.

To allow me to concentrate on spotting as we travelled south, Gill 'volunteered' to write the numbers down for me! There was a mixture of steam and diesel on the Midland main line, but mostly steam at Oxford and Eastleigh. The weather was, by and large, good for the whole holiday and ideal for trainspotting, and mum and dad hardly saw us as I dragged Gill around the island network! There were a few days spent on the beach, but, amazingly, the sand was incredibly hot! On Thursday 19 August the two of us decided to ring the changes by taking the ferry from Yarmouth to Lymington for a trip to Brockenhurst and Bournemouth. We had a good day, despite some early reluctance, but it poured with rain all day – I obviously should have listened!

The great delight during the holiday, of course, was seeing

A damp Ventnor station plays host to No 21 *Sandown* and an inquisitive youngster, complete with Pakamac. Some years later, after this photograph was published elsewhere, the brother of the young lad made contact via my publisher.

the compact 'O2' 0-4-4 tanks, the stalwart island steam locos, hard at work, and I was delighted to see them all at some stage during our stay, including at Ventnor and during a tour of both Ryde shed and Works. The 28th came around all too soon and we were sorry to leave the island – dad took a photograph of Gill on the ferry with a very wistful expression! No D6548 hauled our returning Holiday Special to Oxford, where No D5860 took over for the leg to Leicester.

There were no more outings before the end of August, so thus ended ten full years of my spotting career. The total seen now stood at 15,797, an increase of just 345 over the 365 days, fewer than I had copped on some individual trips in the past! Not surprisingly, the largest increase was in the number of diesels, going from 3,241 to 3,440, whereas only 18 MR and two ER locos had been captured. The largest steam increase was 82 WR and 30 SR (those on the Isle of Wight being a large proportion). It would be nearly two years before I broke the 16,000 barrier!

In damp conditions, 35 'Freshwater' prepares to restart its journey for Ventnor from Ryde St Johns on 24 August 1965.

Chapter 3
1965-1970

My 11th trainspotting year began on 1 September 1965 with attention turned to the Great Central line in Leicester and the recent introduction of 'Britannias' to haul the Nottingham-Marylebone services. A visit to the lineside near Belgrave & Birstall station, then Central station in the city, saw me capture on film Nos 70046 *Anzac*, 70052 *Firth of Tay* and 70054 *Dornoch Firth*. With all still officially allocated to WCML sheds, perhaps the powers that be were not sure of the efficacy of the trial, as they were all transferred away to Carlisle at the beginning of January 1966!

With the spreading electrification on the WCML, a small cadre of 'Britannias' was drafted onto the GCR route in 1965. On 1 September No 70046 *Anzac* climbs out of Leicester towards Birstall with a Marylebone-Nottingham express, picked out by the low evening sun. The transfer was short-lived, however, and the were all moved to Carlisle (Kingmoor) on 8 January 1966.

Seemingly little of note was happening on BR's main lines, but preservation was a growing interest on a number of fronts and an interesting occurrence was a Birmingham-Bristol train on 17 October, double-headed by Nos 6435 and 7029 *Clun Castle*. The former had been saved and was being moved to the private Dart Valley Railway, whereas the fate of the latter was still in the balance, this being in its last months of service on BR. It, too, was to find safety in preservation.

With no organised outings planned, I journeyed to Birmingham on 23 October — the fourth anniversary of my banking career — to spend time at New Street and Snow Hill stations. No 45697 *Achilles* hauled my train from Leicester, but steam was very much in the minority as the day panned out, but I did cop No 48762 at New Street. No 45288 was the motive power for the return to Leicester, and that was to prove to be the last railway excitement of the year, with the sole exception of the highly unusual sight of No D7516 hauling No E6009 through Leicester. Why and where to, I never did find out.

Gill and I were now spending more time away from the railway, not least in enjoying the music of Bob Dylan, whose year it seemed to be, entering the UK charts on 3 April with *Times They Are A-changin'* and having successive hits with *Subterranean Homesick Blues* in May, *Like a Rolling Stone* in August and *Positively 4th Street* in November. His highly influential and acclaimed album *Highway 61 Revisited* was released on 30 August. Leicester City were performing better in the current season, being slightly above midway and ending the year with a 5-0 victory over Fulham at home. Jackie Sinclair scored twice and, after arrival from Dunfermline, had quickly become the top scorer for the team, netting 24 in all competitions over the season. On 15 November the first Freightliner container train ran from London to Glasgow over the WCML, under a project actually conceived by Dr Richard Beeching. The next two years were to witness further expansions within the system.

1966 was a year of the extremes of highs and lows, with the former undoubtedly being the excitement of England winning the football World Cup at Wembley Stadium on 30 July, defeating Germany 4-2 after extra time. Sadly, the immortal words from Kenneth Wolstenholme as fans began to invade the pitch in the closing minutes – 'They think it's all over' – was to echo through the railway world, with news of high-profile closures of the Somerset & Dorset route (7 March) and parts of the Isle of Wight and Great Central lines on 18 April and 5 September respectively. The former had been due to close on 3 January but had been delayed due to problems with bus replacement. July saw the last loco turned out by Beyer Peacock from its Manchester factory – No D7659, for BR. Elsewhere, India (Indira Gandhi) and Russia (Leonid Brezhnev) had new leaders; Ronald Reagan became Governor of California; 'Moors murderers' Ian Brady and Myra Hindley were sentenced to life imprisonment; the breathalyser was introduced on the UK's roads; and Barclaycard became the country's first credit card.

Musically, despite the influence of the likes of the Beatles, Rolling Stones and Bob Dylan, the year's biggest-selling single was *Distant Drums* by Jim Reeves, who had died in a plane crash on 31 July 1964. Second was Frank Sinatra's *Strangers in the Night* and third *Spanish Flea* by Herb Alpert! It was also a good year for the Beach Boys, with their classic *Good Vibrations* at No 1 in November.

As with 1965, my first railway outing in 1966 was not until March, this time on the 6th, precisely 364 days from the previous year. In a private trip by car, with Gill and David, Kirkby-in-Ashfield was the first destination where, out of the 44 locos on shed, 24 were steam – all Stanier 8Fs bar No 92095 (in store) – with the rest being 18 Brush Type 4s and two Type 2s. The diesel side of Langwith Junction was a mix of main-line types and shunters, while the steam element was a small group of eight 'Austerities'. The shed had officially closed exactly a month earlier, on 6 February. The weather was initially dry but dull and, with so many diesels, not conducive to extensive photography! Staveley (Barrow Hill) had closed to steam on 4 October 1965 and thus was completely dieselised, with only the diminutive No D2401 being of any real interest.

Grasping at small straws to continue the steam fix, we ventured to Garnham, Harris & Elton's Lockerford sidings, alongside the main line at Chesterfield, to record Nos 61003 *Gazelle*, Departmental Locomotive 23 (ex-No 61300), 61181 and 61361. I also photographed No D1749 as it passed us on the main line. Westhouses would be open as a steam depot for another six months and it was gratifying to see 22 on shed, again mostly Stanier 8Fs, out of a total presence including diesels of 33. Our final shed was Derby, viewed 'over the wall' from the road adjacent to the station/shed site, where we espied No 60019 *Bittern*. This was our reasoning for visiting this location, as we had planned to photograph the 'A4' on the 'Williams Deacon's Bank Club A4 Tour'. Brought down from Scotland specifically, it hauled the tour from Manchester to Crewe and Derby and return, taking the participants directly into the Works and sheds at the last two locations. It had been a mad dash throughout the day for us to reach Derby in time, then to capture it on film as it accelerated from Derby past Stenson Junction, but we made it and the sun even came out to grace our photographs. Compared to similar events in future years, there were few photographers, and what there were showed concern that they did not impede others. Would that it was so today! Overall, the day had been worthwhile, including 49 cops!

The next outing was a mid-week three-day break for Gill

Grasping at straws to continue the steam fix, we ventured to Garnham, Harris & Elton's Lockerford sidings, alongside the main line at Chesterfield, on 6 March 1966, to record No 61361 together with Nos 61003 *Gazelle*, Departmental Locomotive 23 (ex-61300) and 61181.

Another railtour: on 6 March 1966 No 60019 *Bittern* leaves the environs of Derby and passes Stenson Junction with the return leg of the Williams Deacon's Bank Club railtour journey, to Manchester. There were very few sites at which to capture the moment.\

I returned to Barry, this time by car (in the distance), as a brief holiday with Gill. Lined up on the Docks are Nos 7822 *Foxcote Manor*, 7819 *Hinton Manor*, 7821 *Ditcheat Manor* and 7817 *Garsington Manor*, all except the last going on to preservation thanks to Dai Woodham's policy of scrapping wagons before locos.

and myself, based once more at my favourite B&B in Barry. On Tuesday 19 April we investigated the scrap scene in Newport, first at J. Buttigieg's yard, where we saw Nos 42103, 84002, 82022, 34033 *Chard* and 31858. The nearby yards of John Cashmore Ltd were more populated, with 19 noted in total, including Nos 6856 *Stowe Grange*, 34076 *41 Squadron*, 84000, 92230, 92244 and 92250. The last three had all been withdrawn from Gloucester (Horton Road) the previous December and were only seven years old – such a waste of valuable assets and BR investment! The scrap theme continued the following day at Briton Ferry, where Nos 6110, 5202 5208, 6116, 5241, 7248 and 7249 were noted. Then returning to Barry, there was, of course, the de rigueur visit to the lines of scrap locos. Seventy-two were scattered around the sidings, with a further 103 in and around the Docks. We made another quick stop for yet another photograph of some of the locos there on the 21st, then back home.

By now, with railway attractions disappearing, such as Darlington Works closing on 2 April, my 'extramural studies' were gaining preference for my time and attention, with ten-pin bowling, the local bank football team that I ran, the drama group going from strength to strength – even including some

A team shot of Bank Imperial, the Barclays Bank team I ran in a local league in Leicester. We did receive some stick from the bank for wearing the official badge without permission, and we were not permitted to be known as Barclays, hence the second choice of name! Photographed on a football pitch across the road from Syston station on 17 April 1966, the area is now buried under a housing estate. I am bottom right.

The only occasion when I photographed Bob Dylan. During the disturbing second half of the show on 15 May 1966 (see text) I tried my luck, without a zoom lens, to capture the moment, with The Band accompanying him.

of my Barclays colleagues – and Gill, not unnaturally, wanting to do other things than hang around railways. One of the latter 'diversions' included going to be part of an adoring audience for a second appearance by Bob Dylan, at Leicester's DeMontfort Hall on Sunday 15 May (the day before his latest album, *Blonde on Blonde*, was released in America). Queuing outside, we were interviewed by a television crew. Asked if we would boo him, for turning electric from his acoustic folk roots, as some had done already on the tour, we quickly responded, 'No way!' The first half began, as acoustic, with *Times They Are A-changin'* and ended with *Talking World War III Blues*, to general approval. As the second half opened with *Don't Think Twice It's Alright*, with The Band as accompaniment and Dylan on electric guitar, the show progressed and his performance deteriorated into a noisy cacophony, with several walking out and some shouting 'Judas', and we were almost pushed to eating our words. He still managed an encore, of *It's All Over Now, Baby Blue* – was that prophetic? – and we did stick it out. I took some photographs of him on stage, but, without a zoom lens, he is so small it could almost have been anybody! Six days earlier, Leicester City had ended the season in 7th place after a 2-1 win against West Ham

United at home.

Football took centre stage on 30 July when Gill joined mum and dad at our home in Thurmaston to watch England take on Germany in the World Cup Final, featuring Leicester City's Gordon Banks in goal. The excitement – and the tension – was intense and the latter was obviously getting to Gill at half-time, with the score at 1-1 after Geoff Hurst had equalised Germany's first goal. She could stand it no longer, so upped and went shopping in Leicester! We three masochists stuck it out and were rewarded by seeing the home team persevere, in extra time, thanks to a thrilling hat-trick by Hurst. It was proving to be an enjoyable summer.

With the regular outings now largely a thing of the past, the next fix was the summer holidays. Once more Gill and I joined mum and dad, this time on the North Wales coast, based at Colwyn Bay. While not a railway holiday, we travelled by rail from Leicester on 7 August and many of our other trips were similarly powered; in addition, the line ran parallel and close to the beach at Colwyn Bay itself, leading to many occasions for number-taking! Needless to say, by this time the vast majority of 'main-line' operations were diesel-hauled, but there was still enough steam working the area to make life interesting, with at least one steam cop every day! Far more of our time than of yore was spent on the beach or sightseeing, including to Llandudno, for the Great Orme Tramway and Penrhyn Castle, with its museum that included the preserved No 58926.

A highlight, though, was on 16 August, when we two 'youngsters' left the grown-ups behind to visit the Ffestiniog Railway. By rail to Llandudno Junction, behind No 45447, and thence to Blaenau Ffestiniog, we then caught a bus to Tan y Bwlch, at that time the FR's terminus. Knowing next to nothing about this railway, the narrow-gauge sights and sounds were beguiling, with the relaxed and informal atmosphere being especially appealing, and Gill was especially attracted to the locos. I delighted in seeing and photographing *Linda*, then riding behind her to Porthmadog. Briefly exploring the town, we travelled to Caernarfon by bus, before boarding another train to Bangor and a connection back to Colwyn Bay, behind No 45223. The seeds of a 'love affair' with the FR were sown, but would not take root until my next visit in 1989, with another female companion ... my 11-year-old daughter!

Two weeks later, on 3 September, the last trains ran on the Great Central line between Marylebone and Nottingham (Victoria). Looking back, five decades later, I had been aware that the end was coming for the GCR, alongside which I had stood, sat and spotted at Loughborough, Belgrave & Birstall (next to my grandfather's allotment ... later to become mine) and Leicester, but I had made no effort to visit and photograph until the very last day and the very last trains! I cannot quite understand why this should have been, but it had been the same at the closure of Leicester (Belgrave Road) station. Hindsight is a marvellous thing, but if only I had fully known then... The numbness of losing both was long-lasting. I did make the effort seven days later, however, on 10 September, to see No 4472 *Flying Scotsman* through Thurmaston on the

Incredibly I was the only photographer at this vantage point to record No 4472 *Flying Scotsman* hurrying south past Thurmaston on 10 September 1966, with the Gainsborough Model Railway Society's 'The Farnborough Flyer' railtour.

Gainsborough Model Railway Society's 'The Farnborough Flyer' and was rewarded by sunshine and a decent photograph. Most surprising was the complete lack of any other bodies enjoying the spectacle! When the loco returned again to the main line in 2016, the linesides were swarming!

September/October saw Leicester City record three 5-0 victories – one in the League and two in the League Cup. Reading was first on 14 September, in the League Cup 2nd Round; Aston Villa was next on 24 September, in the league; and Lincoln City the third recipient, on 25 October in the League Cup 3rd Round. Not such goods news were the departures of Derek Dougan (to Wolves) and Gordon Banks (to Stoke City). Some consolation for the latter was the new incumbent between the sticks being Peter Shilton, who had learned such a lot from his predecessor.

Demonstrating just how much the UK's railways and my attraction to them were changing is the fact that my next event was not for three months! It was not until 3 December that Gill and I joined a Jubilee Locomotive Preservation Society railtour from Leicester (London Road) direct to Carlisle (Kingmoor) sheds. It had been literally a toss-up with Roger Thwaites, another keen railway enthusiast and with whom I worked at Barclays, Syston, at the time, as to who would go on the tour – I won! Starting from Leicester in the dark, at 7.22am, I set about collecting the numbers as we tracked north, with Gill doing the honours on occasions. By way of Derby and Sheffield, No 45562 *Alberta* took us to Mirfield, where an engine change introduced No 45593 *Kolhapur* as the train engine that was to take us right into the shed yard at Kingmoor, for us to detrain by steps. On the way north I put my head out of the train to photograph the impressive signal gantry at Preston and succeeded in having an ember lodge in my eye! This was irritating but not too painful for the rest of the journey north and while touring around the shed yard, in the dusk, between our 2.29pm arrival and 3.34pm departure at Kingmoor Through Sidings, but the irritation and pain both increased as the journey home progressed. David and his girlfriend Barbara

joined (unofficially) our train at Derby at 8.25pm and, after arrival back at Leicester at 9.42pm – 58 minutes late – he kindly escorted me to Leicester Royal Infirmary Out-Patients Department, where the problem was quickly dealt with, much to my relief, not least as I still had to drive Gill back to her home near Melton Mowbray!

The various points of the compass and loco numbers had been duly logged, by Gill or me by turn, with steam still in abundance among the diesels;

by travelling from Mirfield to Preston via Burnley and Blackburn, then on to Carlisle, we were to see far a greater variety than if we had traversed the Settle & Carlisle route. Interesting sights included Nos 70020 *Mercury*, 70038 *Robin Hood*, 70008 *Black Prince* and 70029 *Shooting Star* between Preston and Oxenholme; eight in steam on Tebay shed, ready to give their assistance if needed over Shap Summit; No 61278 as the first loco noted on Kingmoor shed; and 17 'Britannias' also present! The return journey was via Leeds (where No 45562 took back the reins) and Clay Cross to Derby, where the 'Jubilee' departed and our journey to Leicester continued behind Nos D5185 and D5299.

So 1966 ended, with my grand total now 15,913, of which 12,341 were steam. It was becoming ever harder to find those oh-so-elusive outstanding cops, not helped by the total of 1,298 steam locos that had been withdrawn over the past year! 5 December had seen the withdrawal of passenger services between Bletchley (Verney Junction) and Buckingham, and the Christmas No 1 was Tom Jones's *Green Green Grass of Home*.

1967 was to become known as the 'Summer of Love', with the ongoing influence of the younger generation coming to a peak with around 100,000 'hippies' gathering in San Francisco, with a seemingly total lack of sexual and/or social inhibition and sparking a welter of alternative lifestyles that would later take root worldwide. Inevitably, the movement quickly spread to London but, to those of us 'in the sticks', it could almost have been another planet, with only minor ripples initially reaching and affecting our lives. What did affect us, however, was the financial crisis as a result of the UK attempting to gain entry to the Common Market, leading to a devaluation of the pound on 18 November. On a happier note, November also saw the launch of the first BBC local radio station – with Radio Leicester going on air on the 8th. Earlier in the year, on 18 March, the supertanker SS *Torrey Canyon* struck Pollard's Rock, off the Cornish coast, with the loss of about 32 million gallons of crude oil, the UK's worst ever oil spill. Also on water, Sir Donald Campbell was killed in January when, minutes after achieving 297mph, his jet hydroplane, *Bluebird K7*, flipped over and crashed on Coniston Water. By contrast, on 28 May Sir Francis Chichester completed his solo circumnavigation of the globe, in 226 days, with just one stop. He was knighted in July.

Musically, 14 January saw the Monkees take over the No 1 spot from Tom Jones and stay there for four weeks, with *I'm a Believer*, but the year's best-selling single was Englebert Humperdinck's *Release Me*, which enjoyed six weeks at the top. Sandie Shaw became the first British act to win the Eurovision Song Contest, with *Puppet on a String*, reaching No 1 in the UK charts on 29 April; Scott MacKenzie rode the hippy tidal wave to see his US hit *San Francisco (Be sure to wear some flowers in your hair)* at the top in the UK for four weeks from 12 August; and 1 June saw the release of the Beatles' eighth studio album, their innovative and incredibly influential *Sgt Pepper's Lonely Hearts Club Band.*

Leicester Central station closed to steam and through trains on 3 September 1966 and this was how it looked for many months thereafter.

On the railways, the year saw further expansion of the WCML electrification as well as the powering of the line between Ryde Pier Head and Shanklin on the Isle of Wight, and Glasgow Central to Wemyss Bay. As a counter to that, the final 'Bournemouth Belle' ran on 9 July, behind No D1924, and BR's last shunting horse, Charlie, was retired at Newmarket on 21 February. On an even sadder note, this was the final full year of steam on BR, and it would see a further 1,329 steam locos withdrawn, leaving just 359 to continue into 1968.

Back in early January 1967 Gill and I discussed holiday plans for the summer and agreed (with some encouragement from me) that we would spend a fortnight in Dawlish. Sadly, however, within days I had broken off our relationship! Even to this day

I cannot fully explain why I suddenly reached this decision, and Gill struggled to have any comprehension of my reasoning and was greatly upset when I left her at her home and drove back to my abode. I wrote to the B&B, cancelling her room but keeping mine, and I would take the holiday on my own.

I gradually returned to spotting trips and the first was back to Kettering on 25 February, where 13 ex-MR locos awaited their fate, including 9F No 92013. On 4 March David and I travelled to Wolverhampton (Low Level) station, specifically to see No 7029 *Clun Castle* on the return leg from Chester General to Paddington as 1X83, the Ian Allan 'Zulu Railtour', to commemorate the last through working between Birkenhead Woodside and Paddington. Booked into Low Level station at 6.35pm, it was dark by the time it arrived and that, together with the throng at the end of the platform, made it very difficult to photograph. On 15 April I was back at Kettering again, this time to record a total of 12, three scrapped since last time but two new ones in their place.

The series of Freightliner routes had expanded during 1966, not least with Liverpool Garston terminal opening, and further route diversification came in April 1967 with a service linking London and Belfast, and in June/July with the opening of terminals in Cardiff and Leeds. By this time Roger Thwaites had taken over the baton from me and had formed his own group of spotters for trips, and I joined them to London on 7 May. I had visited neither Hitchin nor Hornsey before, so was glad to begin our trip there. Once with their own codes (34D and 34B respectively), they were now sub-sheds of Finsbury Park so, on top of the number of diesels always being fewer than the steam they replaced, their offerings were not great in number — eight and 30, all diesels — but the variety was mixed. At just 22 locos, Finsbury Park itself lacked numbers but made up for it in style, not least with the ECML main-line diesels, with two 'Deltics' on display — Nos D9019 *Royal Highland Fusilier* and D9015 *Tulyar* — and 'Baby Deltic' No D5908. Needless to say, without its once huge steam allocation the examples on offer at Stratford was anaemic in comparison to previous visits, but a congregation of 90 diesels was still impressive and the visit was made more palatable with the collection of 13 preserved steam, most housed in a side shed. On show there were Nos 70000 *Britannia*, 30245, 33001, 42500, 30777 *Sir Lamiel*, 63460, 30587, 30925 *Cheltenham*, 63601, 'T9' 120, 30850 *Lord Nelson* and 49395 – strange bedfellows indeed! Outside was No 1008, the former No 50621. Hither Green, Nine Elms, Old Oak Common and Willesden rounded off the day. Nine Elms housed 27 steam and a sole diesel shunter – D3273 – whereas the other three depots were exclusively diesel, electric or both. It was gratifying to see the BR/EE electro-diesels (later to be Class 73) on Hither Green, No 10001 on Willesden, and to have 90 cops, but sad that none were steam! Sadly, No 10001, the ex-LMS main-line diesel, only survived a further seven months, being scrapped at Cox & Danks's scrapyard in North Acton in February 1968.

Two days later, on 9 May, Leicester City beat Chelsea 3-2 at home and ended

As a participant of Roger Thwaites's group trip to London on 7 May 1967, I take the opportunity to capture our leader in the cab doorway of No 70000 *Britannia* at Stratford Diesel Depot. Several other preserved locos were also inside this small shed.

A new vision to me at the time, class leader No E6001 stands on Hither Green depot with sister loco No E6031 on 7 May 1967.

the season 8th in the First Division, level on points with that day's opponents but with a slightly better goal difference. Jackie Sinclair scored 21 League goals during the season, making it two in a row for such a feat in the top flight, having scored 22 in the 1965/66 season. There would only be two other City players – Frank Worthington (1973/74) and Gary Lineker (1983/84 and 1984/85) – to net 20-plus goals in a season before Jamie Vardy achieved it in the 2015/16 season. On 12 May I was at the Odeon Theatre, Nottingham, for a performance of 'The Chuck Berry Show' – at the grand price of 7s 6d!

During the summer of 1966 I had begun writing a novel. Not surprisingly, in view of my predilection for science fiction, it was within this genre, though firmly based on a story grounded in the UK – no aliens or flying saucers! I continued it into 1967 and finally submitted *The Coelenterates* to a publisher; I still have the letter of rejection from Panther Books Limited, dated 20 June 1967. My next step was to contact a literary agent, subsequently resulting in a meeting in London. She was very kind but did not hide the fact that she did not think it worth publishing. Her summation was, 'A nice idea, but it is not long enough. The whole book reads like a first chapter. Go away and try to expand ideas and length.' I went away, but put the manuscript into a file, together with other unpublished writings, not least poetry, that I had also begun writing in 1966.

The next trip with Roger was on 1 July to the North East, where we knew steam was still fighting a rearguard action against the onset of dieselisation. Our first stop, at South Blyth, was a real disappointment, with just three diesels and No 65813 (in store) to greet us. Across the ferry to North Blyth, with fingers crossed that we may find better, the fare was 22 with just four diesels, but it was sad to see 11 of the steam so obviously in store. Tyne Dock and Sunderland were a mix, but with still plenty of steam on show, but it was to be West Hartlepool that gave us the real entertainment, in the form of No 90254. Having jumped the tracks just outside the shed building, it was leaning at a crazy angle, held up by some rather precarious-looking wooden planking! This vision

The staithes at North Blyth were a magnificent sight, especially at low tide, yet despite the smallness in size of the signals and gantries on top, this image from 1 July 1967 gives no real impression of the sheer size of the structure.

Inside the workshop at Tyne Dock shed on the same day, No 65795 has just 14 days of active life left before being discarded from Sunderland shed.

was then boosted by that of No D173 passing the shed on a passenger train – it was my last 'Peak' and, sad to say, my elation was something akin to that experienced at copping *Glorious* at Bank Hall. York (North) closed to steam this month and, not surprisingly, all 12 steam on shed were in store, including No 60019 *Bittern* standing in glorious isolation inside the roundhouse. Happily, Leeds (Holbeck) and Wakefield still held healthy numbers of steam, including Nos 45697 *Achilles*,

Some of the spotters on this trip to the North East are seen taking in the sights at Sunderland and squeezing between Nos 65811 and 65855 inside the roundhouse.

Crazy it seems and crazy it was, but the effect was even greater when first seen at a slightly greater distance through the portal of the West Hartlepool shed building. Just held up by pieces of wood, No 90254 appears to defy gravity on 1 July 1967.

45593 *Kolhapur* and 45562 *Alberta* on the former. The latter seemed to have become something of a dumping ground, with 54 steam, predominantly 'Austerities'. The trip had rekindled something of the old ardour, not least with 30 cops, and this was added to the following day, when David, Barbara (his girlfriend) and 'Chirp' Bird (of Lees fame) made a dash south

In glorious isolation, No 60019 *Bittern* stands forlorn though under shelter inside York North shed on 1 July 1967. It had been withdrawn from Ferryhill (Aberdeen) in September 1966 and was awaiting preservation moves.

by car to Beaulieu Road to capture the very last views of SR steam. No 34095 *Brentor*, 35008 *Orient Line* and 35028 *Clan Line* were all in good health as they handled their expresses for the last time, but *Brentor* was already devoid of front numbers and nameplates. Rumour was that they had been removed to stop theft, but what a disgraceful ending!

On the final day for steam on the Southern Region, a quartet of us are at Beaulieu Road to witness No 34095 *Brentor* heading a Waterloo-Bournemouth express. It was rumoured that the absence of names and front number was to prevent souvenir hunters!

In another view from the last day, to the casual eye everything seems to be normal at Basingstoke shed as Nos 73018 and 80152 stand alongside the shed in the late afternoon summer sunshine.

My summer holiday was coming up, but another trip to Kettering preceded it, on 30 July, to record seven recent arrivals, five of which were captured on film. I had invited 'Chirp' to join me on my holiday, but he was convinced that Gill and I would reunite, so declined. We weren't back together, however, so on 12 August I boarded the train at Leicester alone, bound for the Devon coast. A girl I knew from the bank was catching the same train, so I joined her and her two companions in their compartment. Big mistake! I was intent on recording as many numbers as possible on the way, as well as being sociable with the girls, but we were joined by a trio of pseudo Hell's Angels. They insisted that the blinds all be drawn, which severely restricted my spotting, and they did not take kindly to my alternative suggestions! They were only interested in the girls, but they (the girls) were not particularly keen on the interlopers and tensions mounted as the journey progressed. Eventually I was mightily relieved to arrive at Dawlish and detrain! En route I glimpsed the nascent

At Cohen's scrapyard at Kettering on 30 July 1967, No 76036 certainly looks the worse for wear as it awaits its final demise. New to New England on 19 June 1954, it also worked on the Midland and West Coast main lines up to withdrawal from Chester on 28 January 1967.

preservation site at Ashchurch, but was unable to properly see what was there. This meant little to me at the time, but was to have deeper meaning when I eventually moved to Ashchurch to live in 2007 and found the site long gone.

Staying at the same seafront hotel in Dawlish as some years earlier, I was made most welcome, although the owners were new. I had anticipated a rather lonely holiday, but I quickly made friends with two spotters holidaying from Hull – and also made the acquaintance of 11 different girls in the fortnight, not least through the local night club! With the hotel being on the seafront and the beach the other side of the tracks, plenty of locos were seen every day, even if I did not venture to other locations. I did make a journey, however, to the fledgling Dart Valley Railway on 22 August, behind D1008 *Western Harrier* to Totnes. Nothing was in steam at the Buckfastleigh site, but it was still a joy to witness the collection of preserved locos and to see the potential for the railway. No D826

Jupiter transported me back to Dawlish and the day was most enjoyable.

I returned home on 26 August and left one of the above-mentioned girls in tears as my train pulled away from Dawlish.

Taking a day out from the beach and the girls at Dawlish, I travelled to Buckfastleigh on 22 August 1967 to view the early preservation scene. In glorious sunshine No 1420 stands with an auto-coach, externally attempting to recreate a GWR branch train.

I left another in the same state at Birmingham (New Street), after making her acquaintance as she waited for her train to Weston-super-Mare. We hit it off so well that she very nearly changed trains and came home with me... I am not sure what my parents would have thought! Still high from all this, two days later I drove Roger to Westhouses and Langwith Junction, just 'to see what was there'. Mostly diesels, of course, but it was pleasing to see Nos 47289, 68012, 47313 and 42233 on the former and Nos 63902 and 63842 on the latter. On 3 September Peter was my companion for a trip to Stoke and Crewe. Unfortunately the weather took a turn for the worse

Right to the end, Crewe South shed was a Mecca for spotters, not least because of the number of locos on site. On 3 September 1967 No 70024 *Vulcan* simmers quietly on shed, without name or shed plates, alongside No 48729. The rusty rails tell their own story!

and we were graced with a continual soaking drizzle early on! Stoke had 20 steam and nine diesels and Crewe South 70 steam and 37 diesels. Despite cops being few and far between, it was still good to view the sheer quantity, including Nos 70049 *Solway Firth*, 70024 *Vulcan* and 71000 *Duke of Gloucester* on the latter shed.

Peter was again my co-pilot on 7 October, as I drove us to the North West for another weekend of trawling. Crewe South was still packed with steam, but the runes were well and truly pointing to the elimination of steam from the entire network within months. I was determined to see and photograph as much as possible. From Crewe we travelled north to Northwich – all steam, largely 8Fs – Warrington, Wigan (Springs Branch) and Lostock Hall – all a mix of diesel and steam but with plenty of the latter on view – before bed and breakfast in Blackpool. The local shed was first on Sunday the 8th, all diesel

Also seen on 3 September 1967, class leader No E3001 enters Crewe station with a Manchester-Euston express. New in November 1959, to Longsight shed, it became No 81001 under TOPS and lasted until withdrawal in July 1984.

apart from No 48386 and a wonderfully appropriate apparition of No 70021 *Morning Star* standing proud in the shed yard. Our way back home was then via Rose Grove, Bolton and Sutton Oak – each all steam bar two diesel shunters – Speke Junction, Edge Hill and Birkenhead. The last-named was an incredible sight, with 65 engines in and around the shed – and no bricks! With the volume of steam seen it was almost like being in a time warp, but we were under no illusions.

My year was seen out with visits to Kettering on 28 October – with 23 in the scrapyard this time (four 'Standards' and 19 ex-MR locos) – and once more to the North West on 5 November. Less than a month since the previous visit, there was a transformation, with locos playing musical chairs! Looking back, it is quite remarkable what we encompassed this day, even bearing in mind an early start from Leicester. In order, the statistics were: Crewe South (77 on shed), Crewe Diesel (10), Northwich (31 – up from 24), Birkenhead (12 – down from the

Trips to the North West were increasingly common in the last 12 months of steam on BR. During one trip, No 48024 is pictured snout out from the shed confines at Rose Grove on 8 October 1967. Devoid of

shedplate, it was officially allocated to Oxley (Wolverhampton) and was removed from stock records less than two months after this view.

Not my first visit to Blackpool, but my first to North shed, revealed No 70021 *Morning Star* in the yard on 8 October 1967, again without nameplates but at least bearing a shedplate, showing its allocation to Carlisle (Kingmoor).

65 before!), Edge Hill (52), Speke Junction (81 – up from 66), Sutton Oak (23), Springs Branch (80 – up from 62), Bolton (37), Newton Heath (69), Patricroft (59), Trafford Park (36), Heaton Mersey (20), Stockport (34) and Buxton (25). Having now done the area three times in as many months, and with apparently nowhere to go of any great interest, I hung up my hat for the rest of the year.

Outside of railways, I was promoted to the post of Assistant Securities at the Highfields, Leicester, branch of the bank on 14

November, and the year closed with a performance of Emlyn Williams's *Night Must Fall* by the Thurmaston Methodist Church Players on Saturday 9 December, in which I played Detective Inspector Belsize and Carol Leader was Olivia Grayne. It was another successful production, with a full house.

For the records, my 16,000th cop came with No D6353 at Old Oak Common on 7 May, and my tally at the year-end was 16,281 – 4,903 MR, 2,541 ER, 691 SR, 2,557 WR, 1,677 Standards and 3,912 diesel and electrics. With cops of any sort now reduced to a trickle and there being no hope of any meaningful increase in steam numbers, this would be my last year of keeping such records, but I had the consolation that I had captured roughly two-thirds of my original goal over 12 wonderfully eventful and enjoyable years.

1968 was, of course, the year that BR finally ran out of steam (!), of which more later, but it was also a year that saw death and disturbance outside the railway and in other countries. One of the most charismatic individuals of the 20th century, Martin Luther King Jr, was assassinated by James Earl Ray in Memphis on 4 April, causing a nationwide sense of anger and riots throughout the USA. Just two months later, another US celebrity suffered a similar fate, when Robert F. Kennedy was shot on 6 June, in the kitchen of the Ambassador Hotel in Los Angeles by Sirhan Sirhan, a 24-year-old Palestinian. In Czechoslovakia, following what was known as the 'Prague Spring' when Alexander Dubček was appointed First Secretary of the local Communist Party, Soviet tanks rolled into the country over the night of 20/21 August, quelling the riots and resistance over succeeding weeks and months. Meanwhile, in France there were mass demonstrations and strikes in May, threatening civil war against Charles De Gaulle. In the UK, things were much quieter, but the merger of the National Provincial and Westminster banks was something of a shock to both the public and the financial institutions, creating National Westminster, the UK's largest bank with 3,600 branches. Working for Barclays, I viewed this with interest, as I did the arrival of the first decimal coins – 5p, 10p and 50p – replacing the 1 shilling and 2 shilling coins and the 10 shilling note in advance of full decimalisation in 1971. In the Mexico Olympics, Dick Fosbury made history by winning the high jump gold with his revolutionary 'flop' method.

Musically, 21 singles reached the top spot and they were a strange mix, not portraying any overall genre. The selection included such as Cliff Richard's *Congratulations*, Des O'Connor's *I Pretend* and Scaffold's *Lily the Pink*. I had moved away from buying singles, gravitating more towards albums, but had also developed a love of blues music and, with a couple of like-minded banker friends, I formed the Leicestershire Blues Appreciation Society. I had gone to Leicester's DeMontfort Hall in October 1967 to see a wonderful array of elderly US blues artists. Les was emigrating with his family to South Africa and he gave me his copy of an album by Howlin' Wolf, and I was hooked. I was shortly to begin writing about music for the *Syston Times & Vale of Belvoir Gazette*, syndicated to *Melton Times*, and went on to review records and concerts for *Melody Maker*,

One of the periodic blues shows at DeMontfort Hall, Leicester, sees Curtis Jones on piano, John Lee Hooker on guitar (seated) and Shakey Horton on harmonica. Not everyone favoured electric blues, but this show certainly satisfied the audience.

New Musical Express and several other national magazines, enabling me over the years to massively expand my record collection of blues and other genres. On 29 May I attended 'The First Rock & Roll Show' (!), headlined by Duane Eddy. Eleven of his hits were performed, with an encore of *Some Kind-a Earthquake*. Also on the show were the Walker Brothers, the Quotations and the Other Two. Duane's autograph was this time obtained on a poster for the show. His only single of the year – *Niki Hoeky/Velvet Nights* – was released two days after this show, but to little attention from the public.

On the railway front closures continued, with local passenger services especially suffering, such as Oxford to Bletchley, and Sheffield (Midland) to Leeds (City) on 1 January, Birmingham (New Street) to Derby (Midland), and Leicester (London Road) to Birmingham (New Street) and to Nottingham on 4 March, Stratford-upon-Avon to Gloucester (Central) on 25 March, and Manchester (Exchange) to Huddersfield on 7 October. As in the previous couple of years, my railway fix did not receive any meaningful boost until March, when I returned once more to Barry on the 17th. By now I had changed my car to a red Austin 1100 and my girlfriend to Anna-Maria, of Italian extraction. She worked with David and he had engineered an introduction by way of a works evening meal (in Leicester), which I attended straight from playing hockey near Peterborough – I am not quite sure what I must have smelled like! However, we liked each other and began going out as a foursome with David and Barbara. My trip to Barry, however, was solo, and any loneliness was dispelled with seeing yet more arrivals at the site since my pervious visit, the record in my notebook showing 214 locos on show, including three cops. I also visited Cardiff (Canton), Radyr and Newport (Ebbw Junction) sheds and Cashmore's and United Wagon scrapyards. Needless to say, the only cops were diesels.

12 April saw me pay a by now rare visit to the roundhouse at Leicester (Midland) shed, where I copped two diesels, but I was more keen to see the preserved steam sheltering under the protection of the shed roof. Around the turntable were Nos 4771 *Green Arrow*, 44027, 63601 and 49385. The last two

had followed me from Stratford, and there were plans to house them in a new Museum of Technology in the city, but these came to naught. Three days later, Anna-Maria joined David, Barbara and myself on a trip to the North West to view what steam was still around, beginning at Carnforth. It was a leisurely day, certainly by previous spotting standards, and Anna-Maria took all our excitement in her stride. We finished our jaunt at Lostock Hall, where we saw No D403, a rare beast to us; Preston, with just No 45268 on shed; and Blackpool, where we stopped for refreshment before resuming our journey south, only for Anna-Maria to (accidentally) tip her cup of hot coffee over my hand! I tried to make light of it, as she was *very* apologetic, but it didn't help my mood for the long journey back!

The summer passed with just two more excursions inside 15C (Leicester Midland) shed, on 11 and 13 May, with little to excite. The two dates coincided with Leicester City drawing 0-0 against Stoke, at home, to finish 13th in the First Division, and beating Rotherham United 2-0, again at home, in the 5th Round of the FA Cup. Sadly, they were to lose 3-1 to Everton in the 6th Round. So to the eventful weekend 2-4 August.

Determined to savour as much as possible of the *very last* weekend of normal steam working on standard-gauge BR, Peter and I set sail on the Friday to Patricroft (24 on shed), Bolton (25) and Wigan (Springs Branch) (24). The sun shone and it was almost a carnival atmosphere as we looked ahead to the next few days. Many of the monsters were, happily, still breathing, but the only cops were, not surprisingly, diesel. 3 August was my birthday and the sun still shone as we travelled to Carnforth, where we were just in time to witness No 45342 being driven to the rear of the shed yard as its last movement and left there to work no more! Rose Grove followed, then Lostock Hall and Preston. Lostock Hall was our main destination for the fateful day, the 4th, where all was bustle as the locos that were to be involved in the last day's efforts were being readied. The visiting 'gricers' swarmed everywhere around the shed, and Agfa, Kodak and Ilford must have made a fortune that day! The showpiece was undoubtedly No 70013 *Oliver Cromwell*, and I doubt she had looked any better even when emerging brand new from the workshops! Lots of TLC and elbow grease were being applied to remove any spot or blemish! Eventually they left the depot, as did we, us to go once more to Wigan and thence to Burton on Trent before it was sadly back to Leicester. The steam age, once seemingly so permanent and often unloved or taken for granted, was gone. It would never be the same again. A week later, on 11 August, the now famous '15 Guinea Special' – the end-of-steam commemorative tour – went out with a bang, but it was no replacement.

On 17 September I went to Leicester's Phoenix Theatre to see *The Back Handed Kiss*, starring, among others, Francesca Annis, Carmen Silvera and Douglas Fisher. The following day I was at the bowling alley and who should turn up on the lane next to us but those three! They were obviously novices at the sport, so I spent much time trying to give them instructions,

'Ah, I'm all cut up!' (Sorry, Elvis!) Peter examines a new wheel arrangement of 4-0-0 for No 44829 on Bolton Shed on 2 August 1968. Following a somewhat nomadic life the length and breadth of the WCML, the loco's final resting place was Bolton from 6 January 1968, withdrawal following on 18 May.

The death of another 'Black 5'. At Carnforth on 3 August 1968 the crew of No 45342 have seen their charge into the sidings and the fireman leaves to walk towards his mates. The loco's last duty was earlier that day, from Barrow with 8P76, the 0930 to Carnforth Goods, and it was then left here to die!

On the final day of normal steam on BR, enthusiasts swarm around Lostock Hall shed like ants and Nos 45110 and 70013 *Oliver Cromwell* are primed and ready for their next duties, after which, happily, both would go on to preservation.

chatting to them and obtaining their autographs. I have followed Francesca's career ever since and imagine my surprise when Carmen would later turn to be Edith, Renée's wife in 'Allo 'Allo!

The weeks following the end of steam brought a dreadful feeling of bewilderment, estrangement and downright loss, like losing an arm. What to do without the regular injection of steam? I joined Roger and his group on 16 November on a trip to the infant Keighley & Worth Valley Railway and dutifully logged the numbers there and at Healey Mills, Wath, Darnall, Staveley and Westhouses, but it was not the same. It was not just the dull weather that created the feelings of disappointment and despair.

But things had moved on in my personal life. My writings were developing, I had been interviewed on Radio Leicester about the blues society, a bank account had been opened for it and, early in the new local football scene – where I played on both Saturdays and Sundays – I met and started going out with Paula, the sister of one of my team mates. But even that was to change.

Since moving to the branch at Highfields in Leicester, my routine had become one of giving Linda, a colleague who lived at the other end of Thurmaston from me, a lift to work each day. This ended when I was promoted again, to Charles Street in the centre of Leicester from 6 November 1968. She and Steve, her boyfriend, were friends with me and Paula, so we were invited to her birthday on 22 December. There I saw and talked to an attractive young lady called Judith, who I took to be 14! I quizzed Linda about Judith the following day, to be told that she was in fact 20. I dropped in at Linda's a few days later – for the first and last time! – when Judith phoned; I chatted briefly to her and asked her out. She said 'yes', then I had a problem… I was joining Paula at a New Year's Eve party at her house, organised by her brothers, and I didn't believe in 'two-timing'. A couple of my bank colleagues were also to be there and I told them that I planned to say goodbye to Paula at the party. They looked at me askance and didn't believe me! Would I do it?

On the railways the year ended with the withdrawal of

the final 359 BR steam locos – interestingly, 307 were pre-nationalisation types (301 were Stanier-designed 'Black 5s' and 8Fs), and only 52 'Standards', despite being much younger. However, such was the rump left at the end that the number of diesels withdrawn in the year actually exceeded this! No fewer than 436 were dispensed with, following a decision to rid the system of non-standard types. No D801 *Vanguard* was the first of its class to go (on 3 August), and classes that were decimated during the year (to use their later official classifications) were Classes 28, 23, 21, 22, 15, 16, 17, 14 and 77 – many of which were less than five years old! The three SR dc electrics, Nos 20001-3, all went in the last months of the year, with the last-numbered sent to Kettering for scrap.

Needless to say, after the demise of steam things would never be the same again and, as was probably inevitable, non-railway influences were exerting ever more pressure and interest; however, even with that, 1969 would prove to be another interesting year. On the world stage, by far the greatest event was Neil Armstrong stepping onto the moon from Apollo 11's lunar module on 21 July, with the immortal words, 'One small step for man, one giant leap for mankind.' Another earth-shattering happening, but of a totally different kind, was the murder of actress Sharon Tate on 9 August by Charles Manson and his 'family' in Beverly Hills. Just over eight years later, I was driven to the gates of Ms Tate's home and the place had a real eerie feeling, even after all that time! Continuing in crime, the Kray twins were sentenced to life imprisonment for their part in two gangland killings, after conviction following their arrest on 8 May 1968. The first UK-built Concorde flew from Filton to RAF Fairford on 9 April, piloted by Brian Trubshaw; Tony Jacklin became the first English golfer to win the Open since 1951; and 14 February was a sad day, seeing the death through a heart attack of Kenneth Horne, just as he was about to start recording the fifth series of *Round the Horne*. He was and is one of my all-time favourite comedy performers. *My Way* by Frank Sinatra was the year's top-selling singles, and the Beatles' album *Abbey Road* and Dylan's *Nashville Skyline* were released to critical acclaim. In the railway world, work was begun in January by BR engineers on what would become the celebrated High Speed Train (HST). The BR Board was told to expect a full working prototype within two years, but it took until 1976 for the final product to enter service.

On the personal front, January 1969 began with a blues concert, organised by me, at the Coronation Hotel in Leicester, featuring the local Stone Blues Band. I took Judith – so, yes, I did end it with Paula! – and she impressed me by taking charge of hanging posters in the venue, arranging seating and generally being a great help. On Saturday 4 January we went to London to enjoy '4 Hours of Blues', a concert organised by the London Blues Society and featuring, among others, Chicken Shack. Also there were Mike Raven and Alexis Korner, stalwarts of the British blues scene. The following day saw the end of passenger services on the Edinburgh Waverley-Carlisle route, one I remembered from our visit to Hawick shed. 31 January saw the release of a most unusual record by Duane Eddy – *Break my Mind* coupled with *Loving Bird* – which saw him singing! Living in London in 1968, he had recorded the single for CBS and appeared (twice) on *The Golden Shot* TV show to promote it. On the first appearance, they ran out of time, so Duane just about had time to say 'Hello' and to agree 'to come back next week'! His performance on the second week was eagerly awaited by us fans and he did not disappoint, proving that he had a good vocal presence; sadly, with no chart appearance, this was to be his last UK single release until 1975, although the USA did put out three between December 1969 and December 1972.

1969 proved a busy year for both me and the Leicestershire Blues Appreciation Society (LBAS) – which by now had 90 members – as I began on 7 March a weekly music column in the *Syston Times*, syndicated to the *Melton Times* and *Vale of Belvoir Gazette*, and LBAS put on a number of concerts. 13 March opened the season with 'Mississippi' Fred McDowell, an artist who had come back to fame following the recent UK appreciation of elderly US blues giants who were still around.

I was at work that day and received a phone call from my mother mid-afternoon, to say, 'I have this black man here. What do I do with him?' He and his roadie had turned up earlier than expected! I suggested that she give them coffee and make them comfortable until I came home. She did, but Fred did not seem to appreciate the coffee; he was much happier when dad arrived home and offered him whisky! His performance that evening, in the Leicester Co-op's Charnwood Restaurant, riveting and magical, was made all the better as I had recently proposed to Judith and she had accepted!

Though the power of the railway drug had been much lessened over the past six months, the lure did not wholly go away, and on 7 April I introduced Judith to the delights with an out-and-back trip to March, by way of Kettering scrapyard. Just two steam this time – Nos 48467 and 44816 – and my first sight of diesels there for scrap. Nos D8400/02/03 were a surprise – a little over ten years old – as were shunters Nos D3643, D4090 and D4093, with the latter pair just six years young! Alongside was No D2176, new in 1961 and most recently working at Crewe Works, but this was not to be finally cut up until November 1971! March was full of 63 diesels of varying shapes and sizes, from which I copped 12, including four Brush Type 2s. This obviously rejuvenated my interest and I was to hoover up a few more numbers for the collection on our first holiday together, a seven-day trip to the Isle of Wight. Before this, however, I had the 'delight' of watching, on the TV, Leicester City in their third appearance in the decade at the FA Cup Final at Wembley Stadium. Sadly, in front of 98,117 fans, they lost 1-0 against Manchester City!

En route to the Isle of Wight on 3 May, I noted locos and places on our rail journey, pulled by No D54 between Leicester and St Pancras. Across London, we then boarded our train at Waterloo for Portsmouth Harbour. Judith did not seem to have the 'Gill effect', as the weather was not overly kind to us, although we did manage walks around various parts of the island. Judith never did forgive me, however, for dragging her, in the rain, up the steep hill out of Ventnor to visit the long closed

Judith's first outing with me was to the scrapyard at Kettering on 7 April 1969. I did suggest that she was not properly clad for climbing locos, but she was adamant that she would take a closer view of No 44816!

and derelict station that I had remembered so fondly from sunny days on my previous visit. She stood there incredulous that a grown man could almost be reduced to tears at this desolate and vandalised station site! We arrived home on 8 May by the same route, pulled from St Pancras by No D125, and I managed to garner a total of 17 cops, a mixture of diesels and SR electrics. I was seemingly oblivious that 3 May, our departure day for the south, had been the very last day of services between Rugby and Nottingham on the remains of the old GCR route. As the year

This special publication celebrated Leicester City reaching the FA Cup Final against Manchester City in 1969. For the princely sum of 2s 6d, fans were offered a record of the achievement. Sadly, yet again, Leicester were to be on the losing side!

progressed, there were proposals for closure of Marylebone – a station so quiet that Alan Jackson opined 'the twittering of the birds in the roof is heard' – the four stations between Neasden and Northolt Junction, and for diverting High Wycombe trains to Paddington.

Back home there was much to do. There was planning for the next concert, to be held on 28 May and featuring Tony 'Duster' Bennett and Ian A. Anderson. Both were popular solo artists, singing a mix of blues, folk and R&B, and the former, born in Welshpool in 1946, toured as a one-man band, playing a bass drum with his foot and blowing a harmonica on a rack while strumming his 1952 Les Paul guitar. His album *Smiling Like I'm Happy* had been released in 1968 to critical acclaim. Ian had released his first album, *Stereo Death Breakdown*, at the time of his appearance for us and songs from this went down well. Another matter taking much time was organising the agreement and rental for the bank flat above the branch in Sibson Road, Birstall. On the basis that Judith and I would need somewhere to live when first married, I moved in in June, together with Guy, with whom I had worked in Syston. He was to live there until Judith moved in after our wedding, and we two single men were to quickly learn the arts of cooking and keeping house, as it was basically a three-bedroom house minus the front room, which the bank had used, with an extension, to produce the local branch office. Roger was to utilise his artistic

During one of the early concerts put on by the Leicestershire Blues Appreciation Society, I pose for the camera as Judith seems overawed to be in the presence of Tony 'Duster' Bennett and Ian A. Anderson, at the Co-op Hall, High Street, Leicester, on 28 May 1969.

skills on the walls of the hall, while I did the same on the lounge wall!

3 July saw the release of *Five Leaves Left*, a first album by new singer/songwriter Nick Drake. I was at this stage receiving albums for review from a number of record companies, to be covered in my newspaper column. This was to expand over the next couple of years, receiving up to 50 albums a week, writing for *Melody Maker*, *NME*, *Sounds*, *IT* and a number of other national publications, some majoring on the blues. I received Nick's album and Judith, Guy and myself were instantly hooked, by his songs, his lyrics, his melodies and his guitar styles and tunings. He was to make two further albums – *Bryter Layter* (1971) and *Pink Moon* (1972) – but none made any real impact, despite critical acclaim. A sufferer from depression, he died on 25 November 1974, just 26 years old. Incredibly, his albums have never been out of catalogue and at the time of writing (2016) he is more popular than ever. Ever since that first album release he has been one of my all-time favourite artists and one whose music I would take to a desert island.

My last railway outing of the year was on 21 July, with another trip to London, noting 'Baby Deltic' No 5903 together with three shunters at Kettering awaiting their trip to Cohen's scrapyard. Two separate visits to King's Cross during the day saw me cop three 'Brush 4s' but, sadly, with no sight of a 'Deltic' on either occasion.

On Sunday 24 August Leicester followed the transatlantic trend by holding a free concert, on Welford Road recreation ground. In bright sunshine – and me responding by wearing my light blue 'Jimmy Reed' cord trousers – a crowd of around 1,200 watched and enjoyed Grizelda (a local group) open proceedings, followed by Moth, Black Widow, Ned Ludd, Clay Cross Blues, Berkeley Squares and Jody Grind. Bridget St John was due to appear but at 9pm the heavens opened and the event was closed. There were immediate clamours and plans for a second, but, to my knowledge, that never happened.

The weekly blues meetings of LBAS above the Chameleon coffee bar in Leicester's King Street and reviewing now took much of my time, but there were moments to treasure. During one meeting an American gentleman entered the room, enquired who we were and what we were doing, saying that he was attracted by our music, especially the Mississippi John Hurt tracks that I had played and he had heard downstairs. It turned out that he had known John and he proceeded to tell us stories about the great bluesman – truly gems to savour. Blues were also to occasion my next railway liaison. Over the weekend of 20/21 September, the London Blues Society ran the 2nd National Blues Convention, at the Conway Hall in Red Lion Square, WC1. At least 24 artists and experts were booked to appear, including elderly bluesman Bukka White and Nick Perls of Yazoo Records, a highly respected US blues label. A very informal affair, Judith, Guy and myself thoroughly enjoyed ourselves and I took the opportunity to meet and talk to Nick Perls, together with John Peel, Ian A. Anderson, Mike Leadbitter, Mike Raven (who invited me to sit in the studio for one of his BBC Radio blues shows), Alexis Korner and Robin Heath – a young white blues pianist, who would come to Leicester to perform for us the following year. The opportunity was again taken of popping into King's Cross, and this time there were eight 'Deltics' present! A week later, I was transferred from the Highfields branch of the bank to Charles Street, Leicester, to take up a position as Head of Securities, under the management of Gil Hunter, one of the best managers I ever came across.

As if all the September blues excitement was not enough, Judith and I attended The American Folk, Blues & Gospel Festival '69 at the DeMontfort Hall in Leicester on Sunday 2 November. It was a delight to see Albert King, John Lee Hooker, Otis Spann, Champion Jack Dupree and the Stars of Faith. Through my publication outlets, enabling reviews of the concerts at this hall to be published, the management agreed to let me have free tickets (for the two of us) for any concerts in which we were interested. We used the facility copiously over the next decade!

I had not lost interest in Leicester City amongst all this hustle but, as they had been relegated at the end of the 1968-69 season to Division 2 by just 1 point, the appeal was not so great. However, they had been doing much better in this lower division and had reached the 5th Round of both the FA and League Cups before being beaten by, respectively, Liverpool on 11 February 1970 and West Bromwich Albion on 5 November 1969. Allan Clarke obviously did not like the idea of playing below the top flight and he was transferred, after just one season, to Leeds United, who had been League Champions at the end of the 1968-69 season.

October 1969 had seen the launch on BBC TV of *Monty Python's Flying Circus* and into and through 1970 the show's popularity grew, bringing classic sketches and ideas such as 'The Dead Parrot sketch', 'The Ministry of Silly Walks' and the 'Spanish Inquisition', all of which have retained lasting appeal and notoriety. The first Boeing 747 landed at Heathrow Airport on 23 January 1970, and Apollo 13 was launched on 11 April; it failed to make a lunar landing as an oxygen tank exploded but, after the near disaster, the crew returned to Earth six days later. England, the World Cup holders, were knocked out in the Quarter Final in this year's event; and on 19 June Edward Heath surprisingly found himself as Prime Minister after the shock defeat of Labour by the Tories. In the singles charts, it was a sort of interregnum, between Flower Power and Glam Rock, but albums brought some kudos, with *Bridge Over Troubled Water* by Simon and Garfunkel and *Led Zeppelin II* hogging the limelight. However, the deaths of Jimi Hendrix on 18 September and Janis Joplin on 4 October (both connected with drugs and both 27 years old) brought a sombre end to the musical year. O. V. S. Bulleid also died this year, on 25 April, aged 87. Line closures continued with the ending of passenger services between Kidderminster, Bewdley and Hartlebury on 5 January, locals from Skipton to Carlisle, all passenger services between Bourne End and High Wycombe, and from Lowestoft (Central) to Yarmouth (South Town), all on 4 May, and Barnstaple to Ilfracombe on 5 October.

On a happier note, 1970 was the year of my marriage to Judith, but before that there was another concert to produce, this time at Vaughan College, in St Nicholas Circle in Leicester on 28 February, when LBAS proudly presented Arthur 'Big

Boy' Crudup. For the uninitiated, he was the composer and original recording artist of *That's Alright Now Mama*, later to be made world famous by Elvis Presley. Sadly, as he told me on the night, he received no royalties from the newer recording and little in the way of spin-off fame. He was supported on our bill by Robin Heath, a young pianist I had met in London. The performances were excellent but the size of the audience was disappointing, not least as the venue was more expensive than the Co-op! The night ended with Arthur sleeping at my flat, as he had nowhere else to go. I did not tell the bank, but I doubt they would have been impressed! On 5 March, Judith and I were joined by friend Brian Chambers on a trip to the latest Lanchester Arts Festival concert. Lesser-known groups Mighty Baby and Juicy Lucy were pretty uninspiring, but the headline act, Love, led by founder and singer Arthur Lee, was superb, fully living up to their international reputation.

As can be judged, my patterns of interests were changing, but the legacy of steam was still in my blood. I now had no great desire to continue long, purely spotting tours, trying to clear the diesel fleet, and my gaze was turning towards the nascent preservation scene. I still collected the numbers seen on my travels, not least during a two-day trip to London, starting at Liverpool Street on 21 March and visiting King's Cross and Paddington. Cops were few, totalling two, three and three respectively at the three locations! Judith and I married at St Michael's Church in Thurmaston on 7 May, with a reception at the White House (!) in Scraptoft. We were to honeymoon in Portugal, staying with Judith's aunt, who had married a Portuguese. David Try, our best man, drove us to London for our overnight stay in a hotel (recommended by a contact in the record industry), then we flew out the next day to Lisbon after a day spent sightseeing in London. We arrived at Lisbon Airport nearing midnight and couldn't see Judith's bag on the carousel. Airport staff were decidedly thin on the ground and none spoke English when we tried to solicit help. With no aid forthcoming, we went outside and hailed a taxi; Judith then suddenly saw her bag being carried by another woman! She went off chasing it, while I sat with the taxi door open and one foot on the ground, to stop him driving away! We finally made it to our hotel, only to find that my bank customer travel agent had booked us a suite but with twin single beds. Not what we had envisaged for the second night of our honeymoon!

The following day we flew north to Oporto, to meet up with the family. Needless to say, railways were not the first thing on my mind but, on the drive to the family home in Riba d'Ave, we passed over a level crossing. Judith's six-year old cousin Liz (christened Elisabete, as the Portuguese authorities would not allow an English spelling!) said that they were 'always' stopped by trains and assured us that we would see lots as we travelled around. Sadly, the truth was not so promising, and on one occasion, when we waited by a crossing for a train, it was some considerable time before one came and I was facing in the wrong direction with my camera when it final arrived. I was granted one spotting trip, however, at Santa Tirso on 18 May, when Judith's Aunt Betty took us to the local station after shopping in the town. It was about 90 degrees in the shade as we walked nearly a mile from the town to the station, to find that the next train was not for nearly an hour. We therefore walked up the hill to the town, had a quick coffee, then went back again, where we ignored the notice forbidding us entry to the platform without a ticket and to keep off the line, to photograph the steam loco No E85 and its crew polishing it on our behalf. Thereafter we only saw one further train, as we were on our way to the airport to come home; but the holiday was most enjoyable, not least due to Liz's antics, fighting her place against her elder brothers Philip and David in their football matches in their garden, and her delight with my goatee beard. She would sit on my knee and assert, in her Portuguese twang, holding her little fingers like scissors, 'I am going to cut zis beard off!' Shortly after my return to work, I saw Anna-Maria at the drive-in window – by this time Barclays had taken over the old Martins Bank drive-in premises in Charles Street. I went to talk to her and she seemed pleased to see me, but not so pleased to hear that I had recently returned from my honeymoon!

This was one of the very few occasions that I saw trains in Portugal, while on honeymoon. Ignoring signs to the contrary, I walked off the low platform to photograph No E85 and its crew at Santo Tirso station on 18 May 1970. A pleasure to see steam once more in normal service.

On 26 June we made another journey to London, this time to see the truly venerable blues singer Son House at St Pancras Town Hall. I recorded numbers on our way there and back and popped into King's Cross (again) to cop five and see three 'Deltics' – Nos 9008 *The Green Howards*, 9000 *Royal Scots Grey* and 9013 *The Black Watch* – all now devoid of the 'D' in their numbering. 3 July saw me spread my writing wings, with my first reviews published in the 'infamous' national underground paper *International Times* (IT), including one of the Son House concert. This had the effect of encouraging yet more record companies to send me albums for review. Many of my published pieces were under the name 'Michael J.', to hide my efforts from the bank, the name using my first Christian name and taking inspiration from the black American human rights activist 'Malcolm X'. During August we spent two days in Cornwall with David Try and his family, visiting Penzance shed and, on the way back home, Staverton and Ashburton on the Dart Valley Railway.

During a trip to Penzance in August 1970, to stay with David, our best man, and his family, Judith accompanied me to Penzance shed, now long since fully dieselised. No D804 *Avenger* and D1054 *Western Governor*, standing outside the shed building, reflect the care that BR so often did not give to its motive power!

On our way back from Penzance we called in at Ashburton, to glimpse what was to prove to be the temporary northern terminus of the Dart Valley Railway. No 4555 stands in the station, with other stock in the siding to the left.

Chapter 4
1970-1975

The next outing was to a preservation site – Tyseley – on 13 September 1970, and we drove there in my new (to me) Triumph 1300, bought for the princely sum of £610 the previous month. After quickly scanning the operating shed, I concentrated on the cluster of steam locos on show, including Nos 30777 *Sir Lamiel*, 30925 *Cheltenham*, 45428, 1501, 7029 *Clun Castle*, 45593 *Kolhapur*, 30120 and 50621. Thankfully, the sun shone and the 'Castle' and 'Jubilee' were top-and-tailing

Our first trip to Tyseley Open Day on 13 September 1970 was graced by glorious weather, which certainly brought out the best of the preserved items on display. 'T9' No 120 (ex-30120) receives attention on and off, its livery contrasting with the Pullman car behind.

coaching stock, giving rides, so there was something for Judith to see and photograph. She was becoming enamoured of steam, but had no time for diesels! Back in Leicester, No 60800 *Green Arrow* had been added to the roundhouse collection, but the elderly and long-preserved Nos 118 and 158A were moved into an old fire station on London Road, to the south of the city centre. With absolutely no railway links whatsoever, it was indeed a strange place to house them! On Wednesday 23 September Judith and I went to see Canned Heat at the DeMontfort Hall but, during the afternoon, I managed some time off work to go to interview Bob 'The Bear' Hite, the lead vocalist of the group, so-called because he was a mountain of a man! Sadly, perhaps reflecting the recent death of group member Al Wilson, the show was an overloud disappointment.

I November saw another collection of American 'Folk, Blues and Gospel' artists at the DeMontfort Hall, with Sonny Terry and Brownie McGhee the stars; and on the 6th LBAS organised another concert at Vaughan College, this time featuring a young (then merely 32!) but up-and-coming US black bluesman, Larry Johnson. He was to bring Dave Kelly with him, a British equivalent. Our audience was even smaller for this one, but they sat patiently waiting as show time approached. 7.30pm came and went. An hour later and we had to make a decision – it was the wrong one! With some of the audience drifting away and no form of telephone contact, we gave up and told the caretaker to close the hall. I later learned that the performers had arrived 30 minutes later, complete with Jo-Ann Kelly, Dave's sister – an artist I had been trying to book for months! They were not amused at a wasted journey, and the booking agent was none too pleased either. This was my last concert for the Blues Society. The regular coffee bar meetings also folded and we kept the Society going for a brief period in my flat, but the end was not unexpected.

By this time, such was the diminution of interest in spotting trips, or going out of my way to find and collect numbers, that my notebooks collated those engines seen by month rather than by day until the end of 1970. The Christmas No

I was Dave Edmunds's *I Hear You Knocking*, which spent seven weeks at the top from 28 November; on the album front, the soundtrack to *South Pacific* was the equivalent, reigning for 13 weeks from 13 October. Having just missed instant promotion back to the top flight in the previous season, Leicester City were riding high, hovering close to the top, where they would finish at the end of the season, 3 points clear of Sheffield United.

1971 saw my outings reduced to the extent that numbers collected were now all lumped together between January and July, with the only notation of any locations on 31 March, when I travelled to London for the weekend for a bank course reunion and a brief visit to Rayleigh, the home of one of the group. Numbers were quickly collected at King's Cross – two 'Deltics', Nos 9004 *Queen's Own Highlander* and 9007 *Pinza* – Liverpool Street, St Pancras and Bedford. Elsewhere on the railway, 4 January saw the withdrawal of passenger services

To show our support to the fledgling Great Central Railway, we undertook a sponsored walk from Abbey Lane Sidings, Leicester, to Loughborough Central station and back (roughly the distance of a marathon!) in 1971. Approaching Kinchley Lane road bridge, I am joined by Peter for our portraits to be captured for posterity! *Judith Stretton*

between Taunton and Minehead, October recorded the same for Buckfastleigh-Ashburton on the 4th, and Barry Island-Barry Pier on the 18th. One sad event was the sale of Brush's No HS4000 *Kestrel* by Hawker Siddeley Group to Russian railways for £127,000. It was exported in July after conversion to the 5-foot gauge.

Off the railway, the UK converted to decimal currency on 15 February; Rolls-Royce went into administrative receivership 11 days earlier, on 4 February; the *Daily Sketch* closed and merged with the *Daily Mail*; Idi Amin seized power in Uganda through a military coup on 25 January; and Stanley Kubrick's film of Anthony Burgess's novel *A Clockwork Orange* was released in New York City on 19 December; it came to the UK on 13 January 1972. The biggest-selling single of the year was *My Sweet Lord* by George Harrison, followed by Rod Stewart's *Maggie May*. Third was one of the most irritating singles of all time (in your author's humble opinion!) – *Chirpy Chirpy Cheep Cheep* by Middle of the Road. On a personal front, a young lady was transferred into the branch where I worked and we quickly became close friends. She and her husband often joined Judith and myself to go out as a four, and she and I found ourselves growing very close. Judith was aware, as we had a very open and honest marriage, and she accepted the situation. The affair lasted for three years, but we kept in touch thereafter until her death from cancer on 9 May 2009.

Judith and I had joined the Leicester Film Society in 1970 and had seen many very enjoyable films. Emboldened by this, we bought tickets for the Leicester University 'Film Weekend', running from Thursday to Sunday, 18-21 February 1971. We attended the first and last days, providing quite a contrast. Thursday screened *Ladies and Gentlemen – Leonard Cohen*, which was a thoroughly entertaining 44 lunchtime minutes, but sadly not all of Sunday's fare was as good. I did enjoy The Goons' *The Running, Jumping, Standing Still* film at 7.00pm, but the film at 8.14pm – *The Inauguration of the Pleasure Dome* – was, without a doubt, the most boring and tedious film I have ever had to sit through and the longest 38 minutes of my life! I couldn't wait for it to end!

Through LBAS I had made friends with Bob Fisher and, making use of the contacts made through my music writings, we would begin making half-yearly trips to London, to 'do the round' of the record companies, coming back home with armfuls of albums, T-shirts and all manner of other goodies! On one of these trips, Bob and I were treated to drinks and lunch at a Soho pub, where we were introduced to David Bowie's publicist, the group Lindisfarne and Howard Werth, guitarist and vocalist of the group Audience. When the pub closed, we were taken to a private club in (if memory serves) Greek Street, and introduced to Foster's lager – then still fairly new in this country. After one, two or three drinks – my memory is rather sketchy – I am told that I verbally abused Clive James, who was sitting nearby, walked to the gents across the flight path of a darts match, and phoned a record company to organise free entry to Ronnie Scott's Club for that night, together with a front row table and free drinks and smokes if we wanted them, to see the featured artist of the night. I 'came to', after a four-hour mental blank, as we were walking towards the club, and can remember the rest of the evening, including passing Marty Feldman on the stairs down to the gents. I looked at him and nodded a greeting but, with his eyes, I could not tell whether he was looking at me or not! It was through these record contacts that Judith and I had front-row seats for Monty Python's performance in Coventry in 1971, at the Lanchester Arts Festival, an event that we enjoyed for several years, with me reviewing for various periodicals. On this memorable night, one of the sketches ran on past what had been seen on TV and the Pythons came off stage and along the front row to the exit doors – still performing the whole way – and I had the 'honour' of having had John Cleese tread on my foot!

The next opportunity for spotting came on a canal holiday, when Judith and I joined Peter and his wife Pam for a fortnight's narrow boat trip from Llangollen. Setting out on 31 July, we first encountered and were suitably amazed at the crossing of Telford's magnificent Pontcysyllte Aqueduct. At 336 yards long and 126 feet above the valley floor, at Trefor near Llangollen, the waterway is just wide enough for a boat, which frequently tapped against the side with the deck about a foot above the parapet on one side! Breathtaking is the only word for it. We headed for Macclesfield and Peter and I had noticed that we came close to railway lines on a number of locations. It was amazing how many mealtime stops seemed to coincide with such places! We saw a number of electrics on the WCML, including Nos E3149, E3128, E3160 and E3106, together with several D4xxs (later Class 50). Nos E3112, 439 and 412 were seen at Kidsgrove, 5048 at Chirk and E3088 at Litchfield. The undoubted highlight of the two weeks, however, even beating the aqueduct, was travelling (both ways) through the single bore of Harecastle Tunnel at Kidsgrove, 2,926 yards long and completed in 1827. Boaters initially made their way through by 'legging', lying on their backs on top of the boat and propelling themselves with their feet on the tunnel roof! Fortunately we had an engine, but it was still slow going, pitch black with just the boat's headlight to show the immediate few yards ahead. Needless to say, the tunnel allowed traffic in only one direction at a time. Two years after our visit, it was closed for four years, to cure subsidence problems!

The next exciting thing for Judith and me was to be 8 September, when we moved into our own house, our first real home together, a three-bedroom bungalow in Birstall, Leicester, costing £5,538, just £62 within our budget. We were there for five years and thoroughly enjoyed the building, the garden and our neighbours. Back in the First Division, Leicester City signed Keith Weller from Chelsea, Jon Sammels from Arsenal and Alan Birchenall from Crystal Palace. All would become useful scorers for the team and the last-named would be a club ambassador for many years by 2016. On 7 August City beat Liverpool 1-0, at home, in the Charity Shield match, with Steve Whitworth scoring the only goal – his only goal for the club in more than 350 appearances! By the year end, the team was midway in the League and would stay there to the close of the season. 14 October saw my first published work in *Frendz* magazine; 1 November witnessed a superb concert at the DeMontfort Hall by Leicester's own group, Family; and seven days later both

Judith and myself had to stand on our seats at the same venue among a sell-out crowd of screaming pre-pubescent females to see T. Rex!

1972 was a year of ups and downs, the latter very much to the fore in the first month. On 9 January the liner *Queen Elizabeth*, by then renamed *Seawise University*, ready for its new life after sale, was destroyed by fire in Hong Kong harbour, close to the end of a £5 million conversion into a floating university; 28 January saw the beginning of the demolition of Leicester's Belgrave Road station and the nearby Catherine Street viaduct, another local landmark; on 30 January British soldiers shot 26 unarmed civilians during a protest march in the Bogside area of Derry, Northern Ireland, creating what would become infamous as 'Bloody Sunday'; and on 9 February the UK Government declared a state of emergency as a result of a miners' strike, which limited coal supplies and in turn caused periods of electricity blackouts of up to nine hours. Ironically, in the year when coal stocks were low, the ban on main-line

Totally closed to traffic for nearly a decade, the former GNR Belgrave Road station in Leicester had been taken over by Vic Berry's scrap business when seen on 3 October 1971. Originally intended as a through station, plans changed and this grand structure was built to show off the (unrealised) intentions of this incursion into Midland territory. *Paul Anderson*

Following closure of the line east from Belgrave Road, the tracks were ripped up and the rest of the land and station areas left to nature. Thus is the view north from East Norton in September 1973, with the station abandoned and evidence of recent rainfall abundantly clear.

steam was lifted! Passenger services to go included Wareham to Swanage on 3 January, Wolverhampton (Low Level) to Birmingham (Snow Hill) on 6 March, and Paignton to Kingswear on 30 October. Video games were gaining a following, and Atari released *Pong* on 29 November, to great acclaim. It is now merely a museum piece!

On a much brighter note, the 4th Lanchester Arts Festival was to provide what would turn out to be a most memorable evening on 3 February, at the Locarno in Coventry. For the princely sum of £1 the audience was entertained by, among others, Slade, Billy Preston and Chuck Berry. Still very early in their public career, Slade struggled to whip up any real enthusiasm, whereas Billy Preston was far more skilled with his set and, finally, Chuck Berry was to completely steal the show. His performance was recorded and would be featured as the second side of his next album, including his party piece of *My Ding-a-Ling*, which would enjoy four weeks at No 1 as a single

Just to the north of the previous view, the erstwhile track crossed an attractive viaduct. This still stands in September 1973, seen from a vantage point just to the west of East Norton station, but in later years it disappeared with landscaping of millions of tons of earth!

later in the year. Already running late, the theatre management tried in vain to persuade him to leave the stage, but he employed his 'duck walk' to avoid them, delighting the fans. The exhortation to clear the hall, to allow in a second set of fans to see Pink Floyd, was met by loud chants of 'F... the Floyd'. Eventually order was restored, but the hall was not cleared before 11pm.

Being press accredited, Judith and I stayed in situ on the balcony to await the second show. I had noticed three gentlemen sitting in a roped-off area on the balcony, just in front of where we were, but it wasn't until Pink Floyd walked on stage, at around midnight (!), that I recognised David Gilmour as being one of them! Also for £1, this was a first public performance of *Dark Side of the Moon*, booming out through quadrophonic speakers, stunning everyone in the hall. Long before the album burst into the public consciousness in 1973, this was something the like of which we had not heard before. Truly, a treasured moment. Judith and I would relive the experience, but without the uniqueness of it all, when Pink Floyd appeared at DeMontfort Hall just seven days later. March was a good month for us for concerts, with Rory Gallagher on the 9th, Jethro Tull on the 14th and, with work colleague David Hall this time instead of Judith, who was not feeling well, Captain Beefheart and his Magic Band on the 30th. May brought the Beach Boys to Leicester, and August saw my first reviews for *Cream* magazine.

On 25 March I had a day out in London and collected numbers on the rail journey, but my first real outing was on 28 May, when I took Judith to relive my steam days spotting at Essendine. It was a dull and occasionally damp day, Judith was not impressed with the diesels flashing by, and was plainly bored as I indulged in nostalgia, remembering 'A4s' and 'A3s'. After a couple of hours and only seeing eight trains, none of which were photographed but three of which were 'Deltic'-hauled – Nos 9015 *Tulyar*, 9008 *The Green Howards* and 9011 *The Royal Northumberland Fusiliers* – we made our way back home. On a happier note, March also saw Secretary of State Peter Walker decline the application to close Marylebone station; in May, Freightliner hauled its millionth container; and in June the prototype HST was completed.

1972 was to see major strides in the railway preservation movement, with the Dart Valley, West Somerset and East Lancashire railways developing, and the Ffestiniog Railway aided by a compensation cheque of £65,000 for the loss of its original route to Blaenau Ffestiniog to facilitate a power station reservoir. Indulging in this popularity, Judith and I made a visit in October to the Severn Valley Railway at Bridgnorth, being up close and personal with 8F No 8233, as well as Nos 600 *Gordon*, 3442 *The Great Marquess*, 70000 *Britannia*, 80079, 45110, 1501 and 813. Fair weather, a look around the town and an enjoyable lunch left Judith fully satisfied!

This trip took place less than a month after another promotion for me, this time as Head of Securities and Foreign departments on 20 September, moving to the Gallowtree Gate branch. Sadly, my manager, one of the most senior in the

We planned a day out to Bridgnorth on the Severn Valley Railway and to Tyseley in October 1972. The day was cold and increasingly wet! Bridgnorth station is quiet here, with no trains running, but open to visitors.

Stanier 8F No 8233 stands at the back of the engine shed at Bridgnorth in October 1972, with the crossing gate drawn tightly against entry. Judith is huddled, right, against the cold in her fur coat!

Nottingham District of the bank, did not see eye-to-eye with the way I ran the departments. His probation appraisal stated that 'I have seen no evidence of leadership, ability or initiative'! Needless to say, the bank was not amused and I was moved (demoted) in 1973. My staff disagreed with him and threatened to walk out on strike at his report and the end result ... so much for no leadership!

Our second visit to Tyseley was not so enjoyable weather-wise, being cold and wet for much of the day, but No 1247 (ex-68846) was on show but devoid of any hordes clambering on and around it.

1973 was the year of BR's new 'Total Operations Processing System' (TOPS), whereby all operating stock was to renumbered, with the relevant 'class' forming part of the new number. If there had been a slow strangulation of my faltering interest in number-taking, this was the death blow. I had no enthusiasm for transferring all my collected numbers into a new book, or for learning a whole new system. In addition, I was transferred to the bank's Belgrave Road, Leicester, branch on 13 March, and this took me completely away from handy railway access. I still idly wrote any recognisable numbers seen, but they were few, consequent on my few railway outings. Examples were 11 and 25 May, on the rail journey to and from Weymouth for our fortnight's holiday in Guernsey, when all I recorded was No 6520 on the way south and No 6521 on the return. When I saw electric loco No 87003 on 15 September, on my way home from a trip to the Kettering scrapyard, I did not recognise the class, let alone the whole number – I gave up! This was the last year of the decade that I would collect numbers, other

Having raised some funds for the new GCR, it was natural for us to continue to support it by visiting. On 25 April 1973 the yard between Loughborough station and the road bridge to the north is bare and empty, with newly arrived No 34039 *Boscastle* the focal point of any attention.

On the same day another recent arrival, Stanier 'Black 5' No 5231, receives some TLC in the platform at Loughborough Central station. Surviving to the very end of BR steam, the loco would soon be revived, to give rides to happy visitors.

than those I might recognise when visiting sites such as the Great Western Society at Didcot on 23 September, where we went for a day out with Judith's mother, father and sister. The previous week, on the 16th, we joined an outing organised by friend David Muggleton – another Barclays employee – to Bressingham, where I was delighted to see No 46100 *Royal Scot* in steam, together with *Thundersley* and Nos 42500, 46233 *Duchess of Sutherland*, 70013 *Oliver Cromwell*, 32662 and 1217E (ex-65567). By this time my best man and his wife were living in Coleford in the Forest of Dean, so visits to them incorporated a trip to look at the nascent Dean Forest Railway at Parkend.

Elsewhere, Britain joined the Common Market in 1 January, and the same month saw the signing of the Paris Peace Accord by all parties in the Vietnam War, leading to the withdrawal of US troops on 15 August (but the war did not end until 1975).

As one of the highlights of our trip to the Bressingham Steam Museum on 16 September 1973, it was especially pleasing to see iconic loco No 6100 *Royal Scot* in steam, parading back and forth in fine external condition.

Widening the net a little a week later, on 23 September we made a family visit to the Great Western Society site at Didcot. Among the delights here was watching No 1466 (a member of my favourite class of loco) giving rides on the short running line.

22 January was a special day for the emerging preserved Great Central Railway, with the arrival of No 34039 *Boscastle*, the first former main-line steam at Loughborough. Noel Coward died on 26 March, aged 73, followed by Pablo Picasso on 8 April, J. R. R. Tolkien on 2 September, and Bobby Darin on 20 December,

Some idea of the growing popularity of preserved railway sites can be judged by this vista of the crowds in Didcot shed yard, as seen from the train pictured in the previous shot. The increasing use of cameras was a welcome boost to the likes of Kodak, Ilford and Fuji!

aged just 37. On 5 May Sunderland became the first Second Division team for more than 40 years to win the FA Cup, beating Leeds United 1-0, and Princess Anne and Captain Mark Phillips married on 14 November. The football season ended on 28 April, with Leicester City finishing 16th in the First Division, drawing 0-0 in front of 56,202 fans away at Liverpool, who were that season's champions. During the season, City had turned out in an all-white strip, for the only time in their history.

Our concert attendances began on 29 January, with Leicester's own Family performing at the DeMontfort Hall. The following month my first article in *Let it Rock* magazine was published, an investigation into the provision (or otherwise) for local groups and/or musicians and musical outlets for them in and around Leicester. On 2 February we were again at Lanchester Polytechnic for its latest Arts Festival, to see Genesis in the midst of their 'Foxtrot Tour', publicising the release of their latest album, *Foxtrot*. A bonus for us that night was finding ourselves standing next to Peter Gabriel, front right of stage, as he left the group during an instrumental piece. The same month saw another first, my article in *Cream* magazine entitled 'Will the Twang be the thang again?', extolling the virtues of Duane Eddy's music and decrying the lack of instrumentals generally but, more specifically, his lack of inclusion in the reissues market. Another memorable concert took place on 11 June when, again standing on seats, as were all the fans in the stalls, we witnessed the event that was David Bowie as Ziggy Stardust. This was followed by Genesis on 18 October, and part of this Leicester show was recorded for inclusion on a forthcoming live album. A departure for Judith and me was to be guests at a Ravi Shankar concert at Birmingham's Town Hall on Sunday 25 November.

Tragedy beset the railway on 19 December, with ten fatalities and 94 injured when the 1718 Paddington-Oxford train, with around 650 passengers on board and hauled by D1007 *Western Talisman*, derailed between Ealing Broadway and West Ealing. In one of those cases where fact seems stranger than fiction, it was caused by an unlocked battery box door swinging open and striking a point motor, moving the points under the locomotive at 70mph. On a much happier note, Judith and I purchased a water bed on 28 December for £130. Looked on with some suspicion by our friends – 'What if it leaks?' – it gave us many years without problems!

1974 was another year of change. 28 February witnessed the first General Election since the war not to produce an overall majority, leading to a hung Parliament and, ultimately, to a second election on 10 October, in which Harold Wilson secured a majority of just three seats! The first ever professional football match on a Sunday took place on 6 January; I changed cars again, this time to a Renault 12, bought from a friend for £845; county boundaries were reorganised, leading to the loss of Rutland, Cumberland, Westmorland and Huntingdonshire; the first Ceefax teletext transmission was on BBC on 23 September; and the first McDonalds restaurant opened on 1 October, in Woolwich, South London. Elsewhere, heiress Patty Hearst was kidnapped on 4 February; Richard

They said it couldn't be done, but hardy volunteers at Loughborough were not to be beaten. Shortly after arrival on site on 27 April 1974, they set to work to bring No 71000 *Duke of Gloucester* back to life. It would take not a few years of hard work!

Gradually stretching its wings, the GCR progressively restored the line to the south. In May 1974 *Littleton No 5* has reached the temporary terminus at Quorn and prepares to run round for the return journey to Loughborough.

Nixon resigned as US President on 9 August; and Lord Lucan disappeared, after the death of his children's nanny on 7 November. On the railway, things were relatively quiet, with more new locos than withdrawals, but the latter incorporating the first batch of 'Westerns' to be dispensed with. 6 May saw the full electrification of services between Euston and Glasgow,

Visiting our best man and his wife in Coleford, in the Forest of Dean, in June 1974, we were taken to the nascent Dean Forest Railway site at Parkend, where No 5541 has obviously received some attention, despite the work having to be done in the open air.

mostly operated by the new Class 87 locos, built specifically for the route.

Musically, our concert highlights were Gentle Giant and String Driven Thing at King's Hall, Derby, on 21 March – both excellent but the latter group taking the plaudits for us – and another guest attendance at Birmingham's Town Hall to see a return to live performing by Van Morrison. Initially seeming to be very nervous, both he and the audience livened up with a performance of *Here Comes the Night*, after which the concert really took off. 11 May saw my first full-page article – as opposed to record and/or concert reviews – for *Melody Maker*, on James Taylor, in the paper's 'Rock Giants from A-Z' series. On 22 June we witnessed Procul Harum and Zzebra putting on a concert by Procul Harum and Zzebra. Once again, the 'support' group – Zzebra this time – turned out to be the most refreshing and exciting. In a third visit to Birmingham's Town Hall in a short time we saw Tangerine Dream on 30 October,

Outwardly fully restored, No 4150 stands in a siding in another part of Parkend. Built at Swindon Works in 1947, it served eight different ex-GWR sheds in its 18 years of life prior to withdrawal on 11 July 1965. It later went on to the Severn Valley Railway.

but the event for me this year was the return of Duane Eddy for a brief UK tour.

In July Judith and I went to see his show at Bailey's Night Club in Leicester, on the first night of a five-day stint, and managed a brief interview with him afterwards, in the dressing room, from which came my review of the night for *Melody Maker* and, later, an article on him for *New Musical Express* in its 'The Guitar Book' special, published in November. It had been suggested to me – by a contact at Capitol Radio in London – that I should write Duane's biography. He (Duane) kindly agreed to discuss the idea and we met the day after the Bailey's show at his hotel; over tea and biscuits, he sanctioned the proposition and confirmed that he would help. Judith and I spent more time with Duane and his friend Deed during their tour, ending up with an invitation to visit him at his home in Los Angeles. While in the UK he recorded some tracks for Tony Macaulay, an established songwriter who, apparently, harboured an ambition to work with Duane. Of these two events, more later.

The year ended with Mud's No 1, *Lonely this Christmas*; my record and concert reviewing were taking ever more of my time, with the number of albums sent to me for review increasing each month; and Leicester City were struggling to stay in the First Division, losing 2-0 to Leeds United, at home, on 28 December.

There are times in life when events happen that seem so innocuous at the time but will have major influence later. Such was the relatively unheralded arrival of Margaret Thatcher as Conservative Party leader and, thus, Leader of the Opposition on 11 February 1975, defeating Edward Heath in a leadership contest. Seventeen days later there was a crash of another sort, when an Underground train failed to stop at Moorgate station and smashed into the wall at the end of the tunnel; 43 died and a further 74 were injured. There were two other fatal derailments, near Watford Junction on 23 January and Nuneaton on 6 June. On a happier note, the Senior Citizen's Railcard was launched on 1 April – not as a joke! – and, two months later, oil production began at the Argyll & Duncan Oilfields, Britain's first, in June, initially moved by tanker to the Isle of Grain refinery. Probably the highlight of the year, certainly for enthusiasts, was the Rail 150 celebrations, culminating with a cavalcade of steam between Shildon and Heighington on 31 August. Elsewhere, the APT-E achieved a new speed record, reaching 152mph between Swindon and Reading. My lack of interest in number-taking at this stage was amply demonstrated in April when, as part of the bank's Nottingham District Ten-Pin Bowling Team, I joined colleagues on a return journey from Grantham to Newcastle and did not collect one number! I know we were hauled north by a 'Deltic', but have no idea which one. David, our captain, was avidly collecting numbers, but I was more interested in playing pontoon. I won £13 on the way north and lost it all on the way back!

On 14 February a new single was released by Duane Eddy, on GTO Records, a relatively new label and the first single release by him in the UK for six years. *Play Me Like You Play*

Your Guitar and *Blue Montana Sky* were the first two releases from the tracks recorded for Tony Macaulay during the 1974 UK tour, employing girl vocalists, echoing earlier hits by Duane, and it entered the charts on 15 March, staying there for seven weeks and reaching No 9. This was followed by an album of new material, imaginatively entitled *Guitar Man*, and an album of old releases to cash in on his new prominence, called *Legend of Rock*. My reviews of the two were blessed with a more-than-half-page feature and a photograph of the man himself in 24 May's edition of *New Musical Express*. A tour of the UK accompanied these releases – with the backing band including Rob Townsend on drums, who Judith had gone to school with in Leicester – and Judith and I saw performances at Wolverhampton, Birmingham Barbarella's (where the microphones kept failing!), Nottingham Playhouse in June and Leicester DeMontfort Hall and London's New Victoria Theatre in July. There were one or two incidents during this tour that were not positive to Duane, so 'The Duane Eddy Circle' was formed, following a meeting and discussion with Duane at the Leicester theatre. Set up to keep fans in touch with their star, I was pleased to be asked to be part of the three-man committee, the other two being committed 'twangsters' Mike Richard and Mike Lancaster. Initially a single-sheet 'letter', by 2016 the Circle's publication had grown into a fully grown and well put together magazine. My 20th spotting year was ending on a high.

Chapter 5
1975-1980

My 21st year of trainspotting started really well, especially for Judith. She was at the time one of the many that were attracted to David Essex, so when we were invited to a party after his show at the DeMontfort Hall on 30 September she was over the moon. With Essex being at No 1 with *Hold Me Close* and Gerry Francis being Captain of England's football team, their respective managements had arranged a Subbuteo match between them at the Holiday Inn in Leicester. Judith and I and one other couple were the only people outside of the camps of these two stars to be invited, and she thoroughly enjoyed chatting to David Essex and receiving a signed photograph from him. She had it under her pillow for months afterwards! Although David Essex had enjoyed success with his singles, he was not among the best-sellers for the year. Ironically, and perhaps for the first time ever, three artists filled the top slots for both singles and albums sales, though in differing order. The Bay City Rollers had top singles sales with *Bye Bye Baby* (2nd in the album sales), with Rod Stewart second with *Sailing* (3rd in album sales), and the Stylistics third, with *Can't Give You Anything (But My Love)* (top album sales).

Elsewhere, the first broadcast of *Fawlty Towers* was on 19 September, the first of just six shows in the first series (the second wasn't until 1979). The Duke of Edinburgh opened the National Railway Museum in York on 27 September, and on 23 November 'The Drain' (the Waterloo & City line on London's Underground) lived up to its name when it was flooded by a burst water main that kept it closed for a month. Kate Winslet was born on 5 October and two world-class sportsmen followed in December – Ronnie O'Sullivan on the 5th and Tiger Woods on the 30th. Sadly, Graham Hill, twice Formula 1 World

Champion, died on 29 November, aged 46. But the highlight of my year was undoubtedly our trip to America.

Judith and I had been saving for a grand holiday prior to starting a family and had thought of Kenya, but the invitation from Duane came at the right time and we gladly accepted. On 10 October we departed from Heathrow and flew 'over the pond' to Boston Airport, where we changed planes and continued on to Los Angeles, being mightily impressed by the sheer size of the country and the Rockies in particular. We collected our bags and went outside the airport to await Duane's arrival and were astounded to see Lee Marvin casually strolling around among the crowd! We spent three wonderful weeks with Duane and Deed and were treated to a great many surprises, including Disneyland, Universal Studios – where I was chosen to do a small piece of acting! – an eventful two-day

I hadn't expected any contact with railways during our trip to America in October 1975, so was surprised and gratified when we were taken to Griffith Park in Los Angeles in October to see the collection of ancient preserved steam locos, with no restrictions on close attention or even access to footplates. Here is Stockton Terminal Eastern Railroad No 1.

trip to Carmel – where we were instrumental, including my photographic evidence, in the police capturing a couple who had tried to break into Duane's car – and to experience the sights of the giant Sequoia trees in the National Park. Our first experience of Mexican food was also a delight. Not expecting anything linked to railways, I was delighted when we visited Griffith Park on 19 October, where a host of locomotives stood neatly placed for photographs and for close inspection. We became used to the warm, fine weather while there and it was a real shock to arrive back in London, at 6.10am on 1 November, after a non-stop flight over the Pole from Los Angeles, to find the temperature approaching 30° Fahrenheit lower than what we had left!

We had recently joined the Haymarket Theatre Club in Leicester and began 1976 by enjoying Alan Ayckbourn's *Absurd*

A couple of days later we were treated to a guided tour of Universal Studios, where we saw several items recognisable from films, including 'Psycho's House', and where Judith had the opportunity for a little weightlifting! I also had a brief acting appearance alongside a mock-up of a San Francisco trolley car!

Person Singular on 23 January. This month was historic, seeing the first scheduled flights by Concorde on the London-Bahrain route. Elsewhere, Harold Wilson announced his resignation as Prime Minister on 16 March, while in the USA Jimmy Carter was elected as the new President. The Sex Pistols came to public attention with their performance at the Marquee, in London, on 12 February, as support act for Eddie and the Hot Rods; Second Division Southampton won the FA Cup, beating Manchester United 1-0 on 1 May; and the Montreal Olympics began on 17 July. My reviews, live and disc, continued, with March being a particularly busy month: we saw Sailor on the 1st at Birmingham Town Hall, Robin Trower at Birmingham Odeon Theatre on the 2nd, 10CC at DeMontfort Hall on the 6th, back to Birmingham Town Hall on the 15th for Thin Lizzy, and DeMontfort Hall for Diana Ross on the 16th! It was sometimes difficult to find time to write the reviews and find outlets for publication!

On 2 April there was a full house for a superb concert at Birmingham's Barbarella's club by John Miles, riding on the cusp of his singles hit, *Music*. Thursday 13 May brought Leonard Cohen to the DeMontfort Hall, and the next night the Rolling Stones to Leicester's Granby Halls. Both were excellent concerts, and after the former I was shepherded by CBS staff into Cohen's dressing room to undertake an interview. It was not the easiest I have ever done, beginning with 'Yes … no … yes … no …',.but it developed into what the CBS minder said afterwards was, 'The best interview I have heard with Leonard. You weren't afraid to ask interesting and searching questions!' I still have the tape of that interview! April also saw my article in Barclays Bank's *Spread Eagle* magazine of our trip to stay with Duane, followed by my reviews of the Rolling Stones show in the June issue and Leonard Cohen in July's. I finished the year with an article on W. C. Fields.

But the year will be remembered for the heat wave that lasted through June to August, and the hottest average summer temperature since records began. The UK suffered a severe drought, at its most severe in August, leading to heath and forest fires, crops failing and even some ancient villages reappearing as reservoirs came close to drying up. It was during this searing heat that Judith was big with child and struggled to cope with the temperatures and bulging stomach on two separate occasions.

The first was our holiday in Yorkshire. Supposedly a (gentle) walking holiday in the North Yorkshire Moors, based at Sleights, things did not quite work out as planned. On our way north from Leicester on 19 June, we called at York, visiting the town, then the NRM. Outside the station we heard a steam whistle! Hurrying onto the platform, to our amazement we saw No 60103 *Flying Scotsman* standing light engine, after working in from Leeds at the head of the LCGB's 'The Fells & Dales Railtour'. Chatting to a couple of enthusiasts, we learned that a special was due in shortly. Sure enough, only moments later Nos 790 *Hardwicke* and 92220 *Evening Star* entered the

We had planned a walking holiday in and around the North Yorkshire Moors but, in the infamous hot summer of 1976, we found more railways to enjoy than mere walking! Arriving at York station on 19 June, I was astounded to find No 4472 *Flying Scotsman* in one of the platforms taking water!

station, double-heading the LNER Society Railtours' 'The Gresley Centenarian' from Leeds. Pure serendipity, as I had no foreknowledge of the two tours, both of which used Nos 790 and 92220 at some stage. Immediately the old enthusiasm and excitement returned, and even Judith was caught up in it as we rushed around the platforms with our cameras.

On our way to Sleights, we paused at Kirkham Priory signal box and level crossing and were invited into the box after photographing a passing DMU. During the next 14 days we walked the moors, travelled extensively around the North Yorks Moors Railway, then visited the Keighley & Worth Valley Railway – not exactly a walking holiday! Sunday and Monday 20-21 June we spent time at Levisham, photographing No 1247 (ex-68846) on the trains (and, as Judith remembered it, negotiating a 1-in-2 slope down into the valley there to capture the first shot) and at Grosmont and Goathland. Late in the day

Moments later we were at the northern end of York station to witness the arrival of *Hardwicke* and No 92220 *Evening Star*, double-heading on the LNER Society Railtours' 'The Gresley Centenarian' from Leeds.
Judith Stretton

263

on the Sunday we moved to Sandsend, where I photographed the old station site. Now in private hands, the line long closed, the station buildings looked in remarkably good condition. On the K&WVR we visited Haworth, Oxenhope and Keighley before making our way back to Leicester.

On 20 June we explored the North Yorks Moors Railway. No 2005, in LNER Apple Green livery, stands on shed at Grosmont on giving some welcome colour highlight to the scene.

The second occasion was at Grace Road, Leicester, on Sunday 15 August, for a cricket match between Leicestershire and Yorkshire (featuring Geoffrey Boycott). As guests of one of our customers at the Belgrave Road branch of the bank, we had a large tent in which we could shelter from the sun, but Judith preferred to sit outside in the shade of the tent, opining that the air inside was just too humid! Whether the exertions of this and the holiday had any affect I do not know, but our first-born, Adam, hurried into the world on 2 September, one month early! However, his haste was not without some purpose. Dad's birthday was 4 July, mine was 3 August and Adam's 2 September,

Top: An hour or so later Judith, six months pregnant, stands in Grosmont station, patiently observing No 1247 as her spouse, the photographer, composes 'the perfect shot'!

Middle: We are now on board, to witness No 1247 crossing over the points as it exits from Grosmont Tunnel, heading for Pickering.

Bottom: After the train ride, we motored to Goathland, where this portrait of the station and stock was taken.

To end the day on 21 June 1976, I was desirous of seeing part of the long-closed (5 May 1958) Sandsend station on the line between Whitby and Redcar. It was truly gratifying to see that the impressive structure, on the hilltop, was obviously in caring private hands and still with its platform.

Gradually making our way back home to Leicester on 26 June 1976, we enjoyed a visit to the Keighley & Worth Valley Railway and are here on board our train leaving Keighley station behind No 41241.

very sequential and an imperative for him to have a son on 1 October at some stage in the future!

Within days of his birth, the bank approached me to join one of its Inspection teams in another District. While this would have been promotion, it would mean me travelling away from home a lot. I explained that I was not keen on moving so soon after Adam's birth, so declined the offer. I took a risk, turning down promotion, but they accepted the reasoning. However, they did not give up, coming back with a move south, to a branch not far outside London, three weeks later than the Inspection job! With some reluctance I accepted, much to the displeasure of Judith and both sets of parents, and in October moved to be Appointed Accountant at Little Chalfont in Buckinghamshire. After a few weeks in a hotel, travelling back to Leicester at weekends, I found a house that we liked in Amersham-on-the-Hill, moving in during 1977. We bought this three-bedroom detached for £23,250 (having sold the Birstall bungalow for £13,800). The disparity of prices for virtually the same thing was to severely strain our finances, not least as the area in Buckinghamshire was inherently more expensive than Leicestershire. However, looking back four decades, the prices do not feel outlandish!

Elsewhere, 1976 was to be the momentous year when, on 9 August, the first High Speed Trains (HST) were introduced on the Western Region out of Paddington, then, designated as Class 253, they began 125mph schedules from 4 October; sadly, on the other side of the coin, the much-beloved (by us on the Midland Main Line) 'Thames-Clyde Express' ceased to run through to London on 1 May, being truncated thereafter at Nottingham, although its named status had actually ceased exactly two years earlier, when electrification reached Glasgow. There were 16 chart-toppers in the year (including a Demis Roussos EP, *The Roussos Phenomenon*!) with the Christmas No 1 being *When A Child Is Born* by Johnny Mathis. Leicester City were straddling the middle of the First Division, with Frank Worthington as top scorer, including one during City's best win of the season, 4-1 at home to Arsenal on 23 October.

Needless to say, as my new branch was literally a hundred yards away from Chalfont & Latimer station, and the old Metropolitan line ran yards behind the rear of the bank, as 1977 dawned I fairly quickly examined what was on offer. I was sad to discover that a mix of BR DMUs and London Underground trains was all there was – no loco haulage at all. With alternatives some miles away, at Gerrards Cross to the west or Hemel Hempstead to the east, I became a virtual railway hermit, seeing only glimpses during walks or drives, or when chain-sawing logs in the wood to the rear of our house, close to the Amersham-Aylesbury line. Other than family snaps, the camera was mostly asleep until 1981, with only brief excursions, such as three shots of No 63395 at a distance near Grosmont on 4 July and two close-up shots of the railway layout in the model village at Bekonscot on 13 July 1978. The first, on dad's birthday, was in the early days of what was planned as

Our 1977 holiday, including ten-month old Adam and my parents, again to the North Yorkshire Moors, was cut short by severe stomach upsets in both child and grandmother, but we did manage one day out to watch trains; this one, hauled by No 2238, is heading south near Grosmont on 4 July, dad's birthday.

a fortnight's holiday back in North Yorkshire, again staying in Sleights. Sadly, both Adam, then nearing his first birthday, and his grandma had violently upset stomachs, leading us to severely cut short our stay.

1976 saw 18 different No 1s, with Paul McCartney's *Mull of Kintyre* being the Christmas hit. As well as continuing my musical writing, I was also still preparing for the possibility of writing Duane Eddy's biography, and in May I joined fellow Duane fan Mike Lancaster to interview saxophonist Jim Horn during his brief stay in London. Not only had he earlier been one of Duane's Rebels, but he was also a much-sought-after session musician in America, having played on records by the Rolling Stones, Neil Sedaka, the Righteous Brothers and Ike and Tina Turner; also, incredibly, when Mae West was making an album, he was asked along, for, as he put it, 'She wanted some horn parts!' Later in the year I did a second interview with Clifford T. Ward, the first having been some four years earlier. He was easy to talk to and I thoroughly enjoyed his very English-sounding records – and still do. The biggest news of the year in the music industry, however, was the death of Elvis Presley on 16 August, the precise cause of which has never been positively identified.

Elsewhere, it was the year of the Queen's Silver Jubilee; Virginia Wade won the Women's Singles title at Wimbledon, her first and only Wimbledon title and, at the time of writing, the last British woman to achieve this; *Star Wars*, *Jaws* and *Close Encounters of the Third Kind* were the most successful films; 2 April saw Red Rum win the Aintree Grand National for the third time (1973, 1974 and 1977, having been second in 1975 and 1976, the only horse ever to achieve this); ex-PM Anthony Eden died (14 January) as did singers Marc Bolan (16 September, aged just 29) and Bing Crosby (14 October), and actor/comedian Charlie Chaplin on Christmas Day. 'Ladies Only' compartments were abolished on the UK's railways in January, and the prototype HST power car was withdrawn, after only two years' service, whereas the first ER set – No 254001 – entered service from 7 September. The Ffestiniog Railway made further strides towards re-reaching Blaenau Ffestiniog, its new temporary terminus at Lyn Ystradau, alongside the 'bête noir' reservoir, opening on 25 June. Leicester City had a dismal start to the 1977-78 season, winning only two and losing 14 out of the 23 matches up to and including New Year's Eve.

1978 was a year that would prominently feature the name of Argentina, with the country hosting and winning the football World Cup – 3-1 against Holland – in Buenos Aires on 25 June, and the stage show *Evita*, starring David Essex and Elaine Paige and featuring Eva Peron's cri de coeur *Don't Cry For Me Argentina*, opening in London on 21 June, becoming the hit of the year. It ran until 18 February 1986, clocking up 3,176 performances! The oil tanker *Amoco Cadiz* ran aground off the coast of Brittany on 16 March, resulting in the largest oil spill of its kind in history. On 4 May I bought my second Renault 12 Estate – £1,545, prices still rising! – and the Right Rev Eric Treacy died on 13 May, aged 70. Redland opened its stone terminal at Mountsorrel on 19 June.

For Judith and me the highlight of the year was the birth of our second child. Just after midnight on 27 August Judith's waters broke and I dashed next door to ask our neighbour to babysit Adam while I took Judith to the hospital. Like her brother, Tammy was early, but only a week this time and not four like Adam, so it was a case of rapidly gathering clothes, etc, ready to go to Amersham Hospital. It was fortunate that it was Amersham, as Tammy was obviously in a hurry and was born shortly after 2am; we only just made it to the ward and very nearly beat the midwife! I dread to think what would have happened if we had been booked into High Wycombe!

By this time Leicester City had played their first match of the season in the Second Division, after having been relegated on 29 April as bottom of the First. Under new manager Jock Wallace, they started well and up to Christmas, but then things slid and they finished the season 17th out of 22! The year also saw developing interest in Duane Eddy, with the launch in April of the US arm of the fan club and the first Duane Eddy Convention on 8 October at the Clarendon Court Hotel in London. I was pleased to write a review of the event for the next available issue of the Circle newsletter. The following month, on 9 November, Duane performed at the Winter Gardens, Margate, on the first night of a European tour headlining with Jerry Lee Lewis. Judith and I saw him later, on Sunday 19 November, at the Rainbow Theatre in Finsbury Park, London, where I was commissioned by the tour organiser to walk round the theatre wearing a newly designed Duane Eddy T-shirt! Later in the month Duane recorded new versions of 20 of his hits for Ronco Records, with members of the Circle welcomed into the studio to watch him at work and even contribute one or two 'rebel yells'!

With the flurry of excitement of the last three months behind me, my more senior position within the bank, our increased family and its commitments, and the lack of any real railway interest on the line into Amersham meant that other than family snaps the camera was to all intents abandoned into 1979. Neither did the 'Winter of Discontent', with strikes causing petrol and food shortages, help the privations from my salary struggling to keep pace with the cost of living so close to London. With this background, Margaret Thatcher swept into No 10 Downing Street as Prime Minister after success at the General Election of 3 May. However, this did provide grist to the mill for *Not The 9 O'clock News*, first broadcast on 16 October and featuring Rowan Atkinson, Griff Rhys Jones, Mel Smith and Pamela Stephenson.

One highlight for me was the bank's Oxford District Annual Sportsmen's Dinner. Organised by sports sections in turn, it was the task of the Ten-Pin Bowling Section, of which I was organiser, to provide a speaker for the event on Friday 16 February, at Elms Court, Botley. After some correspondence I was fortunate to book Brian Johnston, the celebrated broadcaster and cricket commentator. I collected him (in atrocious weather!) from Oxford station and acted as host during the evening. He was booked to speak for around 30 minutes, but spoke, without any notes whatsoever, for double that, thereby missing his proposed train back to London. He was unconcerned and was quite happy to answer questions

Your author, and event organiser (left), poses with two 'celebrities' at the Barclays Bank Sportsmen's Dinner, hosted by the Ten-Pin Bowling Section at Elms Court, Botley, Oxford, on 16 February 1979. Oxford District Local Director Alan Hodgson stands on the right, while broadcaster and cricket commentator Brian Johnston is centre. The latter gave a wonderful speech, without notes and speaking way beyond his booked time! *MJS collection*

and wait for me to extract myself from duties to return him to Oxford station, to catch a later train. My letter from him afterwards is a treasured possession! Nine years later I was again in charge, for what would be the last such dinner for the Oxford District and the first to be open to ladies!

My only railway outing came early in April. Billeted in an ex-convent in Ashdown Forest, East Sussex, for a two-week management course, one of the course leaders took a group of us appropriately interested to visit the Bluebell Railway at Sheffield Park on 18 April. Nothing was obviously in steam, but with the evening sunshine glinting off polished parts it was a joy to see Nos 30064, 34023 *Blackmore Vale*, 31323, 31263, 9017, 33001, 30847, 30096, 31027, 31178, 80100 and 30541. Two months later I visited my nearest preservation centre, at Quainton Road, but nothing excited me enough to point the camera! The only other railway photographs were of *Linda* at Porthmadog on 6 July, during our trip to North Wales doubling as a holiday and an opportunity to visit Judith's brother.

For me the latter part of the year was graced with the second Duane Eddy Convention, on Sunday 21 October, at the Cora Hotel in London, where I was pleased to give an illustrated talk on Duane. Steve Douglas, one of Duane's early saxophonists,

Taking time out from a bank course in East Sussex, a group visited the Bluebell Railway during the sunny evening of 18 April 1979. No 30064 stands at the head of the yard, with stock in a variety of stages of restoration behind.

was a special guest at the event and I met him a couple of days beforehand to interview him for my proposed biography of Duane. On 29 December Leicester City beat QPR at home 2-0, midway through a season that would see them become Second Division champions.

1980 and the start of a new decade – what would it bring? The first thing it brought for me was an interview with and a subsequent article on Neil Innes, published in April. Famed as a member of The Bonzo Dog Doo-Dah Band and *Rutland Weekend Television*, he had recently had an album and BBC TV show entitled *The Innes Book of Records*, but he was also the creator of *The Rutles*, a spoof documentary on the Beatles, featuring George Harrison, Mick Jagger and Paul Simon, and I was keen to talk to him about this. His was a very creative character and the afternoon at his home was most enjoyable; and he posed for photographs, including one with his outrageous pregnant female gorilla costume! In May the Oxford District's Ten-Pin Bowling team became the first in the bank's history to enjoy a bowling tour against other districts. Over three days, eight of us – four men and four ladies – travelled to Manchester, Hull and Leeds to play teams from Liverpool, Manchester, Radbroke Hall, York, Leeds and Nottingham. Our

I have been fortunate to interview a number of 'famous people' over the years but, undoubtedly, one of the most entertaining was Neil Innes. Famed for his participation in the Bonzo Dog Doo-Dah Band and composer of the brilliant music for *The Rutles* spoof documentary on the Beatles, here he is literally at home with his pregnant female gorilla costume in January 1980! *MJS collection*

scores were inconsistent, our excuse being the toll taken by the travelling, although the after-match social treats afforded by Liverpool and York teams were probably a greater cause! One highlight was the sight of shirt-sleeved policemen daintily tip-toeing through spreading sewage as they battled to sort out an overturned tanker at a roundabout outside the motel where we had been enjoying a meal!

Elsewhere, on 6 January rail fares rose by 20%, and by the end of the month the first two 'Deltics' were withdrawn – Nos 55001 *St Paddy* and 55020 *Nimbus*. The APT made its main-line appearance at Euston on 11 February, but derailed at 100mph near Carnforth on 18 April! 20 April was the sad day when the ex-GCR bridge (No 328) over the Midland Main Line at Loughborough was removed; 'J. R. Ewing', played by Larry

By the time of our visit to Bridgnorth in 1980, the SVR had developed by leaps and bounds and had much more to offer. On 5 July 'Black 5' No 5000 and No 6960 *Raveningham Hall* are prominent among others in the shed yard.

Hagman, was shot in the episode of *Dallas* broadcast in March; the Iranian Embassy Siege, in South Kensington, took place between 30 April and 5 May, finally ending after SAS troops stormed the building; Mount St Helens volcano dramatically erupted on 18 May, spewing a massive debris avalanche that reduced the height of the mountain by more than 1,300 feet and killed 57 people; and the Moscow Olympics opened on 19 July and were boycotted by the USA in protest at the Russian invasion of Afghanistan!

Just a week earlier, we were once again in North Wales for the family holiday and I was photographing the Ffestiniog Railway again, at Tanygrisiau, the new 'temporary' terminus, Tan y Bwlch and Dduallt. On our way north, on 5 July, we called in at Bridgnorth to see the progress since our previous visit, and were greeted by Nos 45000, 80079, 4930 *Hagley Hall*, 3205 and 43106; then, on the 15th, on our way home, we again dropped in to the Welshpool & Llanfair Railway. My interest in the nation's railways was being to some extent re-ignited as my 25th spotting year closed. It would increase to a blaze once more as the years progressed.

En route back to Leicester from a holiday in North Wales, we passed the site of the Welshpool & Llanfair Railway at Llanfair Caereinion and pulled in for a very brief pit-stop! Seen from the car park, *Joan* sets off with a train for Welshpool on 15 July 1980.

Chapter 6
1980-1985

Into my 26th trainspotting year, I was anticipating the
culmination of more than six months of work and negotiation
to see the release of a new Duane Eddy LP. Earlier in the
year I had the privilege of being asked by RCA Records in
London to compile an album of Duane's music. There had
been similar collections before, but they so often appeared as
though thrown together, without much thought, so, although
the material must perforce come from the RCA stable, I
felt strongly that it should be a proper, carefully thought-out
collection. One of my wishes was to see some unreleased
material included – which Duane had expressed a desire to see
available – as well as some hits to encourage the wider market.
I settled on 20 tracks, with four 'virgin' cuts – including one of
my favourites, *Sunday Morning Rain* – five hits, and the rest less
frequently heard tracks. We needed a title. Wanting something
that would catch the eye, fellow fan Mike Lancaster (who had
originally approached RCA with the idea) came up with *20
Terrific Twangies* –.and it worked! Released on 14 November
1980, RCA hoped for sales of 5,000 in the first year, but it sold
that many in the first two weeks, and 15,000 in the 12 months!
I hoped Duane's contract with RCA would result in some
royalties for him! Gratifyingly, it received much publicity and
all-round praise.

Elsewhere, I spoke to actress Felicity Kendal early in
September, with a view to an interview. She was happy with the
idea but, sadly, it was not to be. I did, however, interview Radio
1 DJ John Peel for the bank's magazine and the article was
published in December. The planned introduction of the APT

was 'postponed indefinitely' on 6 October, then 12 October saw the temporary withdrawal of rail services over Barmouth Bridge, due to the discovery of a marine boring worm in the supporting timbers. However, the saddest day, meeting with worldwide shock, was undoubtedly when John Lennon was shot dead on 8 December, in New York, as he returned to his apartment. Back in the First Division for the 1980-81 season, Leicester City struggled and on 27 December lost 4-0 away to Southampton.

For me, 1981 was truly a year of change. Having been totally immersed in the music industry, I had long since given up buying, or even reading, the railway press, although I did keep half an eye on my local scene. Due to increased pressures at work – I was promoted from 1 May within the branch at Little

Over the years since the BBC began broadcasting Radio 1 in the late-1960s, John Peel became a sort of folk hero for his championing of a wide variety of music styles and artists that would not otherwise have received airplay. It was a pleasure and honour, therefore, to interview him at Broadcasting House in September 1980.

Chalfont from Appointed Accountant to Manager's Assistant, still the number two within the office but, with increasing staff, the duties were more challenging – and the constant domestic ties with two small children, Judith and I were not able to go to concerts as we had in earlier days. I did manage to escape to a few music industry 'bashes', being only 26 miles from the centre of London and with Bob Fisher, my old friend from Leicester, now working in the industry, but my outlets for music writing were falling away and the music scene had changed beyond recognition since punk. My contributions to *Melton Times* finally ceased with the last publication on 3 July – they had fluctuated from weekly to monthly throughout the years since March 1969 – and my efforts had ended for *Melody Maker*, *NME*, etc. I had begun review articles for the *Buckinghamshire Advertiser* and *Black Music* magazine, and these did continue for a few years. Thus, the door that had opened towards the end of steam was now closing; interestingly, both concentrations of attention had lasted 12 years – 1956-68 and 1968-80.

Having been lured back to photographing railways, I began toting the camera wherever and whenever possible. Nothing special, but historic from the vantage point of 2016, a four-car DMU set leaves High Wycombe and passes the semaphores as it heads for Banbury on 3 October 1981.

As if by magic, in a newsagents in Little Chalfont early in January I spotted a brand-new magazine, *Railway Reflections* – '32 pages of previously unpublished photographs of the nostalgic days of British Railways'. It felt like the answer to some unspoken prayer. Making contact with Hugh Ramsey, the Editor, who lived not too far from me, we became friends and the dormant enthusiast within me stirred. A passing comment from Hugh that things change so swiftly that we should be recording it all, for tomorrow it could be gone, was all I needed. I thought back to all those scenes at Leicester that I had not photographed, as they were so commonplace (or so it seemed), and for which I would now give a ransom, and the light bulb in my brain shone brightly. Like embers caught by a sudden breeze, I was fanned into a new blaze of enthusiasm. I had direction again. By the year end I was pleased to see some of my photographs appearing in the magazine.

Elsewhere, Bill Haley died from a brain tumour on 9 February, aged just 56; there was an assassination attempt on Ronald Reagan on 30 March, as he left a speaking engagement; and Bob Marley died from a malignant melanoma on 11 May, aged 36. The famed electrified Woodhead route, linking Manchester and Sheffield, finally closed, with the last freight running on 18 July (passenger services had ended in 1970), and the same date saw the Welshpool & Llanfair Railway extend its route south from Sylfaen, to finally again reach Welshpool, but sadly only on the outskirts at Raven Square. The wedding of Prince Charles and Lady Diana Spencer took place in St Paul's Cathedral on 29 July, and on 26 November Shirley Williams won the Crosby by-election for the Social Democratic Party, overturning a 19,000 Tory majority. *Tainted Love* by Soft Cell was the highest-selling single, and the end of the year saw mass withdrawals of the 'Deltics', leaving just four – Nos 55022 *Royal Scots Grey*, 55002 *The King's Own Yorkshire Light Infantry*, 55009 *Alycidon* and 55015 *Tulyar* – which nominally survived to 1982, but only by a matter of days. I finally became emboldened by the media ballyhoo and took Adam and Tammy (aged 5 and 3!) to stand on a very cold road bridge in Slough on 28 November to watch No 55016 *Gordon Highlander* pass on BR's 'Deltic Devonian' railtour. Not understanding the meaning of it all, they were, not surprisingly, bored and cries of 'Can we go now?' were frequent, as the train was late!

As the year progressed, I became increasingly aware of the constant changes on the nation's railways and scarcely a week went by, it seemed, without some startling announcement or plan, with shifts in corporate thinking, whole classes of motive power disappearing, and changing views on namings, liveries, slogans, main-line steam running, etc. *Rail* magazine (initially *Rail Enthusiast* until 1988) was launched as a monthly (later fortnightly) early in the year, at a time when the Government was grappling with hyperinflation, industrial unrest and high unemployment and things did not look good for the UK's railways, with no money or encouragement to modernise. I had seen the birth of the 'Deltics' and was now witnessing their demise just 20 years later! Urgency was becoming increasingly

A disappointingly poor shot – my fault for choosing the location – but again historic. No 55016 *Gordon Highlander* accelerates past Slough at around 1000 on 28 November 1981 with British Rail's 'Deltic Devonian', a railtour tribute to the end of the 'Deltics'.

apparent. More happily, my photography had benefited from changes of cameras, more latterly to Canon, and my photographic eye was improving, together with upgrades in film stock. Though still not extensive, my railway photography expanded, often in conjunction with visits to locations for other purposes. So, No 69523 was captured at Quorn on 20 August and a selection of current traffic at High Wycombe (3 October), Berkhamsted (11 October), Gerrards Cross (17 October) and Slough (for the 'Deltic' on 28 November). The year ended with violent storms in December, bringing snow and record low temperatures, such as -25.2°C at RAF Shawbury in Shropshire!

1982 opened with BR being split into new business sectors on 4 January – InterCity, London & South East, Provincial, Parcels and Freight. It was also under attack on the industrial relations front, with 17 days lost to strikes in the first six

During an uncertain period, with closure hanging over it, Marylebone station stands not uncommonly quiet, as two commuters casually stroll towards the camera on 22 November 1982.

weeks! All this, together with continuing Government pressure to reduce its deficit, a revival of interest in conversion of railways into roads, interest from the National Bus Company in constructing a new coach terminus in central London, and antipathy towards rail by Mrs Thatcher, led to a review by Sir David Serpell set up in May and his highly controversial report on 20 December. One of his proposals was to slash the rail system to just 1,630 miles, including turning over the lines out of Marylebone to buses! Happily the report was rejected, not least through the efforts of BR Chairman Sir Peter Parker, but there were other attempts at savagery (see below in 1983).

The year started quietly for me, with just two photographs at Aylesbury when passing through on 24 February, but this blossomed on 10 March when en route from Southend to Nottingham, on another bowling tour, I managed to persuade Ian, my driver and fellow team member, to make a slight detour and call in at March depot. The late-afternoon darkness sadly prevented photographs, but I took the 24 assembled numbers, though they meant nothing to me at the time! It was sometime later that I established what was what, and discovered, to my delight, that No 40176 had previously been D376 ... and I copped it, one of only three needed from that class! So, a promising start, but my photographic skills still needed polishing. Largely 'point and shoot', I wasn't caring about exactly what was in the frame and, without the romance and sheer aesthetic appeal of steam, modern traction required a whole new approach. I made a conscious effort to analyse where I was going wrong and, with hopes of possible publication, this aspect would become ever more important. I fairly soon learned that the basic picture had to be inherently pleasing without the train, which would become the icing on the cake. I also decided to revisit b&w, as lighting conditions were not always conducive to good colour shots and slides had a lower tolerance of poor light. I had still been using the Pentacon SLR bought second-hand in 1969 and it was showing its age. Scraping together the necessary, I bought a Canon AE1-Program – then the latest model. The automatic function would be the answer to my prayers, I thought. Wrong again! I persevered and experimented and things did improve. A visit to the GCR on 21 March would be my next chance, then a revisit to Leicester shed in April.

Before that, however, on 2 April attention was drawn to the invasion of the Falkland Islands by Argentina and the UK's reply, sending a task force the 8,000 miles to fight back. Although aged 38, I did wonder, if the contest continued, whether I might be called up to fight! Having avoided Conscription by two years, would I now be called into the military? Elsewhere, the year had begun with three million unemployed, the first time since the 1930s; Laker Airways went bankrupt on 5 February; the DeLorean Motor Company – famed for the 'gull-wing' car – also went into receivership this year; and the 20p coin was introduced. Prince Charles opened Milton Keynes Central station on 14 May, and the FR finally regained access to Blaenau Ffestiniog on 25 May. Service and line closures had slowed over recent years, but on the relatively small list for 1982 passenger services were withdrawn from Newcastle to Carlisle and Sheffield to Leeds on 4 October, with March to Spalding following on 28 November. In the FA Cup tie against Shrewsbury Town on 6 March, Leicester City used *three* goalkeepers, when Mark Wallington went off during the match with a thigh injury. Outfield players Alan Young and Steve Lynex both tried their hand and obviously succeeded, as City won 5-2. City reached the Semi-Final but lost 2-0 to Tottenham Hotspur at Villa Park on 3 April.

Visiting Leicester shed on 11 and 18 April, it was interesting to see that only one loco, No 08695, was common on both dates. Interesting, also, that No 08618 was there on the later date, as this was the first diesel shunter allocated to the shed; it later went to Gateshead, from where it was withdrawn in September 1990. Between these two dates, we went as a family to visit friends in Brentwood, during which I was taken lineside for a brief photo session. Within a week in May I was at Watford Junction on the 8th and 15th, to see Judith safely on and off for her week's break in North Wales. When there on the second date, I snapped a '501' unit in the terminal platforms. Within months all the buildings on the platforms had been demolished, in preparation for development!

Visiting friends in Brentwood, I was offered a visit lineside at the local railway. York-built in 1962, four-car No 309622 and a sister unit form the eight-coach 1F58 Liverpool Street-Clacton working on 4 April 1982. Ten years later, the unit was withdrawn and cut up at the MC Metal Processing plant in Glasgow.

An updated view from the 'Birdcage', overlooking the yard of the erstwhile 15C shed, featuring Nos 20087 and 20151 among others on 11 April 1982. The layout of tracks from the old roundhouse is still visible, centre right. In 2016 the depot is happily still in active use but this view is now impossible, due to the growth of trees on the embankment above the yard.

Above left: The staple fare in 1982 on the Metropolitan route to Amersham was BR DMUs alongside London Underground stock. The former is here represented by a four-car set as the 1210 Marylebone-Amersham service passing Amersham Common on 14 April. The LU line to Chesham is to the left.

Above right: Also seen at Amersham Common on the same day, and looking rather like a large grey caterpillar, the 1240 Chalfont & Latimer to Chesham service heads towards its destination, before the days of 'Technicolor' reached the Underground stock.

While Judith was away, I drove to Quainton Road on 11 May, where Tammy slept in the car as I photographed some of the preserved locos, and visited Slough on the 14th. At Hemel Hempstead on the 29th, I and the children were at the station while Judith was in town shopping. As well as other trips (shopping and to see the family) to Hemel and Leicester, pictures were also gathered at Swanage on 28 July, during our fortnight's holiday with Judith's mum. As well as the elimination of the 'Deltics', I became aware that my long-familiar 'Peaks' (by then Class 45) were also to be removed from the Midland route by HSTs, so on 15 August I took the kids with me to Sandridge, to shoot one or two of them before the end. Sadly, having to stand at the edge of a cornfield and keep an eye on two small children, my illustrative anticipation was not fully realised.

A trip to Didcot on 5 September, for the children's birthday

During a visit to the Buckinghamshire Railway Centre on 11 May 1982, I took the opportunity to examine and photograph Quainton Road station, built in 1868 by the Aylesbury & Buckingham Railway in what was then (and still is largely) underdeveloped countryside.

The BR-designed 'High Speed Train' (HST) is one of the best ever designs for express travel on our railway system, and still gives front-line service 40 years after introduction. On 14 May 1982 WR set No 253012 speeds past Slough forming a Paddington-Bristol service.

Above left: Dropping Judith off at Watford Junction on 15 May 1982, to catch a train for Buxton, I grabbed the chance of photographing No 501108 and a sister unit waiting in the terminal platforms to form a working to Euston. Within weeks the awnings and other paraphernalia at these suburban platforms had been stripped away, and the '501' units had also gone within three years!

Above right With the purchase of a second camera I was able to take b&w and colour when out and about, depending on circumstances and weather conditions. On dull days, the former was preferred, as here with No 45122 heading past Thurmaston on 20 June with an up express. The first of what became Class 45, as No D11, new from BR Derby on 1 October 1960, and allocated to Camden shed, it was withdrawn from Tinsley on 27 April 1987.

treat, with some of their friends, was followed by Amersham (to see *Sarah Siddons*), Thame, High Wycombe, Thurmaston, King's Cross, Liverpool Street and Birstall between late September and the year end. By this time I had begun reviewing for *The Railway Magazine*, initially of Transacord LPs of train sounds, but this would progress to videos, then books. Also, I had my second LP release from RCA, this time a selection of blues tracks, many previously unreleased, under the title *Vintage Blues*. It was reviewed, in French (!), in *Soul Bag*, a French magazine. I was also contributing to *Black Music* magazine.

1983 started out with me paying a visit to 15C (its BR shed code and my shorthand for Leicester Midland shed) on three consecutive days, 1-3 January, during an extended stay in Leicester with the family for New Year and mum's birthday on the 3rd. There were 28 on shed on New Year's Day, with eight

You don't know what you have until it's gone! The station, goods shed and adjacent yard at Loughborough (Midland) were well known to me from 1955 onwards, and little did I know that within just a few years of this 22 August 1982 picture all the right-hand half of the view would be blitzed and transformed and, later still, the station would have its platforms greatly extended in this direction!

cops, including HST power car No 43084 seen passing the shed yard on the Midland line. On 2 January there were three fewer, but with 11 new arrivals, and the 3rd was as the previous day plus No 25190, giving a grand total of 37. I was intrigued by the site of half a dozen Class 56s, and was by now sufficiently knowledgeable to recognise that Class 46s were on the way out, so was glad to see No 46017 present on all three days. My trip on the 2nd included a look at a number of GCR sites, including what had become of Leicester Central station, as well as photographing No 506 *Butler-Henderson* recreating a mail bag drop at Quorn.

The next outing was not until 27 February, when David and I travelled to Burton Coggles on the ECML to witness a northbound run (Peterborough-York) by No 60103 *Flying Scotsman* on the SLOA's 'The Flying Scotsman Pullman'. It had snowed heavily prior to the day and this led to a very wet and messy walk to the embankment, where we intended to

On return visits to Leicester I would inspect various well-known locations to see what changes had occurred over the years. In little over a decade from final closure, the Leicester Central station site is transformed, with industrial units on the left occupying the old platforms area, while some of the old buildings survive to the right.

A visit to the ever-expanding GCR captured No 506 *Butler-Henderson* recreating a Royal Mail bag snatch at Quorn on 30 October 1982.

take our photographs. Several enthusiasts were on the west embankment, on the assumption that the train would pass on the main line. When it finally arrived, some 15 minutes down, it was on the slow line, closer to the embankment and slightly less advantageous for photographs. Cries of 'She's on the slow!' led, rather stupidly, to many of the throng immediately dashing across all four running lines – complete with extended tripods! – to the east side, seemingly paying no heed to the 125mph HSTs that were constantly passing! It was merely luck that prevented a trip and/or a fatality – and they were then on the wrong side for the sun! 4 March saw me on an errand for the bank into central London, by rail from Amersham and visits to both Broad Street and Liverpool Street, passing the time until my trip back with a message from Head Office. Two days later, I was at the GWS site at Didcot, to record the visit of No 92220 *Evening Star*, and at Butterley on the 23rd but I was not wholly satisfied. I missed the old lure of the working railway and not knowing what was around the corner. David had different ideas,

Celebrating its 60th birthday (with an appropriate operating code of '1G60'), No 4472 *Flying Scotsman* operated the Peterborough-York leg of the SLOA's 'The Flying Scotsman Pullman' railtour on 27 February 1983, seen here passing a bitterly cold Burton Coggles.

favouring steam, and we were to have many discussions on this subject over the years!

Elsewhere, the feared Serpell Report on the state and long-term future of BR was released on 20 January; Shergar, the 1981 Epsom Derby winner, was stolen in Ireland by masked gunmen on 8 February and never seen again; and the new £1 coin was introduced on 22 April, to replace the previous note and add weight to trouser pockets! On 19 April I bought a Peugeot 305 Estate for £3,730, needing a bigger car for the family. As spring turned to summer, I had seen publication of my article on the life and career of David Essex (sadly, I have forgotten for which magazine!), and the UK had another General Election, on 9 June, when Mrs Thatcher won a landslide majority against the Labour Party led by Michael Foot. Rumours of threats to the Settle-Carlisle line were confirmed on 18 August, when an announcement was made to that effect, and the Penzance sleeper service was relaunched as the 'Night Riviera' on 11 July, but would hit the headlines for the wrong reasons on 23 November when train engine No 50041 *Bulwark* derailed on its arrival at Paddington. What would become famous as the 'Brink's-Mat Robbery' occurred on 26 November at Heathrow Airport, while *Karma Chameleon* by Culture Club was the biggest-selling single, with Michael Jackson's *Thriller* the top LP, breaking records throughout the world and producing five hit singles. 14 May was a happy day for Leicester City fans, as a draw at home against Burnley on this last day secured promotion to the First Division, together with QPR and Wolverhampton Wanderers. Gary Lineker had had an excellent season, scoring 26 goals, including one penalty.

Back on the numbers trail, I was again in London on 22 April, at Liverpool Street, Broad Street and Waterloo. The latter was a first for me; now used to the TOPS numbering system, I enjoyed seeing Nos 33012, 33030, 33013, 50017 *Royal Oak* and 33118 during my brief visit there. Interspersed among a number of trips to Watford Junction between 30 April and 11 June, I joined David for a trip to Aynho on 5 June, to see and photograph a steam special. Having trekked the mile or so to our chosen location to the north of Aynho station – a farm bridge that we shared with a herd of cows! – we learned that the trip had been cancelled. The day was hot and we did not appreciate the long trek back to the car, but hoped to find some solace with a visit to the GWS at Didcot. There were many opportunities for satisfying photographs here, and I was happy to cop No 50001 *Dreadnought* on an express passing the site. However, I was missing the tours and memories of yore. Making my own short sorties was one thing, and I did derive pleasure from them, but I yearned once more for the organised expeditions. I was to obtain some satisfaction on 16 June.

Barclay's Oxford District Manager's Assistant's Club arranged a trip to Swindon Works and, although working at the other end of the district, I made sure of my place in the group. Most of the other participants were only loosely interested in railways and the engineering within the Works – probably they were enjoying a day away from work! – but there was one who was as keen on collecting the numbers as I was. Unlike cousin

Graduating to more concerted efforts for railway photography, rather than the ad-hoc occasions of late, I was at Liverpool Street on 22 April 1983 where, among others, I captured No 37050 waiting to perform the honours as the 1650 express to Ipswich.

While I had previously toured scrapyards to mourn the passing of steam, I was now faced with a similar set of emotions as I saw familiar faces about to die. No 46038 (the former D175) awaits its fate in Swindon Works yard on 16 June 1983.

During the same tour Class 08 Nos 08795 and 08778 are seen receiving attention inside Brunel's famous 'A Shop'. Lauded by enthusiastic visitors, it was not so by the workers within it, with frequent complaints of it being cold, draughty and with a roof that leaked!

David, Paul was interested in the modern scene and, like me, he had his camera with him. We were 'on pain of death' not to take pictures in the scrapyard – BR was sensitive to its image! – but our guide never seemed to be looking at the appropriate moments. Secretly snapping added a certain frisson to the afternoon. Although not as productive as in steam years, the Works did yield 60 locos, including several 08s, 25s, 40s, 45s and 46s. Just five 08s were cops, mostly the more elderly ones, together with Nos 03022 and 40176.

By this time I had been commissioned by a railway publisher to put together a photographic book. Wanting to see what images David could offer, I travelled to Nottinghamshire to see what he had. One thing that he did offer was a trip to Toton shed, where a friend of his worked. To a proper shed at last! I was in seventh heaven, not least as we were surrounded by nine different classes of diesel as well as the recently introduced Class 58s, new to me. With an innovative body design and new Railfreight livery, they were the subject of a number of my photographic studies, but by far the outstanding presence was No 40122, just inside the shed, being prepared for reinstatement in original green livery as D200, the precursor of the large class. Toton had been given the job of restoration and although the shed foreman turned to us at the sound of my camera shutter, he was satisfyingly sympathetic to our feelings and allowed the shots. Also on shed was No ADB968002 – the former D8237. Truly it had been a very worthwhile visit.

Our family holiday this year was in Buxton, a place that I had not visited since steam days. With the spotting bug now deeply biting, I made nightly pilgrimages to the old LNWR

This sight, during a tour of Toton depot on 17 July 1983, was a complete surprise and the click of my camera's shutter brought us to the attention of the Foreman, in the blue coat. Fortunately he was sympathetic to our appreciation of the work to restore No D200 (still 40122 at the time) to original condition for main-line runs. We were even allowed a closer inspection of the hand painting! *David Richards*

station – the Midland version alongside had been demolished by this time – to see the new shed and the site of the nascent Peak Rail preservation movement, which had Nos 47406, 48624 and 92214. The old steam shed, slightly out of the town, had long since disappeared. Class 37s, 47s, 40s and 45s all appeared during the holiday. On 10 August I dragged Judith and the kids to Dinting, another preservation site, to the east of Manchester, where I saw No 46115 *Scots Guardsman*, *Hardwicke*, and No 58926, among others. Ostensibly as a birthday treat for Adam and Tammy (!), I dragged us all, together with mum and dad, on a railtour on 29 August. I had made contact with the organiser of the LNER Society – has was one of the customers at my branch – and had booked on the trip to York, joining it at Hemel Hempstead at 7am. By way of Nuneaton behind No 86221 *Vesta* (with a reversal and change of locomotive to No 47328), Leicester, Derby and Sheffield, I found the trip fascinating, not least the sight of No 84003 at Derby, but the others were mostly underwhelmed! A pleasing surprise at York was the sight of No 5305 (a Stanier 'Black 5', restored to ex-LMS black livery) steamed up and ready to depart on that day's

Another holiday in Buxton provided another view of the fledgling preservation movement on the site of the old Midland Railway entrance to the town. No 48624 is akin to a kit of parts on 11 August 1983.

I never saw many of these stylish Swindon Cross Country DMUs, so was pleased to capture this portrait as we settled for some lunch next to the line in a field near Grindleford. No M51955 leads this eastbound service on 12 August 1983. New in August 1960, it was incinerated at Mayer Newman's furnace in Snailwell in November 1984.

'Scarborough Spa Express'. The photos I took were fortuitous, as the loco failed 5 miles out of York! Having enjoyed our day out in York, No 45108 hauled us back to Nuneaton, where No 86004 took over for the run south. A most satisfying day for yours truly.

With two young children, neither Judith nor I wanted any more, so on 2 August – the day before my birthday! – I signed to have the relevant medical procedure, commonly known as 'The Snip'. It was booked for High Wycombe Hospital but, unfortunately its operating theatre was out of use, so the surgeon asked if I minded having the procedure done in his office! I stretched out on his table, and he was assisted by a nurse who had never attended the procedure before – it could all have been from an episode of M*A*S*H! The rest of the year was taken up with a variety of odd trips to all manner of places for all manner of reasons but, always, with camera at the ready. Thus I took the opportunity of quickly investigating what remained of the shed at Oxford on 13 October, when

Our day out in York is nearly over, as our (delayed) return LNER Society special drifts into the station behind No 45108, to the relief of many, on 29 August 1983. The return home was uneventful but sufficiently speedy, via Sheffield and Leicester, that we were 'right time' at Nuneaton, where the diesel was replaced by electric for the final sprint south.

we went to the station to meet Judith's cousin Liz, who was to stay with us for a few days; then on 23 December I dashed by car from Little Chalfont to Hemel Hempstead in my lunch hour to record wrong-line workings. News had reached me that a freight had brought down the wires in the station area on the slow lines, and in consequence paths had to be found between expresses for locals and freight trains, with inevitable delays. I only had 35 minutes to record the scene, so it was all go, but it was well worth the trip. I made this journey on several occasions. History was made on 4 December, when Leicester City played their first ever Sunday match. Away to Nottingham Forest, they lost 3-2!

1984 was an eventful and truly momentous year for me. Judith's mum died in the middle of her two-week holiday in Wales (her father had died in 1980), while I was at home, looking after Adam and Tammy and writing my book on Duane; my first book – Steam on Shed – was published and I undertook my first book signing session; and I became a born-again Christian! The latter was not something I was searching for; indeed, I had moved almost as far away from God as I possibly could when he 'grabbed hold of my collar' and effectively said, 'I want you!'

Elsewhere, the Sarajevo Winter Olympics, held on 8-19

February, saw the world-beating performance by Torvill and Dean to Ravel's *Bolero*, gaining complete 6s for their outstanding routine; what became infamous as the year-long miners' strike began with a walkout at Cortonwood Colliery on 6 March; and on 17 April WPC Yvonne Fletcher was fatally shot in a protest outside the Libyan Embassy. Sir John Betjeman died on 19 May and Eric Morecambe died of a heart attack nine days later, at 4am on 28 May, after taking six curtain calls at the Roses Theatre, Tewkesbury, the previous evening. The IRA bombed the Tory Party's HQ at Brighton's Grand Hotel on 12 October, killing four and narrowly missing Mr and Mrs Thatcher. The ongoing famine in Ethiopia was highlighted in a BBC TV broadcast on 23 October, in which Michael Buerk shocked viewers by visuals and his description of 'a biblical famine in the 20th century' that was 'the closest thing to hell on Earth.'; prompted into action, Bob Geldof swiftly organised 'Band Aid' and the single *Do They Know It's Christmas?* was released on 3 December.

On the railway scene, BR(WR) moved its headquarters to Swindon (but would close the nearby Works the following year!); closure notices were posted for Marylebone station, following BR's report on the proposal the previous year; 5 January saw the first run of an HST with a telephone on board; a derailment on 1 May of the 2310 Garston-Glasgow Freightliner service demolished the River Calder bridge in Carlisle and closed the diversionary route permanently; and 8 June saw the beginning of the 'Sprinter' revolution, with No 150001 formally handed over to BR at York Works. On 17 July a dramatic collision was staged by CEGB – at a cost to them of £1.5 million – between No 46009 and a loaded nuclear flask wagon at Old Dalby, to prove that there was no danger in the rail transfer of nuclear waste; and HST power cars Nos 43002 and 43003 broke the UK diesel speed record over 100 miles, averaging 112.8mph over a run from Paddington-Bristol on 30 August. On 20 December fire broke out deep within Summit Tunnel, on the Calder Valley route between Manchester and Leeds, after the derailment of a freight train; it took four days for the fire to burn itself out!

I was now learning to keep my ears and eyes open for news of developments and to keep my options open by visiting as far and wide as possible, even to places seemingly offering little. Thus it was that on 4 January, opportunistically strolling the short distance from work to Chalfont & Latimer station, I was rewarded with the sight of two sets of as yet undelivered stock for the Victoria Line, being given brake test runs. Loaded with sand bags, to simulate passengers, they used this Buckinghamshire line as there were decent runs between stations where they could slam on the brakes with little danger

A casual stroll of 100 yards from work at lunchtime brought me to Chalfont & Latimer station, and lo and behold what an unexpected sight on 4 January 1984! An unnumbered Victoria Line test train enters the station, filled with heavy bags to simulate commuters for braking tests!

One of Leicester's iconic girder bridges, at Braunstone Gate, is seen on a quiet 11 March 1984. A remnant of the former GCR, it had been a footpath since closure in 1969 but, early in the 21st century, despite

much local protest, the City Council swept away both it and the pub to the left of the far pillar to allow DeMontfort University space to expand. It is widely doubted that the action was absolutely necessary!

of overshooting or colliding with anything. After this, my first railway outing was an LNER Society trip to Glasgow on 3 March.

This was back to pure trainspotting, with me joining the special at Hemel Hempstead, Hugh at Bletchley and David at Rugby. Pulled by No 86243 *The Boys' Brigade*, we sped north, all of us contributing to collecting all the numbers we could, through Northampton, Crewe, Blackburn, Hellifield and onto the Settle & Carlisle route. With closure notices posted, it was widely rumoured that 1984 was to be its last year and we all felt we had to make an effort to travel the line before it was too late. On the outward run we were graced with glorious sunshine, providing breathtaking views of the snow around Ribblehead – although it was mighty cold leaning out of the carriage window for photos! After Carlisle the run was over the G&SW route to Glasgow, where we had time to ourselves and had chosen to visit Eastfield shed. Taking a taxi from Glasgow Central station, we were amazed, during a brief halt in the traffic, by the sight of a car blazing merrily in a side street. Passers-by and, indeed, children playing near to it seemed to be totally unfazed. When quizzed, the taxi driver merely commented that this was a poor part of the city and it was an everyday occurrence! After that, the woman who stopped our return journey at Preston because she had smelled burning and thought the train was on fire was tame by comparison!

Arriving unexpected at Eastfield, the foreman was suspicious of my blanket permit for Scottish sheds but, after a donation to the railwaymen's fund, he allowed us to tour the depot. There were 46 engines on view and, just before rain set in, we were able to photograph – and in Hugh's case video – the shed scene. Although wholly diesel, it was nevertheless 'reality', and it was to be my last views of Class 27s in working order, although I did not know it at the time. It was also my first sight of 'ETHEL 3' (the former No 25319), a loco especially modified to provide electric train heating. No 86225 *Hardwicke* headed our return train. Now with 36-exposure 35mm film, it was salutary to look back on our trips to Scotland two decades earlier with one 12-exposure b&w film! With faster film speeds another bonus, as well as having bought a second Canon AE1-P – one for colour and one for b&w – I was rapidly increasing the number of photographs taken.

On 12 April I was again moved by the bank, this time to the Flackwell Heath branch, on the outskirts of High Wycombe. This initially created a predicament, as Judith needed our car to take the kids to school, so how was I to travel to work? Happily, the junior at Little Chalfont was changing his motor bike and offered his old one to me. Never having ridden one before, he delivered it to me a couple of days before my change of branch, with a very brief lesson on how to ride it! It was only 125cc, but it still seemed a speedy beast to me! Practicing up and down the road outside our Amersham house, I rapidly found out that what had been the rear brake on my bicycle was the clutch on the motorised version and it would not stop me – all very different! I had to very speedily come to terms with that as I was to travel through the Amersham and Beaconsfield rush hour in the mornings. 30mph initially felt like

A change of office gave me the chance to see the 0622 Wolverhampton-Paddington service, the sole remaining loco-hauled roster on the ex-GWR main line through High Wycombe, on my way to work. On 19 April 1985 No 50050 *Fearless* does the honours, powering away from the Wycombe stop and passing Loudwater.

the wind, but I negotiated the traffic and over the weeks built up more confidence and speed. I quickly learned that the 0622 Wolverhampton-Paddington passed through High Wycombe around the time that I was making my way to my new branch, so I began pausing my journey at either Beaconsfield or Loudwater to see it, usually headed by a Class 50. It was the only remaining loco-hauled train on the former GWR Birmingham-Paddington main line. There were strange looks from the locals, as I stood there in my leathers, camera in hand, like some alien recording the scene! My first recording was No 50017 *Royal Oak* on 16 April.

On 12 May I journeyed to Quainton Road to see Nos 25076 and 25245 double-heading the homeward leg of BR's '10 Counties' railtour. Originating at St Pancras, this duo had taken over at Walsall and returned the train to its ultimate destination at Marylebone. It also incorporated the last day of services into Bedford St Johns station. Just days later I received copies of my first published book – *Steam on Shed* – which included colour and b&w shots of many of the steam sheds between 1A (Willesden) and 89A (Shrewsbury). I was contracted to a book signing at the local book shop in Amersham on 9 June. It was a very hot day and over a 2-hour period I felt disappointed at only selling and signing 12 copies but, having thus commented to the shop manager, he said, 'On a day like this, people don't want to come book shopping. If it makes you feel any better, we recently did a signing with Frank Muir, for his latest book, and we only sold *two* copies!' Being chosen as part of the 'Editor's Choice' for the Railway Book Club, 15,000 copies were printed … and it sold 14,700! The local press was interested and small features appeared in *The Buckingham Advertiser* (three times, including a double-page spread in September!), *Wycombe Star*, *Chiltern Newspapers*, *Bucks Examiner*, *Leicester Mercury*, *North Leicester Weekly* and *Barclaynews*. The whole process had been relatively trouble-free since being contracted, and I thought this was to be the first of many more to come. However, things did not turn out that way.

Contracted to write 70,000 words for my biography of Duane Eddy, I began on 2 June, planning to complete 5,000 words per day over the two weeks while Judith was away and the kids were at school, and was going well when Judith's mum died during the middle weekend. I had to ask the publishers for an extension, to which, in the circumstances, they agreed. I eventually wrote 84,000 words, which were faxed to Duane by one of my neighbours and he would fax corrections by reply. Sadly, by this time the publishers had been taken over and the new owners did not want to publish it! We had disagreements over its title, the editing (in which they wanted to change quotes from interviews and even the spelling of record titles!) and certain legal discussions that ended with me having to pay them for the work that they had already done in order for me to have my material returned to me. Consequently, *Twangs for the Memory* did not see the light of day.

Railway trips were now increasingly solo affairs and I began to utilise the motor bike for ease of travel to profit from visits to Taplow in my lunch hour, to record as much as I could. I also continued to make use of any available opportunities, such as what proved to be my last visit to Broad Street on 7 June, by rail from Watford Junction, as well as to Liverpool Street, St Pancras, Euston, Camden, Willesden and Paddington. At Watford No 86238 was on the 'Manchester Pullman' and No 87027 *Wolf of Badenoch* headed the 'Royal Scot'. One-off specials were always interesting, such as No 31117 and Inspection Saloon KDW150266 forming 'The Wedding Belle' at High Wycombe on 23 June, chartered by Tony Parkins, then Chairman of the Rail Tour Operators Association, to transport him and his new wife from High Wycombe to Shrewsbury after their wedding. Then there was No 1054 on the 'Wilson's Brewery 150th Anniversary' special, seen by Tammy and myself at Manchester Victoria on 1 August, as we took a day trainspotting during our holiday in Buxton. There was another pairing with David on 15 July, when we toured Toton shed, then visited the Midland Railway preservation site at Butterley, where I was pleased to see and photograph No D4 *Great Gable* in 'as delivered' green livery without yellow front ends, as well as Nos 13085, 12077, D2959, 1708, 68012, 44932, 80080, 4072 and 16440. The preservation theme continued on 6 August, when I saw Nos

Top: Another iconic structure that has been swept away in the name of progress is the delightfully designed Broad Street station, still in use when seen on 7 June 1984, with the steps leading up to platform level.

Middle: On that upper level at Broad Street, Nos 501186 (left) and 501159 wait for their next duties on the route to Richmond on 7 June 1984. Opened by the North London Railway on 1 November 1865, the station closed on 30 June 1986, at which time the Class 501 fleet were also dispensed with.

Bottom: What a romantic way to whisk your new wife away on honeymoon! 'Crew Cut' No 31117 heads away from High Wycombe on 23 June 1984 with 'The Wedding Belle' special. New from Brush as No D5535 in June 1959, it became 31117 under TOPS in March 1974, before being withdrawn from Crewe Works in March 1987 and cut up at Doncaster Works in September 1988.

While Adam and Judith explored the Derbyshire countryside on 1 August 1984, Tammy and I took a trip to Manchester Victoria, where we were in time to witness the arrival of No 1054 (ex-58926) and Inspection coach, forming the 'Wilsons Brewery's 150th Anniversary' special.

After bringing the 1308 from Buxton into Manchester Piccadilly, the crew that will take it out again prepare to board on 1 August 1984. Forming the 1418 return trip, it comprises 1958-vintage Class 104 No M53598 (closest to the camera) with Class 108 Nos M59390 and

M53542. The '104' was withdrawn in December 1986 and scrapped at Vic Berry's Leicester scrapyard 13 months later.

How 'Peaks' should look, in BR green, with grey stripe and *no* yellow front ends! Restored to virtually as-new condition, No D4 *Great Gable* stands on shed at Butterley on 15 July 1984.

The years 1984/85 were to see the closure of the 'Leicester Gap' of semaphore signals on the Midland Main Line. On 30 September 1984 the old order is still in place, with Leicester North signal box and a glorious signal gantry, but the invader is taking shape on the extreme right in the form of the new Leicester Power Box, which would sweep all this away. The same view in 2016 is so bare!

47406, 92214 and 48624 again at Peak Rail's Buxton site, and Quainton Road on 26 August, with Nos 7715, 41298, 9466 and various other items on show.

1984 was also the year that I made my first visits to Vic Berry's scrapyard in Leicester, 30 September being the first of many over succeeding years, as I was given permission by the man himself to have free range of the site to take photographs. This was to prove valuable to my photographic library, but also

I was honoured to be granted unfettered access by Vic Berry to his Leicester scrapyard and went there on numerous occasions. On one of the early visits it was interesting to see a selection of discarded WCML electrics. No 83011 is very close to the end on 4 November 1984.

to my sense of enjoyment. Vic had bought small BR shunter No 03069 and it was a joy watching this shunt various items of stock around the yard. On 4 November there were ex-WCML electrics Nos 82006, 83011, 83001, 83007, 83010, 83002, 83008 and 82002 – to my knowledge the first appearance of such motive power in Leicester.

1985, the final year of this first volume, was a year of ups and downs. Released the previous December, Jennifer Rush's *The Power of Love* became the year's biggest-selling single; 10 January witnessed the launch of Sir Clive Sinclair's C5 vehicle; 54-year-old Mikhail Gorbachev became the youngest ever leader of the Soviet Union on 11 March; Dr Beeching died on 23 March, aged 71; and Saturday 11 May saw the worst fire in UK football history, with 56 killed in the Bradford City conflagration, followed 28 days later with 39 people – mostly Italians and Juventus supporters – killed in Heysel Stadium, Brussels, in hostilities between Juventus and Liverpool fans. *Brothers in Arms* by Dire Straits was released on 13 May and became the year's best-selling LP; Boris Becker, at 17, became the youngest ever Wimbledon Men's Singles champion on 7 July; 13 July was the momentous day that the 'Live Aid' concert was held simultaneously at Wembley Stadium in London and the John F. Kennedy Stadium in Philadelphia; and another positive move was the quiet abandonment of the Marylebone closure proposals, after strong opposition from many quarters.

For the near-20 years since the demise of steam on the ex-Great Central line out of Marylebone, BR had staunchly and stubbornly refused to admit preserved steam into the terminus, trotting out a number of reasons why it was not possible. Suddenly, in 1985, it suited their purpose, in order to help publicise the issue of a set of railway stamps. Thus it was, on the bitterly cold late afternoon of 12 January 1985 that Tammy and I stood on the ice of Beaconsfield's platform to witness No 4498 *Sir Nigel Gresley* steam sedately through at the head of Pullman Rail's 'The Thames-Avon Express' – 45 minutes late! In ensuing months the loco's resplendent blue livery would be seen on Sunday specials to Stratford-upon-Avon, as would Nos 35028 *Clan Line*, 46229 *Duchess of Hamilton*, 30777 *Sir*

In 1985 BR did a volte face over steam into Marylebone when it suited them, to publicise an issue of stamps featuring railways! Also as part of the publicity, No 47500 *Great Western*, duly adorned with facsimile stamps and an appropriate headboard, drifts through Beaconsfield on 22 January 1985, with a rake of Pullmans in tow.

Lamiel, 34092 *City of Wells*, 4422 *Mallard* and 4771 *Green Arrow*. It was impressive to see the numbers of armchair 'gricers' and/ or photographers who suddenly crawled from the woodwork, their interests reawakened. It became ever more difficult to find a free photographic vantage point!

My lunchtime and ad-hoc local outings continued, but on 12 March I again stole away from our party of bank ten-pin bowlers, in Manchester for a day on another District Team tour, to visit Piccadilly and Victoria stations, together with a quick trip with a local spotter to Newton Heath shed. Seemingly still as busy as in steam days, I concentrated on photographs rather than number-taking on this occasion, partly as we did not have permits, and was pleased to capture No 56066 on crew training. Also on shed were some of the former St Pancras 'Bed-Pan' units that had been sent north for conversion to parcels vans. Two days later our tour was in Leeds and I took

Following the steam relaxation into Marylebone, a multitude of steam specials followed, many to Stratford-upon-Avon. One such was an evening 'wine & dine' special on 30 April 1985, headed by No 35028 *Clan Line*, complete with 14D (Neasden) shedplate, 'Golden Arrow' headboard and British and French flags!

Another of the steam duties, this time in the opposite direction, sees No 46229 *Duchess of Hamilton* on 4 May 1985, southbound at Saunderton on the SLOA's 'The South Yorkshireman', initially diesel-hauled from St Pancras, but steam-hauled from Sheffield to Marylebone and running 50 minutes behind time.

Change was in the air in the 1980s, both with the replacement of types of motive power and rolling stock and a rethinking of some routes. Encompassing both aspects is No M65461, standing in the terminal platforms at Manchester Victoria on 12 March 1985 forming a service to Bury. Within a matter of years this route was transformed from heavy rail to tram status and these '504' units, built in 1959 specifically for the route, were withdrawn.

the opportunity to visit City station and saw a variety of motive power. The following day I went to Toton while the rest of our team sampled the bar in Ilkeston Bowling Alley.

On 6 April Judith was off for another break in North Wales, so a few days later, with Adam at school, I took Tammy with me to Tring station, ostensibly to see the APT on test. Setting up my camera on the platform, the station master was interested and updated me with its progress and even provided coffee while we waited. My time was limited and the APT was becoming ever later, so at 1330 I had to call it a day. We piled into the car and drove away from the station, only to see it roar through as we did so! It was due back in the evening and, having ascertained its due time, I arranged to be back for photographs. I was there in time, but the APT was *early*! It approached as I arrived at my vantage point – I had no time to do anything but

Another visit to Vic Berry's yard, on 6 April 1985, shows No 03069, bought from BR by Vic specifically to shunt the yard, resting between duties, with the beginnings of the famed piles of coaches and, later, locos on the left.

On 10 April I took Tammy with me to Tring, in the hope of seeing the APT on one of its test runs. Sadly, it was running late and I ran out of time. The last thing I photographed while there was No 81005 on an up parcels working. Already relegated from top-link rosters, it was withdrawn on 20 February 1989.

stop the car, wind the window down, grab the camera and snap, through the window, with no time to check speed, exposure, composition, etc! I was fated never to see it running again.

The next major outing was a family trip, including mum and dad, to Reading Depot Open Day, as part of BR's 150th celebrations of the GWR. We were rewarded with hot and sunny weather and an appealing mix of events and motive power, not least a brief run behind preserved steam loco No 5572 alongside the main line. Two weeks later I was at Victoria, on my way to a week's Barclays course at Ashdown House in East Sussex, by way of the 'Gatwick Express', then onward train journey to Hayward's Heath. I travelled behind No 73122 as the 1600 departure for Gatwick. A bus was provided to take us from Haywards Heath to the house, which had until relatively recently been a convent. It had also been filmed as part of the TV drama *Colditz*! Not exactly the usual environment for red-

The Reading Depot Open Day on 1 June 1985, in celebration of 150 years of the GWR, was a delightful day in all respects, especially the weather and the items on display. Adam and Tammy thoroughly enjoy their moment 'driving' A38W, watched by mum and grandma!

Another holiday in Buxton gave me the opportunity to capture Nos 45058 and 20140 in the sunshine of 21 July 1985, standing proudly outside the engine shed. Negatively affected by changes in traffic locally, the shed buildings were abandoned and, finally, demolished in 2016.

On the same day we enjoyed a ride on the first 'Peak Rail Rambler' to New Mills Central, my only visit to this location. While we were there No E54009 entered the station with a Sheffield-New Mills Central service, closely watched by Adam (right). Note the crowd waiting for the return run of the 'Rambler' to Buxton on the other platform.

blooded management trainees to concentrate and learn… No 73116 pushed my return train from Gatwick to Victoria on 21 June.

Our family holiday was back to Buxton, beginning on 20 July. The following day we enjoyed sampling the first year's 'Peak Rail Rambler' from Buxton to New Mills Central and back, for my one and only visit to this latter station. My daily visits to Buxton depot saw a constantly changing variety, with, seemingly, virtually none of the locos spending more than one day on site. The sight of Class 20s still hard at work was very pleasing.

My final visit of this 30th year was a return to Toton with David, on 18 August. Sixty-three locos on shed was most satisfying, with several cops and a wide variety, from 08s to 58s. Although no longer keeping detailed logs of totals seen through the years, as I had in steam days, I was still just as keen to underline those seen and to plug any gaps wherever possible.

So my 30th trainspotting year ended on 31 August. I was still writing – for *The Railway Magazine* mostly – but also for *Railway Reflections* and even St Leonard's Parish Magazine in Chesham Bois. Leicester City had survived two years in the First Division, but top goal-scorer Gary Lineker left to go to Everton (then the First Division champions) by the end of the 1984-85 season. City began the new season with a win against Everton, 3-1 at home on 17 August, but thereafter wins were few and far between and the team only survived in the First Division by Ipswich losing to Sheffield Wednesday on the final day. Also, at this time, Chris Green was approaching his second anniversary as supremo in ScotRail. He was making a name for himself, and we shall learn more of him in Volume 2.

And so, leaving the best until last! Having photographed so much on my travels, I am here captured on the other side of the lens with an appropriate sign, near Chesterfield, on 28 August 1967.

Books by John Stetton

Solo

ISBN	Title	Year
0 7137 1440 9	Steam On Shed (1984)	(1989)
1 85241 007 8	Leicestershire Railway Memories	(1990)
1 85241 006 X	30 Years of Trainspotting	(1994)
1 85794 019 9	Closely Observed Trains	(1995)
1 85895 141 0	Past & Present – Ffestiniog Railway	(1995)
1 85895 109 7	Past & Present – Leicestershire & Rutland [non-railway]	(1996)
1 85895 091 0	Past & Present – The Ffestiniog & Welsh Highland Railways	(1998)
1 871608 49 X	Illustrated History of Leicester's Railways	(1999)
1 85895 142 9	Past & Present – Welsh Highland Railway	(1999)
1 85895 135 6	Past & Present – Bodmin & Wenford Railway	(1999)
1 899624 40 6	Festiniog in Camera – 100 Years 1871-1971	(2000)
1 85895 166 6	Past & Present – West Somerset Railway	(2001)
1 870119 70 3	Colour of Ffestiniog [– first wholly colour book]	(2002)
1 85895 206 9	Past & Present – Dean Forest Railway	(2003)
1 85794 174 8	Steam Locomotive Shed – Vol. 3 The Ray Ruffell Collection	(2003)
1 85895 218 2	Past & Present – Swindon & Cricklade Railway	(2003)
1 85794 216 7	The Last Years of British Rail 1990-94	(2003)
1 85895 233 6	Past & Present – Welsh Highland Railway Vol.2	(2004)

With Peter Townsend

1 85794 274 4	Railways & Recollections – 1956	(2006)
1 85794 275 2	Railways & Recollections – 1964	(2006)
1 85794 276 0	Railways & Recollections – 1973	(2006)
1 85794 277 9	Railways & Recollections – 1981	(2006)
1 85794 278 7	Railways & Recollections – IoM	(2006)
978 1 85794 291 0	Railways & Recollections – 1957	(2008)
978 1 85794 292 7	Railways & Recollections – 1961	(2008)
978 1 85794 294 1	Railways & Recollections – 1975	(2008)
978 1 85794 320 7	British Railways STEAM The final Years 1965-1968	(2008)
978 1 85794 337 5	Railways & Recollections – 1955	(2010)
978 1 85794 338 2	Railways & Recollections – 1961 pt2	(2010)
978 1 85794 330 6	The Fall & Rise of BR STEAM	(2010)

The trainspotting memoirs series so far...

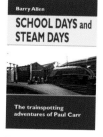

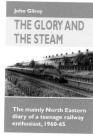

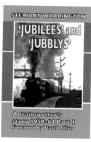

Further details can be found on our web site at:
www.nostalgiacollection.com